Stone Lake is the first translation and study in a Western language of the poetry of Fan Chengda, one of the most famous Chinese poets of the twelfth century. For the nonspecialist reader the main attraction of the book will be the translations of Fan Chengda's poetry, which make up almost half of the text and include poems on such familiar themes as the Chinese countryside, peasant life, Buddhism, and growing old. The more technical part of the book contains a biography of the poet, a discussion of his affiliation with poets of the generation before him, a detailed analysis of his style, and discussion of the major themes of his work.

Cambridge Studies in Chinese History, Literature and Institutions
General Editor, Denis Twitchett

STONE LAKE
THE POETRY OF FAN CHENGDA (1126–1193)

Other books in the series

Glen Dudbridge The *Hsi-yu Chi*: A Study of Antecedents to the Sixteenth-Century Chinese Novel

Stephen Fitzgerald China and the Overseas Chinese: A Study of Peking's Changing Policy 1949–70

Christopher Howe Wage Patterns and Wage Policy in Modern China, 1919–72

Ray Huang Taxation and Government Finance in Sixteenth-Century Ming China

Diana Lary Region and Nation: The Kwangsi Clique in Chinese Politics, 1925–37

Chi-yun Chen Hsün Yüeh (A.D. 148–209): The Life and Reflection of an Early Medieval Confucian

David R. Knechtges The Han Rhapsody: A Study of the *Fu* of Yang Hsiung (53 B.C.–A.D. 18)

J. Y. Wong Yeh Ming-ch'en: Viceroy of Liang Kuang (1852–8)

Li-li Ch'en Master Tung's Western Chamber Romance (*Tung hsi-hsiang chu-kung-tiao*): a Chinese *Chantefable*

Donald Holzman Poetry and Politics: The Life and Works of Juan Chi (A.D. 210–63)

C. A. Curwen Taiping Rebel: The Deposition of Li Hsiu-Chang

Patricia Buckley Ebrey The Aristocratic Families of Early Imperial China: A Case Study of the Po-ling Ts'ui Family

Hilary J. Beattie Land and Lineage in China: A Study of Tung-ch'eng County, Anhwei, in the Ming and Ch'ing Dynasties

William T. Graham, Jr. "The Lament for the South": Yü Hsin's *Ai Chiang-nan fu*

Hans Bielenstein The Bureaucracy of Han Times

Michael J. Godley The Mandarin-Capitalists from Nanyang: Overseas Chinese Enterprise in the Modernisation of China 1893–1911

Charles Backus The Nan-chao Kingdom and T'ang China's Southwestern Frontier

A. R. Davis Tao Yüan-ming (A.D. 365–427): His Works and Their Meaning

Victor H. Mair Tun-huang Popular Narratives

Ira E. Kasoff The Thought of Chang Tsai (1020–77)

Ronald C. Egan The Literary Works of Ou-yang Hsiu (1007–72)

Stanley Weinstein Buddhism under the T'ang

Robert P. Hymes Statesmen and Gentlemen: the Elite of Fu-Chou, Chang-hsi, in Northern and Southern Sung

David McMullen State and Scholars in T'ang China

Arthur Waldron The Great Wall of China

Brian E. McKnight Law and Order in Sung China

Hugh R. Clark Community, Trade, and Networks

Denis Twitchett The Writing of Official History under the T'ang

Stone Lake:
The Poetry of Fan Chengda
(1126–1193)

J. D. Schmidt

Published by the Press Syndicate of the University of Cambridge
The Pitt Building, Trumpington Street, Cambridge CB2 1RP
40 West 20th Street, New York, NY 10011-4211, USA
10 Stamford Road, Oakleigh, Victoria 3166, Australia

First published 1992

Printed in the United States of America

This book has been published with the assistance of grants from the Canadian Federation for the Humanities and the Chiang Ching-kuo Foundation.

Library of Congress Cataloging-in-Publication Data

Fan, Ch'eng-ta, 1126–1193.
[Poems. English. Selections]
Stone lake : the poetry of Fan Chengda (1126–1193) / [translated and edited by] J. D. Schmidt.
p. cm. – (Cambridge studies in Chinese history, literature, and institutions)
Includes bibliographical references and index.
ISBN 0–521–41782–1 (hardback)
1. Fan, Ch'eng-ta, 1126–1193 – Translations into English. 2. Fan, Ch'eng-ta, 1126–1193 – Biography. 3. Authors, Chinese – Biography.
I. Schmidt, J. D. (Jerry Dean), 1946– . II. Title. III. Series. PL2687.F3A6 1992
895.1'142 – dc20 91–34640

A catalog record for this book is available from the British Library.

ISBN 0–521–41782–1 hardback

To Mei-hui, Erika,
and the entire Bakongo Family

Contents

Preface

In the twelfth century Chinese civilization under the Song dynasty (960–1280) attained a ripeness that it rarely if ever equaled in later ages. The thinker Zhu Xi (1130–1200) put the finishing touches on his great synthesis of neo-Confucian thought; Chinese science and mathematics reached the apex of their development; artists of the Southern Song Academy created landscapes and bird and flower paintings of unparalleled refinement, and although the northern half of China was occupied by foreigners, the Chinese capital at Hangzhou was the largest and most cultured city in the world.

It is no wonder then that poetry in the classical language, the favorite literary art of the upper classes, rose to one of the highest levels ever witnessed. *Ci* verse, which had first come into prominence during the waning decades of the Tang dynasty (618–907), reached its climax with authors such as Xin Qiji (1140–1207) and Jiang Kui (ca. 1155–1221), while *shi* poetry, the form that survives in the greatest quantity and that was most highly regarded by Song intellectuals, explored a host of new themes and perfected the many innovations of earlier Song dynasty poets.

Fan Chengda (1126–1193) was one of the three most outstanding *shi* poets of his generation, and although today he is chiefly remembered for one series of bucolic poems that he wrote on the countryside near his home not far from the modern city of Shanghai, the main purpose of this book is to demonstrate how he excelled in practically every type of poetry known to the Song dynasty literary tradition. Since no representative sample of Fan Chengda's poetry has been translated into a Western language before, the original intent of this book was to provide enjoyable translations of some of Fan Chengda's more outstanding poems, but I soon discovered that the translations would be more easily appreciated if they were prefaced by a short biography of Fan Chengda and a critical examination of his literary style. Nonspecialist readers may wish to read the translations first, but even if they have an aversion to literary criticism, they still are encouraged to examine the discussion of Fan Chengda's poetry because they will find quite a number of other poems translated there.

Although it is hoped that the critical section of this book will contribute to our overall understanding of Chinese poetry during the Song dynasty, the translations are obviously of primary importance for this study, and it seems useful to comment briefly about the method of translation adopted. Translation is an art that few scholars of Chinese literature have mastered (to the great loss of nonspecialist readers), and although these translations are certainly not superior to the work of others, every effort has been expended to make them enjoyable for even the nonspecialist reader. Thus, in some cases specialists may complain that they are a bit too free, although, in fact, all of them follow the Chinese originals quite closely line by line, departing from the originals only in certain details such as word order or the translation of a Song colloquialism by an equivalent English expression. Generally speaking, where the translations deviate enough from the literal meaning of the originals to cause confusion for scholars reading the poems in Chinese, the notes provide a more literal translation. In the interest of readability, all the footnotes have been kept short; important literary and historical allusions necessary for the understanding of poems have all been identified, but some allusions that merely involve the echoing of an earlier author have been excluded, particularly when it was felt that their explanation was not necessary for an intelligent reading of a work. In line with most recently published translations, few place names have been identified, and the names of persons have been identified only when deemed essential.

Although many scholars of classical Chinese literature still retain the Wade-Giles system of romanization for Chinese names, it seems peculiar to use one system for books on contemporary topics and another for ancient ones, and, hence, this book adopts the modern *pinyin* system, which is official in China now and used in practically all Western-language newspapers and periodicals. Where confusion is likely to occur, as in the citation of earlier works in Western languages, the older Wade-Giles system is quoted in parentheses. Except where indicated, all dates have been expressed in the Chinese lunar calendar. Although this may seem strange to nonspecialist readers, Chinese poetry is too closely linked to the cycle of seasons and the traditional festivals of the lunar calendar to make conversion desirable.

Finally, the debt of this work to Zhou Ruchang's pioneering anthology of Fan Chengda's poetry, the first annotated selection of his verse, should be obvious to anyone familiar with Zhou's work. Although I have frequently disagreed with Zhou's interpretations of Fan Chengda's poetry, no one can study Fan without referring to Zhou's excellent scholarship. It is hoped that Zhou's detailed annotations of Fan's poems have prevented the translations from erring too grievously, but if any mistakes have crept in, I will be grateful to any critics who point them out graciously.

Acknowledgments

I would like to express my gratitude to Yeh Chia-ying Chao, professor emerita of the University of British Columbia, and Dr. William Schultz, professor emeritus of the University of Arizona, who read through my manuscript and made many appreciated suggestions for improvements. Of course, any errors that remain are my own responsibility and are a result of my failure to take their good advice. This work would have been impossible without the excellent Chinese and Japanese language collection at the University of British Columbia, and I wish to thank the staff of the Asian Library for their unflagging assistance. The translation portion of this book was generously supported by the Council for Cultural Planning, Executive Yuan, Taiwan, Republic of China. I also wish to thank my wife and my daughter, without whose patience this work would never have been completed. It is to them and our Bakongo friends that this book is dedicated.

Part I
Biography and critical study

1
The life of Fan Chengda

Family background and youth

Fan Chengda 范成大 was born on the fourth day of the sixth lunar month, 1126 (Western calendar, June 26, 1126) in Pingjiang 平江, Wu District 吳縣, near the city of Suzhou (Soochow) in modern Jiangsu Province.[1] By the twelfth century this region of China was already a land of watercourses and canals, which crisscrossed the flatlands between the low, mist-enshrouded hills, bringing the water essential for its rich wet paddy agriculture and for transporting its fine silk and renowned handicrafts to all parts of the Chinese empire. The city of Suzhou itself had been an important urban center for more than a millennium and a half, and although the capital city of the Southern Song dynasty was now located in Hangzhou, Suzhou attracted intellectuals from all over China and was well on its way to becoming one of the preeminent centers of Chinese literary and artistic culture.

Fan later claimed that he was a relative of the famous Northern Song statesman and reformer Fan Zhongyan 范仲淹 (989–1052), who happened to come from the same part of China, but later scholars have cast doubt on Fan Chengda's affiliation with Fan Zhongyan's family, and perhaps Fan Chengda's family made up a connection with the more illustrious clan of Fan Zhongyan in order to raise their prestige in the eyes of contemporaries.[2] However, both Fan Chengda's great-grandfather Fan Ze 范澤 and his grandfather Fan Shiyin 師尹 were granted posthumous titles, so it is possible that the family had belonged to the landed gentry class for several generations, in spite of the fact that Fan's father, Fan Yu 范雩, was probably the first ancestor of Fan Chengda who served as an official, obtaining the degree of metropolitan graduate (*jinshi*) in the year 1124 and finally rising to the relatively humble post of assistant in the palace library (*bishu lang*, rank 8a).[3] Although Fan Yu's official career ensured that his sons would have received a thorough grounding in classical literature in preparation for the civil service examinations, the family does not seem to have been especially wealthy, and his later poetry tells us that Fan Chengda personally engaged in agricultural labor as a youth, an experience that may have been unpleasant at the time but helped to develop his great sensitivity for the beauties of the Chinese countryside and peasant folkways.[4]

The years immediately preceding Fan Chengda's birth witnessed political developments that had disastrous consequences for the next two centuries of Chinese history and that had a direct impact on Fan Chengda himself. Even under its first emperors, Song military might did not suffice to overawe its neighbors to the north and west, and the Song army had suffered a number of humiliating reverses at the hands of the Qidan, a nomadic people who inhabited the steppes to the north of China proper, a situation that did not improve even after the attempts of such great statesmen as Fan Zhongyan[5] and Wang Anshi 王安石 (1021–1086)[6] to reform the Song government and military. The last effective emperor of the Northern Song, Huizong 徽宗 (reg. 1101–1126), was an excellent painter and a generous patron of the arts, but he seems to have had little taste or talent for matters of state,[7] although by this time, the Liao dynasty of the Qidan was at an equally low ebb, its emperor as addicted to falconry as the Song ruler was to art.[8]

A new nomadic people, the Nüzhen, soon took advantage of the Qidan decline, and after the Nüzhen ruler won a great victory over the Qidan in 1114, he proclaimed himself the first emperor of the Jin (Golden) dynasty.[9] The Song emperor Huizong must have rejoiced when he received news about the Jin defeat of the Qidan, for now he had an ally in the struggle with his dynasty's hereditary enemy, and in the year 1120 the Song and Jin governments formed a military alliance and then proceeded to attack the Qidan simultaneously from north and south.[10] By 1122 the Qidan emperor had to flee his capital, and his territory was partitioned between the Song and the Jin. The Jin commanders had observed the incompetence of the Song armies and generals during the campaigns against the Qidan, and in 1125 the Jin launched a surprise assault against their former allies, during which they took the Song capital of Kaifeng and captured the emperor Huizong and his son Qinzong, to whom Huizong had just abdicated his throne, along with many other members of the imperial family, in effect terminating the Northern Song dynasty.[11]

The Jin quickly occupied the remainder of north China and set up a Chinese official as a puppet emperor, but in the meantime the ninth son of Huizong, known in history as the emperor Gaozong 高宗 (reg. 1127–1163), had ascended the imperial throne at Nanjing, inaugurating the

Southern Song dynasty (1127–1280).[12] The Jin Tartars did not let Gaozong rest easily and soon drove him from Nanjing into the south of China until at one point he was forced to take refuge with his navy off the Chinese coast.[13] Just when it seemed that a foreign power was to conquer all of China for the first time, the Southern Song dynasty was rescued by the brilliant campaigns of a number of new military leaders, the most renowned of whom was Yue Fei 岳飛 (1003–1141), who repelled the enemy assaults in 1133 and 1134, until in 1135 the now confident Song army was in a position to recover all of north China from the Jin.[14]

Gaozong began to have doubts about the wisdom of such a policy, for he had fallen under the influence of the prime minister Qin Gui 秦檜 (1090–1155), who advised the immediate signing of a peace treaty with the Jin. Historians are divided over Gaozong's motives for restraining his generals at this critical juncture in Chinese history, but it is conceivable that in addition to being wary about a possible defeat at the hands of the enemy, Gaozong did not desire a complete victory over the Jin, for it would have resulted in the return of his father Huizong and his elder brother Qinzong, necessitating his own descent from the throne.[15]

Nonetheless, Gaozong did need his new generals for a while, because the government was plagued by widespread banditry in the south, and the generals were commanded to suppress all local rebellions. These mopping-up operations in the south were so successful that in 1140 Yue Fei initiated a general counterattack against the Jin, defeating one enemy army after another until he bivouacked within range of the Northern Song dynasty's old capital city, Kaifeng, in preparation for the final assault against the enemy. Yet in the same year Qin Gui ordered Yue Fei to abandon his campaign, and in 1141 Yue was summoned back to the Southern Song capital, where he was murdered at Qin Gui's instigation.[16] In the same year Qin Gui encouraged Gaozong to submit to one of the most demeaning treaties in Chinese history, requiring the Song government to pay a huge indemnity to the Jin every year and recognize the Jin state as its superior.[17] During the fifteen odd years of Qin Gui's control of the Southern Song government, most of the other generals who had fought alongside Yue Fei were eliminated, and the scholar officials favoring war against the Jin were exiled from court and removed from office.

The area around Fan Chengda's birthplace was devastated in the warfare between the Southern Song and Jin dynasties, and Fan's family must have suffered considerable hardship during the first years of the dynasty.[18] Nonetheless, events closer to home probably had an even deeper impression on Fan Chengda's youth, for in the year 1143, when Fan was seventeen years old, his father passed away, and shortly afterward his mother (surnamed Cai 蔡) followed her husband in death.[19] Fan had been a precocious child, able to recognize Chinese characters on the painted screens in his nursery shortly after he was one year old, and he had begun his formal education at the age of four, reading widely in Chinese history and the classics by eleven and composing classical poetry with fluency at thirteen,[20] but after the death of his parents, he abandoned all plans for an official career and busied himself with managing the family's remaining property, supervising the education of his two younger brothers, and finding suitable husbands for his two sisters.[21] At the same time, he pursued his own studies at the Jianyan Monastery 薦嚴寺 in Kunshan 崑山 (between modern Suzhou and Shanghai), where he may have had his first contact with the Buddhist faith that inspired much of his finest poetry and gave him much solace during the prolonged illnesses he suffered as a young man and later in life.[22]

Shortly before his parents' death, Fan married a certain Miss Wei 魏, niece of Wei Liang-chen 魏良臣 (metropolitan graduate in 1121), who was a prominent official under the emperor Gaozong and who highly appreciated Fan Chengda's literary talents.[23] Although the full name of Fan's wife is not known, the marriage, which produced two sons and two daughters, seems to have been a happy one, for his wife usually traveled with Fan during his long journeys on official business, and Fan's poetry does not mention affairs with courtesans, a normal and accepted practice for the elite of his time.[24]

Although he may have wished otherwise, a young man with Fan Chengda's talents could hardly have been expected to live in retirement for the rest of his life, and after a friend of the family, Wang Bao 王葆 (1098–1167), who himself led a distinguished official career,[25] reminded Fan of his father's wishes for his son's advancement in the civil service, Fan submitted himself to Wang's tutelage and finally ended his long isolation by obtaining the degree of metropolitan graduate in 1154 at the age of twenty-eight.[26]

The years of study that prepared the way for Fan's success in the civil service examinations were critical for the development of his poetry, too. As we shall see later, much of Fan's earliest verse was modeled on the work of Tang (618–907) dynasty and even more ancient authors, whose creations he undoubtedly read with great care during his years of relative inactivity at home. Although such imitation enabled him to master the poetic techniques that he utilized so brilliantly in later years, the travels that Fan undertook to attend preliminary examinations probably had an equal influence on the development of his poetry. Since Fan resembled many other Chinese intellectuals in his aversion to leaving his native village to pursue a political career, the unwelcome travels that his participation in these examinations necessitated increased his awareness of the contradictions between material success and the spiritual well-being he had cultivated up to this time, as can be seen from the following poem written before 1153:

On the road to Nanxu[27]

I despise these travels, so contrary to my heart's desires:
Again I speed on a lone sailboat that cleaves the waves in its flight.
I strain eyes to espy Wu's peaks behind the roiling clouds;
The moon that bobs on Chu's River[28] chills my traveling robe.
My long song is more mournful than the dripping of tears;
A short-lived dream rushes me back home in a daze.
If I only had a plot of land and a gate I could shut,
I wouldn't exchange a hermit's hut for this bamboo boat![29]

Of course, many earlier poets had written on the same theme, and although one may suspect the sincerity of authors who, nonetheless, strove to pass the examinations and then rise to high office, Fan Chengda seems to have had a real antipathy for public service, an attitude that would seem to account for the small role his public life plays in most of his poetry, in contrast to such earlier Song authors as Su Shi (1037–1101) 蘇軾 or Huang Tingjian (1045–1105) 黃庭堅, not to speak of the favorite Tang dynasty poet during Song times, Du Fu (712–770) 杜甫, most of whose poems can be related to his political career in one way or another. In Fan's case, one feels that if he had not been pressured by Wang Bao and economic necessity, he probably would have been satisfied to remain at home and continue his literary activities and Buddhist studies without interruption.

However, Fan's early travels had another influence upon his development as a poet, which was even more important than increasing his awareness of the hardships of official life:

Walking through the fields at Tang Village on an exquisite sunny day

The hot sun bakes the flourishing plum trees,
Whose dense perfume assails my horse's halter.
Hues of springtide are brewed from clouds and mist,
Calming and freeing both mind and eye.
The willows' brows are brushed with emerald;
Green eyes of the mulberries[30] remain unopened.
This journey I undertake is on no account vulgar –
Just ahead the road climbs atop eight thousand mountains![31]

This time Fan's journey is not an occasion for a complaint about the frustrations of the scholar's life, and this poem demonstrates how Fan Chengda became ever more sensitive to the beauties of the Chinese countryside through his early travels. As we shall see, much of Fan Chengda's greatest nature poetry was directly inspired by the journeys he had to undertake on the public service that he found so onerous.

Early official career

Fan Chengda's official career commenced in 1155 when he was appointed administrator of revenue (*sihucanjun*) for Huizhou 徽州 (Xin'an 新安) in modern Anhui Province, a minor local post, which he assumed the following year, leaving his native place for the first extended period in his life.[32] Fan's talents went unrecognized by his superiors for a long time, and the poetry that he wrote in Huizhou is replete with grumbling over his irksome life there. In a work addressed to a certain Tang Wenbo 湯文伯, who was contemplating retirement from public service, Fan wrote, "Racing along official life's road, one break one's arm easily / A government office anywhere is a citadel of sorrow."[33] Fan summarized his attitude toward his career and his superiors in Huizhou in the following:

After I return from the office at night I use the same rhyme for this poem, which I present to Ziwen

Home from mounds of paperwork, I unsaddle my horse:
I, too, should neigh like a charger released from its reins!
The curled, antique script of my censer's smoke rises straight in windless air;[34]
The moon hangs on a branch in my courtyard, its rays chilling the dew.
I idly muse about the fairy magpies that fill the Milky Way's river,[35]
And peacefully count fireflies that flutter around my well's railing.
Tomorrow morning I must drive myself back to the office,
And force a free-spirited egret to befriend mighty red phoenixes![36]

Finally, only after three prefects had governed Huizhou did the "free-spirited egret" Fan Chengda find a patron among the class of "mighty red phoenixes" in the person of Hong Gua 洪适 (1117–1184), who was appointed prefect of Huizhou in 1159. Fan was particularly fortunate to have been discovered by a man with Hong Gua's background, for not only had Hong occupied important positions in the central government, but he was also a noted literary figure of the age, one of the so-called Three Hong, who also included his two brothers Hong Zun 洪遵 (1120–1174) and Hong Mai 洪邁 (1123–1202).[37] Hong Gua took particular pains in developing his subordinates' administrative skills, and whenever he handed legal documents over to Fan, he always asked Fan how many people were involved and what their names were. Unlike the two previous prefects, Hong did not remain aloof from the lower officials and spent much time with Fan discussing ancient history and current affairs and encouraging him to advance in his political career. It is impossible to determine what Hong thought of Fan's early poetry, but he must have been impressed by Fan Chengda's administrative ability, for he was largely responsible for Fan being granted the title gentleman for attendance (*congshi lang*) in 1160.[38]

Fan Chengda's term of office in Huizhou was important for more than the patronage he received from Hong Gua, because is spite of his many complaints about life there, Fan's poetry underwent a major transformation in Huizhou. The social conventions of the age dictated that Fan had to exchange poetry with both his equals and superiors, and although before Hong Gua arrived on the scene no major literary figure resided in Huizhou, the necessity to conform with the prevailing style of poetry in his social verse ended Fan's relative isolation from contemporary literature, with an incalculable effect on the poetry he wrote from this time on. Although we shall see that many of the characteristics of Fan's mature poetry were already developing before he arrived in Huizhou, his literary relations with other officials helped to consolidate his earlier literary achievements and resulted in the creation of a poetic style that he cultivated with few major changes for the rest of his life.[39]

In the year 1160 Fan returned to his native village, since his term in the prefectural government had expired, but here he encountered Hong Zun, Hong Gua's brother, who had been appointed prefect of the area. Fan's stay at home was to be brief this time, because through the Hong brothers' influence, he was appointed to the Revenue Section of Lin'an (*Lin'an hucao*) in 1162, his first post in the capital city of Hangzhou (at that time called Lin'an 臨安).[40] Fan Chengda's poetry is mute about urban life in what was probably the most populous and cosmopolitan city in the world at the time, but it tells us about the many new friends he made in Hangzhou among whom was Hong Mai, another of the Hong brothers. Fan Chengda's exposure to the court in Hangzhou certainly influenced his attitude toward the politics of the age, and when Hong Mai was dispatched on a diplomatic mission to the Jin in the fourth month of the same year, Fan Chengda presented Hong poems that suggest that Fan was already coming under the influence of those officials who were dissatisfied with the Song government's subservience to the Jin.[41]

Although Hong Mai's mission to the Jin was singularly unsuccessful in promoting the Song cause, it took place at a time when Song-Jin relations had just passed through a crisis and were about to take an even more dramatic turn for the worse. In 1161, while Fan Chengda was residing at home, the Jin attacked Song forces stationed on the border and suffered an unexpectedly disastrous defeat at the hands of the Song army at Caishi 采石.[42] Two months after Hong Mai's mission to the north, the emperor Gaozong abdicated to his crown prince, the emperor Xiaozong 孝宗 (reg. 1163–1190), who in the following year encouraged a debate among court officials about the advisability of holding to the peace agreement with the Jin,[43] with the result that the war party came back into favor, and Yue Fei's old comrade, the general Zhang Jun 張俊 (1096–1164), was summoned to command a counterattack against the enemy.[44] The Song general, Li Xianzhong 李獻忠 (1109–1177), was successful in the first few encounters with the Jin, but in the end, conflicts between Li and another general led to disarray among the Song armies, and in the fifth month of 1163 the Song forces were annihilated at the Battle of Fuli 符離.[45] Zhang Jun was demoted the next year, and the emperor made Tang Situi 湯思退, an adherent of Qin Gui's pacifistic policies, prime minister, signaling an end to any ambitions for reconquering the north.[46] The defeat of the Song army did not precipitate a violent purge of the war party in the capital along the lines of what had occurred after the murder of Yue Fei during Gaozong's reign, but the peace the Song government signed in 1165 with the Jin brought an end to major hostilities between the two states for the next forty some years.

Although the poems Fan Chengda addressed to Hong Mai suggest that he was sympathetic to the war party, Fan's official career was not stymied by the sudden shifts in Song foreign policy during these years, and he rose gradually through the central government bureaucracy to assistant editorial director (*zhuzuo zuolang*, rank 8a), in which position he was responsible for compiling the state-issued calendar, among other duties, until in 1166 he was promoted to vice-director of the Ministry of Personnel (*libu yuanwai lang*, rank 6b), the first position of real authority he was offered. However, enemies at court attacked this promotion as irregular, because of his sudden rise in rank from 8a to 6b, and, realizing the futility of defending himself, Fan Chengda requested that he be relieved of official duties, after which he returned home again.[47] It is also quite possible that Fan's problems were related to the fall from favor of his mentor Hong Gua, who had been serving as prime minister at the time.[48]

However, Fan Chengda was probably relieved to be rid of his time-consuming duties as a central government official, which had made it difficult for him to pursue his literary activities. Although Fan did write some good poetry during the four years of his service in Hangzhou, both the quantity and quality of his verse suffered in comparison with other periods of his life. Most of the poetry composed at Hangzhou is stiff and formal and consists largely of occasional pieces he was obliged to write in response to fellow officials or superiors, including an unusually large number of funeral eulogies.

Moreover, Fan's removal from the central government did not signify that he had actually fallen from imperial favor, because in the year 1167 he was appointed prefect of Chuzhou 處州 (Lishui 麗水 of modern Zhejiang Province). Fan's biographers assure us that he was a model prefect, initiating irrigation and flood-control projects, limiting the exploitation of the people by subordinate officials and clerks, and lessening the tax burden of the prefecture, and although one should take account of the usual tendency to praise famous intellectuals for their devotion to the people, it is quite clear from Fan's poetry on rural themes that he was always deeply concerned with the welfare of the lower classes in society (see the discussion of this question at the end of Chapter 6).[49]

Mission to the north

In the year 1169 Fan was once again summoned back to the capital, and when he reported to the emperor about the reforms he had initiated in Chuzhou, Xiaozong was so pleased that he ordered similar reforms to be carried out throughout the empire. Fan also enjoyed the patronage of the prime minister Chen Junqing 陳俊卿 (1113–1186), who had him promoted to hold three positions concurrently, imperial diarist (*qiju sheren*), expositor-in-waiting (*shijiang*), and junior compiler in the Historiography Institute (*guoshih yuan bianxiu guan*). Although none of these positions involved any real power, Fan had enough influence in court to promote the elimination of certain inhumane punishments for criminals and the further lightening of the tax burden for the area where he had served in Zhejiang.[50]

The most famous event in Fan Chengda's official career took place in the year 1170, when he was appointed grand academician of the Hall for Aid in Governance (*zizheng dian daxueshi*) to head a delegation to the capital of the Jin dynasty. Although the emperor had no desire to engage the Jin armies in battle again, he was particularly keen on having the Jin return the site of the Northern Song imperial tombs at Gongxian 鞏縣 (modern Henan province) to Song control because of the desecration of his ancestors' tombs after the Jin conquest,[51] and he also hoped to eliminate the demeaning ritual in which the Song emperor had to stand in front of the Jin ambassadors when receiving communications from their emperor.[52]

There was considerable dissension in the court about the wisdom of pressing the Jin for such alterations in the status quo, and even those officials who favored change were not unanimous about how the delegation should approach the Jin government. One of the prime ministers, Yu Yunwen 虞允文 (1110–1154), supported a hard line against the Jin, but the other prime minister, Fan Chengda's patron Chen Junqing, feared the possible consequences and resigned from the government,[53] while Li Tao 李燾 (1115–1184), who had originally been appointed to head the mission, quit out of fear for his life.[54]

Before Fan's departure, the emperor summoned him to the court and questioned him about the controversy and concerns that his mission had aroused among the court officials, upon which Fan is said to have answered, "Sending me as an ambassador for no specific purpose [such as conveying birthday or New Year's greetings to the Jin emperor] may appear a provocation to warfare, and if I am not killed, I may be taken prisoner, but I have already designated an heir and put my family affairs in order in case I cannot return, and my mind is at peace." Xiaozong is said to have been so moved by Fan's resolution that he asked, "I am not sending troops to break the peace treaty, so why would they kill you? It is, of course, possible that, if detained as a prisoner, you might have to undergo the hardship of 'feeding on snow and felt,' but if you have any reservations, state them clearly, for I would not wrong you."[55] Fan obviously did not have any reservations, because in the sixth month of that year he set out from the capital.

Fan Chengda was embarking upon a very dangerous mission, indeed, because, as a result of policy disagreements in the court, the official documents he was carrying referred only to the Song petition for the return of the imperial tombs and not to the emperor's request for a change in the protocol regarding his reception of Jin ambassadors. Fan Chengda was supposed to make this request in a personal memorial he would present upon arriving at the Jin court, a practice completely contrary to Jin laws, which forbade any private memorials from the Song ambassadors.[56]

After arriving in the Jin palace, Fan Chengda at first acted in accordance with the accepted regulations and presented the documents from the Song court, but then he suddenly brought out his private memorial and attempted to submit it to the Jin emperor, who was startled by Fan's audacity and angrily reminded Fan that he was in breach of diplomatic protocol. In spite of the tense situation, Fan Chengda refused to back down and said: "If I cannot submit my memorial, I must die upon my return home, so I might as well die here!" The Jin emperor attempted to rise and leave the audience hall, but his courtiers held him back, whereupon he shouted, "Make him bow to me and then force him to leave!" Fan Chengda continued to kneel, and when the Jin emperor asked him, "Why don't you bow?" Fan replied: "If I am able to submit my memorial, I will bow to you a hundred times in thanks as I leave the audience hall." The Jin crown prince wanted to kill Fan on the spot, but his elder brother held him in check, and in the end the Jin emperor was forced to receive Fan's memorial. Fan's courage deeply impressed the Jin emperor, who is supposed to have said that Fan could serve as a model to "inspire the officials of both countries [Jin and Song]," and although the next Jin embassy to the Song court delivered a note of protest, the members of the Jin delegation privately praised Fan Chengda's willingness to die for his sovereign.[57]

Contrary to what one would expect, Fan Chengda's mission to the Jin also bore important literary fruit, for during his journey to and from the Jin court, Fan wrote a series of seventy-two heptasyllabic quatrains, which are generally considered his finest works on a political theme, composed in a style quite different from his earlier verse (see the discussion of these works in Chapter 7). In addition, after his return to Hangzhou, Fan composed the *Lanpeilu* (Record of holding the reins), a detailed prose account of his experiences at the Jin court, which is a useful historical source and one of the more interesting travel diaries written during the Southern Song dynasty.[58]

Fan's bravery won the admiration of the emperor Xiaozong, and after his return to Hangzhou, Fan was promoted to drafter in the Secretariat (*zhongshu sheren*), although he aroused the ire of high court officials by revealing that during his stay in the Jin capital he had learned that the enemy knew about a supposedly secret treaty between the Song government and the Jin's adversary, the Tanguts.[59]

The emperor, too, soon discovered that Fan's audacity could embarrass him just as well as it could the Jin emperor. When in the year 1171 Xiaozong decided to appoint an in-law, Zhang Yue 張說, notary of the Bureau of Military Affairs (*qianshu shumi yuanshi*), an influential military position, no one in the court dared to voice open opposition in spite of general dissatisfaction with Zhang's qualifications. Upon receipt of the instructions to draft the document for Zhang's appointment, Fan ignored the imperial command and returned the appointment documents to the emperor, remonstrating with him not to appoint Zhang Yue. Although the emperor temporarily withdrew Zhang's appointment and urged Fan Chengda to remain in the central government, Fan realized that his position at court was untenable and requested to be relieved of his official duties. He was promptly appointed military commissioner for Guangxi (*Guangxi jinglue anfu shi*), a post that would make use of his courage and organization talents but keep him far from the capital city.[60]

Guilin and Sichuan

Fan Chengda did not immediately travel to his new post in Guilin but first returned to his home near Suzhou and occupied himself with the construction of a villa at Shihu 石湖 (Stone Lake). There he wrote verse and enjoyed himself throughout the whole of 1172, and there the poet Zhou Bida 周必大 (1126–1204) came to visit him for an extended period, during which Zhou wrote enthusiastically about the gardens Fan had laid out around his villa.[61] Much of Fan Chengda's greatest poetry was inspired by his residence at Stone Lake and the surrounding countryside, and it must have been with great reluctance that he finally set off for his new post in Guilin on the seventh of the twelfth month.

The journey to Guilin was long and arduous, and Fan Chengda took his time, stopping in Huzhou 湖州, Yanzhou 嚴州, and Wuzhou 婺州, not arriving in Guilin until the tenth of the third month. Although he composed quite a number of poems about the famous beauty spots he visited on the way to Guilin, the quality of the poetry written during this period is rather disappointing, particularly after the high level his verse had attained during his embassy to the Jin. In general, one notices that Fan frequently falls back on the pre-Song clichés of travel poetry (for example, a poem written when he entered Liling in Hunan concludes with a worn-out reference to the cry of the partridge (*zhegu*), a traditional symbol of homesickness)[62] and that many of the finer descriptive passages in the poems are spoiled by a tendency to moralize.[63] In addition, many of Fan's longer ancient-style poems (*gushi*) suffer from disorganization and a lack of focus (see discussion in Chapter 5).[64] One is tempted to ascribe this decline in the vitality of Fan Chengda's poetry to disappointment over his failed career in the central government, but the journey to Guilin did inspire one of the better-known travel diaries of Southern Song times, the *Canluan lu* (Record of mounting a phoenix),[65] as well as a monograph on south China (not completed until 1175), entitled *Guihai yuheng zhi*, in which Fan wrote on such diverse topics as the minerals, animals, birds, and non-Han tribes of the area around Guilin.[66]

After arriving in Guilin, Fan Chengda attempted to improve the lot of the people of the Guangxi region, which although famous as one of the great beauty spots of China was at the same time one of the most economically backward areas of the empire. When he learned that circuit supervisors had been appropriating the salt tax money of Guangxi and that the local officials had been burdening the people with additional taxes to make up for the lost revenue, he immediately corrected the situation.[67] Fan also dealt firmly with the incursions of various non-Chinese tribes and the banditry that was endemic to Guilin, in addition to carrying out various water conservancy projects.[68]

In spite of his endeavors on behalf of the people, the general impression that one receives from the unusually small quantity of poetry Fan wrote during his two years in Guilin is that he felt isolated from his relatives and friends and depressed over his inability to do anything about China's subservience to the Jin. One can obtain some idea of Fan Chengda's frame of mind during his stay in Guilin from the following poem:

At dawn I go out north of the city

These people live crowded in deep rural alleys,
Concealed behind the verdant trees' dense shade.
They are mountain folk and never rise early,
Shutting their gates tight like fugitives from justice.
Moulting cicadas sob beneath the thick dew;
Starving swallows soar on a paltry breeze,
A trickle of water oozes through a new irrigation channel;
While a stream roars wildly over a broken dike.
Infertile soil plagues these frontier folk,
Nor are they willing to work with any diligence.
They only go through the motions of farming –
Their late rice is sparse as a water buffalo's hairs.
The morning sky brightens for no purpose at all,
And swims around me, soaking my bow and sword.
My official responsibility is to encourage agriculture,[69]
But I can only face the wind and scratch my head.[70]

This poem almost suffocates the reader by entrapping the normally energetic peasants of Fan's verse in a stifling rural atmosphere that even thwarts the cicadas and swallows from pursuing their natural activities and dooms Fan's efforts to improve the people's livelihood. The stream, which is on the verge of destroying the dike necessary for the people's welfare, is the only active object that one detects in this rural scene. Such poetry is far removed from the verse of moral outrage composed at the time of Fan's embassy to the Jin or the tranquil landscape poems of the period before his entry into official service, and the gloom that underlies it may have been responsible for the failure of Fan's creative vitality to revive after his arrival in Guilin in spite of the magnificent scenery around him.

In the tenth month of 1174, Fan was appointed military commissioner of Sichuan (*Sichuan zhizhishi*), and since his assumption of this post required another arduous journey, he at first asked for permission to turn it down, but this was not granted. Therefore, on the eighth of the second month Fan took leave of his friends in Guilin and traveled by boat through modern Hunan Province via Hengyang and Changsha across Lake Dongting and from there up the perilous Yangzi Gorges to his destination in Sichuan, the city of Chengdu.[71] Although the journey was the most perilous he had undertaken in his life, he was following in the footsteps of other great Chinese poets such as Li Bai 李白 and Du Fu and traveling through some of the most spectacular landscapes in China. As we shall discover in our discussion of his nature poetry, Fan's experiences on the way to Sichuan inspired some of his most outstanding nature verse (see the discussion of these works in Chapter 5), for the depression of Fan's Guilin period vanished completely, and the poems that he wrote during his journey through the Yangzi Gorges throb with an energy rare in his earlier works.

The position that Fan occupied in Sichuan was the most powerful that he had ever held in his life, and his friends were duly impressed by the advancement of his fortunes. A congratulatory letter from Wu Jing 吳儆 commented that Fan had "started as a supporting official and now had become a prefectual governor."[72] Another friend, Lin Guangchao 林光朝 (1114–1178), whom Fan had gotten to know well while he was serving in Guilin, wrote that Fan now "controlled all of Sichuan with undivided authority, so completely does the emperor rely on him."[73] Nor did Fan Chengda disappoint the expectations of either the emperor or his friends after his arrival in Chengdu, for in addition to lightening the burden of the poorer classes through a reduction of taxes on wine and rice, he strove to bolster the defenses of the critical frontier area of Sichuan by sending out military expeditions against non-Chinese tribes who had been harassing the border, building new fortifications, and training a special combat force of five thousand young men.[74]

However, Fan Chengda's stay in Sichuan is most renowned in the annals of Chinese culture for his close association with his great contemporary, the poet Lu You 陸游 (1125–1210). Fan and Lu seem to have met for the first time in 1163 when they were both serving in the central government in Hangzhou, immediately appreciating each other's literary talents and discovering that they shared similar political views, which included dissatisfaction with the government's soft policy toward the Jin. Their association in Hangzhou was brief, however, because Lu was soon appointed to a local position, but the two poets met once more in 1170 at Zhenjiang's famous Jinshan Monastery, when Lu You was on his way to take up a post in Kuizhou 夔州 (modern Sichuan) and Fan was embarking on his fateful mission to the Jin.[75]

As we have seen, the years between Fan's return from the Jin court and his journey to Sichuan represent a period of relative stagnation in his literary production. The same years constituted a particularly fertile period for Lu You, who during his service in the Hanzhong frontier area had firsthand experience of the struggle against the Jin, which inspired some of his most renowned verse on patriotism,[76] a theme that Fan Chengda practically abandoned after his return from his mission to the Jin. We have already noted how Fan Chengda's journey to Sichuan rekindled his own poetic creativity, and Lu You had also been greatly stimulated by his travels through the Yangzi Gorges, producing some of his most outstanding nature poetry and one of the finest travel diaries of the Southern Song period, the *Rushuji* (Record of a journey into Sichuan).[77]

One of the more remarkable features of the relationship between Fan Chengda and Lu You in Sichuan was the way in which Fan, now one of the most powerful officials outside the imperial court, treated Lu, who was only Fan's consultant (*canyiyuan*), as a complete equal, freely discussing military and political affairs with him, visiting famous sites in his company, and, of course, exchanging poetry with him. Lu's close friendship with Fan caused him to form a high opinion of Fan Chengda's knowledge of political and military affairs, especially in relation to the Jin, and Lu wrote that "after Fan returned from his mission to the enemy, he was able to describe all the rituals, laws, political organization, architecture, cities, and institutions of their country . . . with as much detail as if he were speaking of the affairs of his own nation, knowing everything in greater detail than the elders and important figures of the enemy."[78] According to Lu, Fan put his political knowledge to practical use in Sichuan, and "as soon as he arrived, Fan set clear standards, increased trust in government regulations, lowered interest rates, benefited agriculture, selected commanders, and manufactured weapons, so that within a few months his prestige overawed the frontier areas, and we had a bumper harvest."[79]

Of course, for both men the most important aspect of their relation was literary, and although only three poems by Lu You to Fan Chengda survive in Lu's collected works, Lu gives an interesting account of Fan's literary activities in Sichuan in a preface that Fan asked him to write for a collection of Fan's poems that Lu printed there:

Fan's subordinates had less and less work to do [presumably because he solved all the political problems so quickly!], and from time to time he accompanied them and other guests from the four quarters of the world to drink wine and write poetry. Fan had already been one of the most famous poets of his age for some time, so before the ink of his poems was dry on the paper, thousands of gentlemen and ladies were already reciting his works, setting them to music, or inscribing them on silk screens and fans, which they presented to one another, something never witnessed since the post of prefect was established in Sichuan. Someone said to me, "When Fan Chengda entered Sichuan from Guilin, he wrote over a hundred poems in between his journeys by wagon and on horseback. These poems, which he entitled *A Small Collection Written on a Journey West*, are especially outstanding, and the people of Sichuan have not had a chance to read them, so why not ask him to publish them?" I asked Fan several times, but he would not allow it, and only after a year was I finally able to do it. Then I printed the poems for him, and he asked me to write this preface.[80]

Although Lu's preface possibly exaggerates the popular interest in Fan's poetry, it provides an interesting view of literary life in Southern Song dynasty Sichuan and shows the close relationship that Lu had formed with Fan during this period in their lives.

Nonetheless, one could hardly imagine two more different poets than Fan Chengda and Lu You, reacting to Sichuan in completely different ways in spite of their intimate friendship. The parting poem that Lu You wrote to Fan when he left Sichuan begins: "I've not been addicted to wine all my life because I love its flavor so much, / But because, when I'm drunk, I can forget my myriad worries. / When the guests leave, and I sober up, I'm alone in my grief, / Brushing away tears of mourning for my country, as I lie in bed" and concludes: "I am relying on you to convey my many concerns [to the emperor], / So he can quicky clean the barbarians' filth from our holy soil!"[81] Although hardly one of Lu You's most distinguished works from his Sichuan period, this poem touches on two of the most important themes Lu developed during these years, namely, his anxiety over the failure of the Song government to recover north China from the Jin and his pursuit of a wild, unrestrained life style, which resulted in his being removed from office in 1176.[82]

During the same period, Fan's Buddhist faith assumed an ever greater role in his life. Although the poetry written from his mission to the Jin until his departure from Guilin mentions Buddhism much less frequently than his earlier verse, his faith seems to have been reawakened by his journey through the sublime landscapes of the Yangzi Gorges and the pilgrimage he undertook in 1177 to Mount Emei, the holy mountain of Samântabhadra (see the discussion of Fan's Buddhist poetry in Chapter 4). Thus, although Fan's Yangzi Gorges poetry is just as powerful as anything that Lu You wrote during the same period, after Fan's arrival in Chengdu, his poetry becomes suffused with a tranquil acceptance of life's vicissitudes that continued from that time until his death.

Later official career and retirement

In spite of the spiritual revival Fan Chengda underwent in Sichuan, it is quite possible that he still had his eye on a prestigious post in the central government, because during his stay in Chengdu he sent up a number of memorials to the emperor discussing the area's military and political problems.[83] In 1177, however, Fan's always frail health took a turn for the worse, and he requested retirement, departing from Chengdu on the twenty-ninth of the fifth month to return home to his villa at Stone Lake. Although the poetry that he composed on his descent of the Yangzi is not as remarkable as his earlier verse, this deficiency is made up by the travel diary he kept, the *Wuchuan lu* (Record of a boat from Wu), which contains some of the finest descriptive prose that Fan ever wrote and deserves a place beside the travel diary by Lu You already mentioned.[84]

In spite of his bad health, Fan submitted at least one more memorial on Sichuan military affairs to the emperor, and after his health had improved, Fan returned to the capital in the eleventh month of 1177 and was promoted to provisional minister of the Ministry of Rites (*quan libu shangshu*).[85] However, the political situation had deteriorated since Fan had left the capital in 1171. In spite of Fan Chengda's earlier objections, Xiaozong's in-law, Zhang Yue, had been appointed to a high post in the military administration, and many of the more distinguished officials such as Yu Yunwen had been eased from their posts in the administration and replaced by men of much lower caliber. Therefore, it is not surprising that Fan Chengda's tenure in Hangzhou was brief; almost as soon as he arrived there, court censors attacked him, and in the ninth month he was obliged to retire from his post.[86]

In the meantime, the post of Prefect of Wuzhou had been offered to Fan, and Xiaozong had sent an emissary to Fan's home with valuable gifts, but throughout the rest of 1178 and 1179, Fan remained at home, taking a trip with his brother Chengxiang 成象 and others to Lake Tai in the winter of 1178, writing almost continuously and welcoming his poet friend Yang Wanli 楊萬里 as a guest during 1179.

Fan had probably met Yang for the first time when they both passed the metropolitan graduate examination in 1154, and, since they considered themselves "classmates," they exchanged poetry fairly regularly (eight poems addressed to Yang are extant in Fan's collected works).[87] In 1178 they renewed their friendship when Fan Chengda passed through

Jingxi 荊溪 on his way back from Sichuan, and although Fan did not spend as much time with Yang as he did with Lu You, there are many stylistic similarities between the two authors, and in the first month of 1178, only six or seven months before Fan visited Yang in Jingxi, Yang had experienced a poetic enlightenment, which resulted in his rejection of Tang and Song poetic masters for the creation of his own individual style.[88] Since the verse the two poets exchanged is rather formal and not typical of their finest work, it is difficult to generalize about the exact ways in which Fan influenced Yang, but it is highly probable that Yang Wanli, who had just discovered his own style at the age of fifty, learned much from the other creations of his classmate that had been printed or were circulating in manuscript. Shortly before his death, Fan Chengda asked his sons to ask Yang Wanli to compose the preface to his collected works, stating that "Yang Wanli [Chengzai] of Jiangxi is my only true friend among my literary acquaintances in the entire world,"[89] and the preface Yang wrote attests to the high esteem in which he held Fan Chengda's works, even after one discounts the inevitable exaggerations of such writing.[90]

Fan Chengda did not accept any new positions until the death of Prince Wei 魏 created a vacancy for the prefect of Mingzhou 明州 (modern Ningbo in Zhejiang province), which Fan then filled in the third month of 1180. Prince Wei had used the port of Mingzhou as a center for importing foreign goods to the imperial court as "tribute," but Fan Chengda did not wish to continue this practice, first of all, as he said, because he did not think it proper that a commoner such as himself should continue a practice begun by an imperial prince, but, more probably, because of the burden it imposed upon the local people. In addition to eliminating this tribute to the court, he asked that the large amount of money diverted for Prince Wei's personal use in Mingzhou be utilized to reduce the local taxes.[91]

In 1181 Fan Chengda was appointed military commissioner of Jiangnan East Circuit (*Jiangnan donglu anfushi*), approximately equivalent to a provincial governor in later times, in which post he was based at Nanjing. During a short trip Fan took to the capital, the emperor honored the poet by presenting him a piece of silk inscribed in the imperial calligraphy with the words "Stone Lake," a gift that Fan treasured for the rest of his life, carving the characters on a rock at his villa.[92] That year, however, Fan was very busy in Nanjing, because a severe famine broke out, and in typical fashion he ordered that military supplies be released to the victims. There were also problems with banditry, and throughout the next year he supervised military operations against the offenders.[93]

The heavy work load at Nanjing soon took its toll, and in the summer of 1183 Fan's health worsened. After making five requests to be released from his duties, he was granted permission to return to Stone Lake. He did not leave his home for official reasons except for one brief period in 1189, when he was appointed prefect of Fuzhou by the new emperor Guangzong 光宗 (reg. 1190–1195), a post he had to refuse after suffering severe abdominal pains.[94]

The years that remained to Fan were frequently clouded by serious illness, but he found much comfort in his Buddhist faith and was almost continually engaged in literary activities, gathering materials for his *Wujun zhi* (Monograph on the prefecture of Wu), one of the most thoroughly researched and elegantly written local gazetteers from the Song dynasty (first printed long after Fan's death in 1229) and composing one of the most celebrated poetic sequences of Chinese literature, *Impromptu Verses on the Four Seasons of the Countryside*, in 1186, the work that many critics view as the crowning achievement of Fan Chengda's poetic career (see the discussion of these poems in Chapter 6).[95]

In addition to writing almost continuously, Fan spent much time entertaining friends that came to visit him at his villa, the most famous of whom among connoisseurs of Chinese literature is certainly the *ci* poet Jiang Kui 姜夔 (1155–1221), who visited Fan in 1187 and again in 1191 for six months. In 1187, Jiang had traveled to Hangzhou, where he was introduced to Yang Wanli, who entrusted him with some of his poems to take to Fan Chengda. Although Fan had served as a high official and was twenty-nine years older than Jiang, he admired Jiang's literary talent so much that he treated him as an equal, exchanging poetry with him and presenting him with a singing girl named Xiaohong 小紅 (Little Russet), who sang Jiang's poetry while he accompanied her on his flute.[96] These visits of Jiang Kui must have been instrumental in stimulating Fan's interest in the *ci* form of poetry, which he had written intermittently through the years, and he had his collection of *ci* poems, *Shihuji* (Collection of Stone Lake) printed in 1192.[97] Although Fan Chengda's *ci* are certainly of minor interest when compared to his *shi*, his accomplishments in this form of verse demonstrate his great flexibility as a writer.

Nor were the last years of Fan Chengda's life lacking in recognition from the authorities, for in 1188 the emperor sent an imperial physician to treat Fan by means of moxibustion and present him cinnabar for alchemical preparations, and later in that year the crown prince presented Fan with the three characters *Shouli tang* 壽櫟堂 (Hall of the long-lived oak) in his own calligraphy.[98] In 1192 Fan was given the title grand academician of the Hall for Aid in Governance (*zizhengdian daxueshi*) and appointed prefect of Taipingzhou, but in the same year Fan's younger daughter died and, distraught with grief, he renounced any further interest in an official position. On the fifth of the ninth month of 1193 (Western calendar, October 1, 1193), Fan himself passed from this world. He was given the usual posthumous honors of an intellectual who had occupied a high position and was buried at his native place with an epitaph written by Zhou Bida.[99] Although Fan Chengda's poems had been circulating in manuscript for years and some of his poems had already been printed, it was left to his children to publish the collection of his verse that he had been editing during the last years of his life.[100] His friend Yang Wanli died two years after Fan, and when Lu You left the world in 1210, one of the most brilliant periods of Chinese poetry drew to a close.[101]

2
The formative period

Early imitative verse

Our biography of Fan Chengda has already touched on the development of his poetry, particularly as it relates to his political career. Before we can attempt to define the mature poetic style of Fan Chengda, which was largely formed by the time he was serving in Huizhou, we must examine the rather complicated path of evolution followed by his pre-Huizhou verse. Our study is greatly hampered by the loss of most of his prose works, in which he presumably discussed his experience as a poet and, perhaps, even the art of poetry in general, a loss not made up by the material in his poems, for, unlike many other Song poets, Fan almost never examines questions of literary theory in his verse.[1] Thus, an investigation of Fan Chengda's early literary development must utilize three kinds of material: Fan Chengda's poems themselves, critical comments about his verse written by his contemporaries and later Chinese critics, and discussions of literary theory by those Southern Song poets who are closest to Fan in style and were known to have been in close association with him throughout his life. The third category of materials must obviously be used with great discretion, because we cannot always assume that Fan Chengda shared the ideas of his friends.

More of Fan Chengda's early poetry survives than that of his two most famous contemporaries, Lu You and Yang Wanli. At the end of Chapter 11 of Fan's complete works, we find twelve juvenilia, written thirty years prior to their rediscovery by Fan, and Fan's inclusion of these rather undistinguished youthful poems along with an explanatory note in his complete works demonstrates that he was not determined to eliminate all of his earlier verse, as Lu You and Yang Wanli were.[2]

Nonetheless, the poetry recorded in the earlier chapters of Fan's complete works suggests that he spent quite a few years searching rather desperately for different models to emulate before he finally succeeded in mastering his craft. The first poem in Chapter 1 of Fan's of works is an outright imitation:

The road is hard

I present you the red-thorned herb that dispelleth sorrow,[3]
The green crabapple's bloom that unites all joy,[4]
The agate dream pillow for fairyland wanderings,
And treasured gauze that drives off cold.
The Milky Way has not yet turned, the moon has not set;
The night drags long as a year and invites springtide carousal.
Only the city remains; where are the men of yore?
If I do not drink this evening, when will I ever know joy?[5]

Anyone whose knowledge of Fan Chengda's poetry is limited to the works included in standard anthologies of Song verse would not recognize this work as his creation, for it is a close imitation of the Period of Division author Bao Zhao's 鮑照 (414–466) series of allegorical ballads (*yuefu*) by the same title.[6] The work's quaintly archaic style is particularly startling, for the reader of Chinese poetry will recall that Li Bai (701–762) was inspired by Bao Zhao's same series of poems to create his even more famous ballads by the same title, prompting one to ask the probably unanswerable question about Fan's motives in imitating the more ancient author Bao Zhao rather than Li Bai himself, who was certainly more popular among Song intellectuals.[7]

But Fan's early interest in the allegorical ballad, an interest that did not entirely disappear later in his life, is not the only surprise in Fan's early imitative verse. For example, Fan imitates Bai Juyi 白居易 (772–846) in seven quatrains, which he entitles "A Continuation [*sic*] of the Song of Everlasting Sorrow," particularly puzzling in that, judging from the later nature poetry that brought Fan fame, one would expect him to imitate practically any poem by Bai other than his highly popular romantic ballad on the tragic love of the Tang emperor Xuanzong 玄宗 (reg. 713–756) for Lady Yang.[8] At first sight, one would not be startled by imitations of Tao Qian's 陶潛 (ca. 376–427) verse among Fan's early poems, in view of Tao's fame as the creator of Chinese bucolic verse, but rather than modeling himself on Tao's better-known poems, Fan chose to imitate a work in the quadrasyllabic form, which was already archaic when Tao wrote it more than seven centuries earlier.[9] Perhaps the most bizarre of these early imitative poems are two works entitled "Song of the Night Banquet" and "Magic Strings," in which Fan is fairly successful at capturing the florid language of the Tang poet Li He 李賀 (790–816) without any hint of Li's famous obsession with death and the supernatural.[10] Almost equally out of line with the normal image of Fan's verse is a long study of Li Bai's ballad poetry, written somewhat later than the poems just mentioned, in which Fan does, in fact, manage to convey some of Li's energy.[11] With the exception of Fan's studies of Wang Jian's verse, which we shall discuss later, these early imitative works leave us with the impression that Fan Chengda was still far from deciding what direction his poetry would follow, and, with the benefit of hindsight, we can say that even when Fan was imitating authors that "should" have had a major influence upon his development, he was usually imitating their work for all of the "wrong" reasons.

Early influence of Chen Yuyi

Although it is difficult to determine exactly how Fan Chengda's imitation of Tang verse influenced him, Fan was not alone among late Northern and early Southern Song authors in turning to the Tang dynasty for inspiration. According to the Japanese scholar Yoshikawa Kôjirô, the most important transitional poet between the Northern and Southern Song, Chen Yuyi 陳與義 (1090–1138), modeled his own work on Tang poetry in an attempt to liberate himself from the so-called Jiangxi school 江西詩派 of Huang Tingjian 黃庭堅, and thus it is hardly surprising that much of Fan Chengda's early poetry resembles that of Chen, who was one of the best known poets when Fan was a young man.[12]

In spite of the many direct imitations of Tang poetry to be found in Fan Chengda's early works, the following is representative of much of the poetry that he wrote in the four or five years immediately preceding his posting in Huizhou:

Early summer (first of two poems)

Early in the morning I leave the city and climb the terraces,
But nothing's left of spring and I might as well go home.
The mulberry branches are stripped clean and the silkworms are aging;
Vegetables' flowers have become pods, but butterflies still come![13]

Although the second line of this poem echoes Huang Tingjian,[14] the avoidance of any difficult allusions immediately sets this work apart from the complex creations of Huang's Jiangxi school, and yet both this poem and its twin (translated on p. 100) display a close resemblance in spirit and style to Chen Yuyi's mature work, which may be typified by the following:

On the road

The rain first stops, then pours down again;
The creek flows straight, then curves away.
The mountain road stretches far into the distance,
And flowers crowd the entire forest.
Two gulls' reflections break the water's surface;
Sprouts of young grass push aside the mud.
The river and land are high, then low;
Men's houses stand – here and there.[15]

All the qualities that Yoshikawa ascribes to Chen Yuyi's verse are present in both this eight-line regulated poem by Chen and the early quatrain by Fan Chengda just quoted. In neither Chen's mature poetry nor Fan's early works do we encounter a world of grand passions or literary bravura, but rather, in the words of Yoshikawa, a "simple lyricism" and "quiet lucidity" reminiscent of Tang poets such as Wang Wei 王維 (701?–761?)[16] and Meng Haoran 孟浩然 (689–740?),[17] among others. According to Yoshikawa, the principal achievement of Chen Yuyi's "new sensitivity" in his descriptions of natural phenomena is an outstanding "success in creating delicate miniatures."[18]

As Yoshikawa has discovered, Chen is particularly skillful at describing changes in nature (Yoshikawa devotes a brief section in his book to Chen's penchant for depicting changes of light), but it would be useful to see exactly how his sensitivity to change contributes to the success of this poem. In the first couplet, Chen describes the change from the pause in the rain to the sudden resumption of the downpour, a transformation paralleled in the second line of the couplet by the river that first runs straight (hence, relatively statically) but then veers unexpectedly off in another direction. In the second couplet, the lines do not echo one another but form a contrast instead; that is, the "motion" of the road that stretches beyond the ken of our vision is in opposition to the brilliant but motionless colors of the flowers. In the third couplet, where the "miniature" quality of the poem reaches its climax, we encounter both comparison and contrast between the two lines, because the movement of the gull's reflections on the water vaguely resembles the "movement" of the grass sprouts, but the bird's movement is obviously more sudden than that of the plants. The fourth couplet returns to the structure of the first couplet with both lines fundamentally parallel again, contrasts being set up within each line between the elevation and lowness of the river and land in the first line, and the houses' "here and there" in the second line. This return to the structure of the first couplet after the modulations of the intervening couplets, with its hint of *aba* structure, successfully closes a poem that otherwise might seem nothing more than a succession of vivid nature images. Yoshikawa is correct when he discusses Chen's new sensitivity to nature, but Chen's poem does not please us just because the author has a great feeling for natural phenomena, but rather because he expresses his sensitivity through skillfully wrought couplets arranged in a clever way.[19]

Parallel couplets are not typical of the quatrain form in which Fan's poem is written, but we notice a similar use of the distinction between motion and rest just as in Chen Yuyi's poem. The ascent of the terrace in the first line contrasts with the proposed return home in the second line, and the weary mulberries, "aging silkworms," and pods on what were once flowers serve as a foil to the butterflies that still manage to exert themselves in spite of the end of the spring season. Although this early work of Fan Chengda is not as skillfully constructed as Chen's more mature work, its delicate, miniature quality is, perhaps, even more striking, for everything is rendered with a detailed lucidity reminiscent of Song dynasty academic paintings of flowers and insects.[20]

In his early poetry Fan Chengda alludes to and echoes Chen Yuyi's verse frequently, and like Chen, Fan was obviously fascinated by the alternatives that Tang poetry provided to Su Shi 蘇軾 and Huang Tingjian (Chen himself stated that in spite of their intense admiration of Du Fu, both Su and Huang had not equaled Du's greatness), and yet in early poems such as the one just translated, Fan had already moved beyond the Tang tradition, assisted at least in part by Chen Yuyi's example.[21] As we shall see later, Fan's skill in describing the subtle changes in nature through cleverly constructed couplets is one of the hallmarks of the most famous poetry of his old age (see discussion in Chapter 6), and Chen's example must have contributed significantly to his development as a poet.

Southern Song poets and Huang Tingjian's Jiangxi school

No Chinese poet beginning to write in the middle of the twelfth century could ignore the influence of Huang Tingjian, the author whose ideas on literature had dominated Chinese verse for more than half a century.[22] Because the late, "decadent" phase of Huang's Jiangxi school emphasized the imitation of ancient masters so strongly, the authors of Fan's generation experienced immense difficulties in their attempts to forge individual styles. As a result of the contradictions inherent in the literary culture of the age, a number of poets contemporary with Fan Chengda underwent literary crises involving the rejection of their youthful verse, usually modeled at least in part on the Jiangxi school. The most dramatic example of these was Fan's good friend, Yang Wanli, who burned more than a thousand of his youthful works in 1162, when he was thirty-five years old.[23] In general, historians of Chinese literature are ambiguous about the relationship of Huang Tingjian to Southern Song poetry,[24] and in Fan Chengda's own case, the contemporary scholar Zhou Ruchang maintains that Fan owes much to Tang poets such as Bai Juyi and practically nothing to Huang Tingjian or even the Northern Song master Su Shi.[25]

At first sight, the evidence would suggest that Zhou is correct. Although we do not wish to enter into a detailed stylistic comparison of Huang and Fan just yet, a reader's immediate impression is that Huang's verse and the mature poetry of the early Southern Song masters could not be further apart. In addition, although we do not have any meaningful comments on Huang's poetry from Fan, possibly because of the loss of Fan's prose works already mentioned, we do have abundant testimony on Huang Tingjian and the Jiangxi school from Huang's contemporaries and friends, Yang Wanli and Lu You, with whom Fan shares many stylistic similarities.

First, let us examine what Yang Wanli has to say on the matter of his earlier development as a poet and the influence of the Jiangxi school in particular. In the preface to one of his collections of poetry, Yang tells us:

> I first imitated the poetry of the gentlemen of Jiangxi, following which I imitated the pentasyllabic regulated verse of Chen Shidao 陳師道 [1053–1101].[26] Then I imitated the heptasyllabic quatrains of Wang Anshi [1021–1086],[27] and, finally, the quatrains of the [late] Tang poets.[28] But the more I studied, the less I was able to write.... Thus, from 1162 until the spring of 1177, I had written as few as five hundred eighty-two poems! In the summer I went to my official position in Jiangxi, and as soon as I assumed my post, I read lawsuits and administered the local revenues, up to my ears in paperwork. From time to time ideas for poems raced back and forth in my mind, but although I wanted to write, I did not have any leisure. On New Year's Day of 1178, I started to write poetry, because I was on vacation and had no official business. Suddenly, I was as if enlightened, and at that moment I took leave of the [late] Tang poets, Wang Anshi, Chen Shidao, and all the gentlemen of Jiangxi, no longer daring to imitate any of them. I was so overjoyed, I tried having my son hold a writing brush while I orally composed several poems, and they came gushing forth without any of the earlier straining.[29]

Yang Wanli's account suggests that his literary evolution can be divided into several periods during which he imitated the Jiangxi poets among others (with the exception of the late Tang poets, he seems to have been more attracted to Song authors than Fan Chengda), culminating in a poetic crisis that eventually led to a rejection of his earlier masters and the creation of his own natural poetic style. The impression of a real crisis in his career as a poet is suggested by the destruction of his earlier verse, an act that is extreme for any author, East or West.

There are numerous hints in Yang Wanli's later poetry of dissatisfaction with the Jiangxi school and its leader Huang Tingjian:

> I am ashamed of those who transmit schools and sects,
> For each author has his own individual style.
> Don't rest your feet beneath Huang Tingjian's and Chen Shidao's fence;
> Stick your head beyond the ranks of Tao Qian and Xie Lingyun![30]

Although this poem could be viewed as nothing more than an exhortation against imitation (it is unlikely that Yang had anything against Tao Qian or Xie Lingyun), the hostility to at least one aspect of Huang Tingjian's verse is clear in a poem Yang wrote about Zhang Lei 張耒 (1052–1112), a poet of the Northern Song, who was noted for his simple style as opposed to Huang's complexity:[31]

> Zhang Lei dared to discuss poetry in Huang Tingjian's presence,
> And Huang praised Zhang's phrases "rinsing the well" and "sweeping flowers."
> But if Huang had only read Zhang's complete works later,
> He would have discovered a natural treasure – something beyond his comprehension![32]

Yang Wanli asserts that Huang Tingjian praised Zhang Lei for the ingenuity of his language but that Huang could never have understood the natural simplicity of Zhang Lei's greatest works because of his own proclivity for complex verse.

Lu You's literary evolution resembles that of Yang Wanli. Although Lu was strongly attracted to the works of Tao Qian and the poems of the *Classic of Poetry* (seventh century B.C. and earlier) as a boy, the most decisive event in his early poetic career was his literary apprenticeship under Zeng Ji 曾幾 (died 1167), who was one of the the leading Jiangxi poets at the time.[33] In a parting poem addressed to Zeng, Lu wrote:

> I heard of your fame when I was only a boy,
> But it seemed you had lived a thousand years before my age.
> When I got older, I began to recite your creations,
> Together with Du Fu's and Han Yu's writings.[34]
> I dreamed of you straightaway every night,
> Shining as brightly as the moon in the sky.

> But then I would rise and sigh again and again,
> For I wished to meet you, but there was no way. . . .[35]

Zeng Ji was a student of Lü Benzhong 吕本中 (fl. 1119), the man who was responsible for the idea of a Jiangxi school of poetry in the first place, and it is certain that Lu You modeled his early verse on the Jiangxi style with the same eagerness that Yang Wanli imitated it at about the same time.[36]

And yet, Lu You's ultimate reaction to the Jiangxi school closely parallels that of Yang Wanli. Although he does not mention a similar poetic crisis and subsequent enlightenment, his present collected works do not contain any poems written before he was thirty years old, and only 139 poems remain between that age and when he was forty-four, a remarkably small number when one recalls that Lu's surviving poems number more than ten thousand. Hence, it is likely that in subsequent editing of his manuscripts, Lu deleted practically all of the works written under the direct influence of his teacher, Zeng Ji.[37] Although Lu You always spoke of Zeng with respect, his later attitude toward the kind of poetry he wrote under Zeng's tutelage was negative:

> I got nothing out of my previous study of poetry,
> And could not avoid begging left-over scraps from others.
> I knew in my heart that I lacked force and vigor,
> And I was ashamed of the undeserved fame I had achieved. . . .[38]

And

> When I commenced my study of poetry,
> I was only concerned with literary embellishment.
> At middle age, I became somewhat more enlightened,
> And my poetic vision gradually broadened.[39]

The references to "left-over scraps" in the first poem and "literary embellishment" in the second are aimed specifically at the approach to poetry espoused by Huang Tingjian and the Jiangxi poets, with their love of erudite allusions and complex diction.

So far we have only examined evidence that would support the view that Southern Song poetry represents a complete departure from the Jiangxi school, but a closer examination of the critical comments of Yang Wanli and Lu You does not permit such a sweeping generalization. In spite of the criticisms of Huang Tingjian, Yang had a great admiration for Huang's poetry that lasted a lifetime. In 1178 when he was fifty-one years old, Yang composed an inscription for the shrine to Huang Tingjian at Yizhou, where Huang died in exile, and in the same year Yang wrote the following poem after rereading some of Huang's works:[40]

Reading Huang Tingjian's poems by lamplight

There is no match to Mr. Huang of Matched Wells,[41]
Whose works are still redolent with past ages' fragrance.
Men of the last century are nowhere to be seen,
But Huang's fame will be transmitted for millennia in print.
If only my poems could be equal to his,
What would I care for either life or fame?. . .[42]

The reader who is familiar with the simple directness of Yang Wanli's poetry is even more amazed to discover that Yang Wanli had a high opinion of Huang Tingjian's mastery of complex allusions. Yang's prose works contain at least two references to Huang's well-known poem "Writing-Brush of Orangutan Fur" (see the discussion in the next section):

When beginning to study poetry one must employ the best language of the ancients, sometimes two words, sometimes three, as Huang Tingjian did in "Writing-Brush of Orangutan Fur": "In all his life how many pairs of sandals / After his death five carts full of books," in which "In all his life" comes from the *Analects* of Confucius; "after his death" refers to Zhang Han of the Jin dynasty, who said: "I wish to be famous after my death;" "How many pairs of sandals" is a reference to Ruan Fu; and "five carts full of books" is an allusion to what Zhuangzi said about Huishi: two lines of poetry, which comprise allusions combined together from four sources.[43]

And

The most marvelous method of poets is to use the language of the ancients without using their literal meaning as Huang Tingjian did in his "Writing-Brush of Orangutan Fur."[44]

From his comments on another poem one can conclude that Yang's admiration of Huang's clever allusions to earlier literature in "Writing-Brush of Orangutan Fur" is not an isolated phenomenon:

Du Fu's poem "Dreaming of Li Bai" reads: "The setting moon fills the rafters of my room / And I suspect it still shines with the image of his face." Huang Tingjian's poem "Bamboo Mat" reads: "The setting sun shimmers on it like the waves on a river / Vaguely, dimly like the face of a person." . . . This is using the language and form of the ancients without using their meaning and is truly "making something new out of the old" and "snatching the fetus to renew the bones"![45]

What Yang Wanli admires so strongly in Huang Tingjian's poem is his skillful reworking of a poetic line by an earlier master. If the Southern Song poets considered their work to be such a radical break with the poetry of the Jiangxi school, as some later critics have suggested, it is, indeed, peculiar that Yang Wanli, the poet generally deemed the most "vulgar" of the early Southern Song and, hence, farthest in spirit from Huang Tingjian, should praise Huang's works so highly, and precisely for the reason that later detractors of Huang and the Jiangxi school attacked them.[46]

Fan Chengda's relation with the Jiangxi school is just as complex as that of Yang Wanli and Lu You, but as we shall see later, an understanding of this relation is crucial to a study of the development of Fan's style after his earliest imitative period. Although Zhou Ruchang has identified many allusions to and echoes of Huang Tingjian's poetry in Fan's work, there is no overt mention of Huang's poems in Fan's surviving collected works until 1173, when Fan was already forty-three years old. Two poems written in this year that mention Huang Tingjian do display an intimate knowledge of Huang's activities, but unfortunately Fan has nothing to say about Huang as a poet other than joking about a name that Huang had given to a spring Fan himself renamed. It was only later that Fan paid Huang the ultimate compliment of writing poems to the same rhymes Huang had used.[47]

Traditional Chinese critics held widely differing opinions about the relation between Fan Chengda's verse and the Jiangxi poetry of the previous generation. Jiang Kui, the famous *ci* poet and close friend of Fan who, as we saw in Fan Chengda's biography, spent extensive periods of time with Fan at Stone Lake, wrote that "the Master [You Mou 尤袤 (1127–1194)] once said to me that men of recent times have delighted in imitating the Jiangxi style, but none of them are 'mild and rich' like Fan Chengda, 'lofty and ancient' like Xiao Dezao 蕭德藻 [fl. 1160], or 'noble and unrestrained' like Lu You, all of whom created their own 'devices', and who had nothing to do with the Jiangxi school," suggesting that Jiang agreed with You that Fan's poetry was largely free of Jiangxi influence.[48]

The early Ming critic Song Lian 宋濂 (1310–1381) seems to have held exactly the opposite view when he wrote that "at the time of the Longxing [1163–1165] and Qiandao [1165–1174] reign periods, the purity and geniality of You Mou, the depth and incisiveness of Yang

Wanli, the vastness and beauty of Fan Chengda, and the abundance and richness of Lu You were all quite remarkable, but they did not steer clear of the well-worn tracks of the Tiansheng [1023–1032] and Yuanyou [1086–1094] reign periods [synonymous with the late Northern Song style of Su Shi and Huang Tingjian]," suggesting that Song Lian believed that the major defect of the early Southern Song masters was that they followed too closely in the footsteps of Huang Tingjian and other Northern Song masters![49]

Only in the Qing dynasty did the scholar Ji Yun 紀昀 (1724–1805) suggest an approach that might possibly reconcile these two diametrically opposite views:

If one compares the collected works of Yang Wanli and Lu You [with Fan Chengda, one discovers that] the vigor of Fan's talent is not equal to Yang's but that he is free from Yang's crudity and the breadth of his vision is not equal to Lu You but he is free from Lu's conventionality. Fan's early poems are clearly derived from mid- and late-Tang poetry. This can be clearly inferred by looking at Fan's note after his "Songs of a Banquet at Night" in Chapter Three of his works, which says "the two poems below are in imitation of Li He,"[50] and the note after his "Songs to Delight the Spirits," which says "the following four poems were written in imitation of Wang Jian."[51] Such poems as his "Ballad of the Lone Swan on West River"[52] and "Lament of the Globe-fish"[53] are impromptu works in the Changqing style [of Bai Juyi and Yuan Zhen.] Poems such as "Jesting about a Villager's Recent Wedding," "Spring Evening, Three Poems," and "Four Paintings of Longshi" are all reminiscent of the late Tang and Five Dynasties, and the influences are easy to trace.[54] But after Fan took on his post of Clerk of Xin'an [Huizhou], his poetry gained gradually in vigor, because he revived the poetic practices handed down by Su Shi and Huang Tingjian, which he controlled by means of his restraint, so that there is no wonder he attained his own style and is worthy of a place as an equal to Yang Wanli and Lu You.[55]

Although one might be inclined to disagree with certain details of Ji Yun's account of Fan Chengda's evolution as a poet, Ji was the only traditional Chinese critic to attempt such a detailed analysis or to support his conclusions by reference to specific poems from Fan's works. As for the first part of Ji Yun's analysis, there can be no doubt about Fan's youthful fascination with mid-Tang and later authors, but with the exception of Wang Jian, it is difficult to say exactly how his early imitation of these authors with their great differences in style contributed to the formation of the mature style that came into being when Fan Chengda arrived at Huizhou.

Ji Yun's contention that Fan was more deeply influenced by Su Shi and Huang Tingjian than by the mid-Tang poets is certainly even more problematical, because it contradicts what You Mou and Jiang Kui, Fan's contemporaries and friends, thought about Fan's poetry, but more important, because Ji fails to support his conclusion with any textual evidence, and as we have seen above, there may be many echoes of late Northern Song poetry in Fan's works, but there are few precise references to the poets themselves. In spite of these problems, Ji Yun's contention that Fan was deeply influenced by late Northern Song verse and particularly the poetry of Huang Tingjian is basically correct, a fact that many later critics do not seem to have understood fully.

Huang Tingjian and tradition

Before we can discuss this question of Huang Tingjian's influence on the formation of Fan Chengda's mature style, it will be necessary to say a bit more about Huang Tingjian's theory and practice of poetry.[56] Of course, each of the poets of the Jiangxi school had his own style of verse, and the whole idea of a Jiangxi school was a creation of Lü Benzhong and not Huang Tingjian, but Huang's theory and practice exercised a great influence on his contemporaries and all the poets Lü included within the Jiangxi School. The generally accepted view of Huang Tingjian's literary theory is summarized by Huang Tingjian's oft-quoted statement on poetic diction:

> To create new language by oneself is most difficult. When Du Fu composed poetry or Han Yu wrote prose, every word they used was derived from tradition, and it is probably because later men read so few books that they said Han or Du created their own language. The literary masters of antiquity were truly able to refine the universe's phenomena. They filled their writing brushes and ink with the ancients' old language, and yet, just like the magic elixir, they were able to transform iron into gold.[57]

Such a theory of poetic diction is completely in harmony with the two alchemical phrases that Yang Wanli quoted from Huang Tingjian above, namely, "making something new from the old" and "snatching the fetus to renew the bones."

It might seem that Huang Tingjian's theory of poetic diction would bring about a poetry consisting almost entirely of allusions to earlier poetry that would totally preclude the author's originality. This was a charge frequently leveled against Huang Tingjian and his followers, but a more careful reading of Huang's comments on poetry suggests that his opponents have not been quite fair to him:

Sent to Chao Yuanzhong (one poem of ten)

When thin waists were in vogue, Chu palace ladies starved;
When broad eyebrows were stylish, they covered half a woman's forehead.[58]
In the realm of brush and ink during recent times,
Poetic writing has turned garish and flashy.
Literature is an art that comes from within,
And has followed no single track from antiquity to the present.
I have always hoped that my friend, Chao Yuanzhong,
Would intimidate these poetasters – like an enemy army![59]

It is not certain what specific authors Huang is criticizing here, but he is clearly attacking superficial worship of contemporary fashion and excessive attachment to outward form. Yet, most important of all, the poem tells us that Huang Tingjian saw poetry as "an art that comes from within [literally, 'an art of the heart,' *xinshu* 心術]" and that an author cannot depend upon antiquity for his inspiration. At first view, this poem would seem to be in direct contradiction with the prose passage we have just quoted, but, in fact the contradiction is only apparent, for although Huang Tingjian stressed the importance of study and imitation of ancient models, he always insisted upon the transformation of these models, a process that he likened, as we have seen, to the alchemical transformation of the base metals into gold.

Such a view of poetry is not all that far removed from the theories of Yang Wanli and Lu You and presumably Fan Chengda, for both Yang and Lu, as we have seen, went through a long period of imitation and study of ancient models before they were able to create their own individual styles. Thus, although modern critics are correct in noting fundamental differences between the style of late Northern Song poets and Fan Chengda and his contemporaries, there are also undeniably close resemblances between the approaches to poetry of Huang Tingjian and the early Southern Song poets.

Of course, similarities in the theories of literature held by different authors are no guarantee that the authors have much in common stylistically, and to prove a link between Fan Chengda's verse and the Jiangxi school one would have to demonstrate similarities in style. Unfortunately for our purpose, traditional Chinese critics have not clearly defined what they mean by a Jiangxi style or even precisely which poets should be included in the Jiangxi school, but whether they like or dislike the poetry of Huang Tingjian, they all seem to agree on the central role complex allusion plays in his verse.[60] To see just how allusion functions in one of Huang Tingjian's poems, let us first examine the work praised by Yang Wanli above, for although the poem is difficult to study in English translation, it is an interesting example of Huang's creation of an original poem by allusion to the earlier poetic tradition:

In answer to Qian Xie's poem on the orangutan fur writing-brush

Loving wine, the orangutan was so drunk it could not move,
And although it can speak, it was careless with its secrets.
How many pairs of clogs can one wear in a lifetime?
After death you leave behind five cartloads of books.
If you wish to see the brush, you must attend a gathering of Chinese and foreign princes;
The brush's accomplishments are recorded in the Stone Channel Library.
With the fur plucked from the orangutan one can rescue the world,
Something that should be explained to hedonists like Yang Zhu![61]

The Qing scholar, Ji Yun, who suggested the strong influence of Huang Tingjian on Fan Chengda, wrote that in this poem "the transformations are marvelous in the extreme . . . it can be considered a model for the use of allusion in poetry describing objects," and, indeed, few Chinese poets have used allusion so cleverly as Huang has in this work.[62]

The first and second lines employ two allusions from the *Huayang guozhi* (about 347)[63] and the late Zhou dynasty Confucian ritual text, the *Liji*,[64] respectively, to explain how the orangutan is captured by exploiting its supposed propensity for wine and carelessness in "speech," an ability that presumably should but does not save it from being taken prisoner. In the third line a clever doubling of allusions occurs, that is, the "second" part of the allusion from the *Huayang guozhi* (the orangutan's supposed love for wearing clogs and the way this, too, is used to capture it) is juxtaposed with an allusion to the love for clogs of the third-century scholar Ruan Fu 阮孚.[65] This overlapping of allusions provides a transition from the capture of the orangutan to the topic of the third and fourth lines, the use of the orangutan's fur in manufacturing the writing brush, and skillfully interweaves two seemingly irreconcilable things, the ignoble behavior of the orangutan, which is captured because of its attachment to such an unimportant object as a pair of clogs, and the clearly noble vocation of a man like Huishi 惠施 (370 B.C.?–310 B.C.?), a philosopher who is reputed to have "left behind five cartloads of books" to posterity.[66]

The idea of the "nobility" of the orangutan writing-brush is continued in the allusions of the fifth and sixth lines (now the emphasis is much more on the *writing*-brush than the *orangutan* writing-brush), for the instrument is present in "the gathering of Chinese and foreign princes" (allusion to a commentary by the venerable Han dynasty scholar Zheng

Xuan 鄭玄 [127–200], the most famous exegete of the Confucian classics)[67] or in the Stone Channel Library, the archetypal library in the most bookish culture of the world (again Han dynasty in date).[68] The serious intent of the poem is continued to the end with an attack upon hedonists such as the Zhou dynasty thinker Yang Zhu 楊朱 (before 300 B.C.), who according to the Confucian sage Mencius (ca. 372–289 B.C., about as venerable as one can get!), "would not have even plucked one of his hairs in order to save the entire world," suggesting the saving powers of literary culture symbolized by the orangutan writing-brush, and yet at the same time recapitulating with incredible cleverness the purely "orangutan" side of the orangutan writing-brush and showing how the orangutan, through his sacrifice of his hair (hardly noble or voluntary on his part) has advanced the cause of the entire human race and its culture.[69]

Although at the end of our analysis, the reader who cannot read the Chinese original might be inclined to ask the perennial question, "But is it art?" no one can dispute the incredible ingenuity of Huang Tingjian's poem. However, Huang Tingjian was not the first Chinese poet to employ allusion skillfully, and although Chinese critics have said little about how his use of allusion differs from other highly allusive authors such as Xie Linyun 謝靈運 (385–433)[70] during the Period of Division or Li Shangyin 李商隱 (ca. 813–ca. 858)[71] of the Tang dynasty, we shall see that it is the spirit behind Huang's allusions rather than the actual use of allusion itself that was so important to Fan Chengda and other Southern Song poets.

Fan Chengda's first Jiangxi-style verse

We have already seen that Ji Yun was one of the few critics to have recognized the full significance of Huang's impact on Fan Chengda, and since Huang's influence is not immediately apparent in Fan's most popular later works, we shall defer our detailed analysis of Huang Tingjian's contribution to the formation of Fan Chengda's style until we have examined the first period in Fan's literary development when we can prove the influence of the Jiangxi school in Fan's poetry beyond a doubt. Before we study Fan Chengda's first works in the style of Huang Tingjian, it would be useful to say something about the periodization of Fan Chengda's verse given by Zhou Ruchang, the only modern Chinese scholar who has studied Fan's works in any detail.

Zhou Ruchang divides Fan Chengda's earlier verse into three periods, the first extending from when he began writing in his middle teens until he started studying for the civil service examinations (ca. 1140–ca.

1152), the second occupying the approximately ten years during which Fan took his preliminary examinations, passed his metropolitan graduate degree, and served at Huizhou (ca. 1152–1162), and the third beginning with his service at Hangzhou (1162).[72] Such a division according to Fan Chengda's political career may seem artificial to the Western reader, but our biography of Fan Chengda indicates that his official life did at times influence the general development of his verse, although most of his poetry did not address political themes.

Nonetheless, the development of Fan's early work cannot be explained satisfactorily by means of the periods that Zhou Ruchang proposes. First, Fan was composing poetry in imitation of Tang authors throughout the first two periods,[73] and even in Zhou's first period quite a bit of his poetry resembles Chen Yuyi's miniaturist verse.[74] Most important, Zhou's periodization fails to take into account the major change in Fan's verse that occurred as soon as he assumed his post in Huizhou (1156).

Although some of the poetry Fan wrote at Huizhou is not as readable as his earlier work, the following is a relatively successful example of the new style he adopted at that time:

Following the rhymes of Tang Wenbo's poem "Moved after rain and cool weather"

Poor scholars like me are always sick and hungry:
From antiquity to the present we have all been the same.
Now my life is safe and my stomach is full:
What more than this could I possibly desire?
Administrative assistant is a low post, indeed,[75]
And I still must worry lest my rice pot go empty.
In these remote mountains the sultry weather makes me ill;
And I lie exhausted, unable to raise my head.
Poverty and disease beset me on all sides:
Human life is an insubstantial dream.

Clouds form at morning, black as ink;
Peals of thunder shake the hills and mountains.
Cascades of water suddenly gush from my eaves;
Frogs and katydids sing in mutual refrain.
The red-capped summer season with his fiery troops[76]
Is routed in battle by the torrential downpour.
The fresh, cool air reinvigorates my lungs,
And I wade in water to climb the city wall's tower.
I will invite the fairy maid of clouds and rain
To twirl her long sleeves in time with Liangzhou's frontier tunes.[77]
Rain puffed by the wind will fill my wine jug,
And a thousand pints will wash me clean of my sorrow.[78]

And yet, I know this can never be,
For my icy hall is as cold as in autumn.[79]
Ideas for my poem burgeon forth from my mind,
And vigorous sentiments enter the silver hooks of my writing.
But the work seems useless when I bring it to completion,
For I wonder how it can ever save me from my life of poverty.

Master Tang, you also live far away from home,
And feel regret, whenever you gaze toward your village.
You began this song, which I barely dare answer;[80]
Together let us compose chants in the mode of Shang.[81]

In contrast to Fan's earlier verse, the mark of Huang Tingjian and his followers is now clearly visible. The work contains more allusions than Fan's earlier verse, and, although they are not as complex as in some of the other poetry he wrote during this period, they still make this poem much more difficult to understand in the original Chinese than the quatrain translated above in our discussion of Chen Yuyi's possible influence on Fan Chengda. Not only are the allusions greater in quantity, but most of them are drawn from "orthodox" poets such as Han Yu 韓愈 (768–824) and Du Fu, authors especially favored by Huang Tingjian.[82] The poem also treats one of Huang Tingjian's favorite themes, the poet's dissatisfaction with official life and his desire to return to his native village.[83]

Nor did Fan Chengda abandon writing pure Jiangxi-style poems later in life, and the following was addressed to his good friend, Yang Wanli, when Fan was serving in Mingzhou (1180), more than twenty years after he left Huizhou:

Following the rhyme scheme of poems sent me by my classmate Yang Wanli, director of the palace library

When will you return from the malarial clouds and misty rain?[84]
In Guangdong you should treat the barbarians like men of China.
Formerly I heard that your poems startled the very gods;[85]
Now I learn you snatched victory's banner from beastly rebels.[86]
The Shao River's stones are ancient, but Shun's panpipes still echo;[87]
Plum blossoms sent from Yu Range wilt, because the post is slow.[88]
The red-stringed zither has always suited the Imperial Shrine;[89]
You musn't try to soar like the ocean roc to gape at Heaven's Pool![90]

In spite of the passage of so many years, this work is even closer to the Jiangxi style than the poem from Fan's Huizhou period just translated, and although Fan does not employ the numerous allusions with the cleverness and dexterity of Huang Tingjian, Fan concludes his work with some witty advice to Yang Wanli, who had recently experienced great success in both his literary and political careers, to keep his place as a "red-stringed zither" (literatus) and not aspire to "gape at Heaven's Pool," that is, rise to a high position in the government.

Such poems may lack the simple lyricism of Fan's earlier nature poetry and of the mature verse with which he is usually identified, but they exemplify one of Fan Chengda's more intriguing contradictions, namely, his creation of two quite distinct styles, the first following Huang Tingjian closely in its recondite allusions, the second finding its expression in the simpler, more direct poems that have ensured Fan's everlasting fame to posterity. The poetry that directly imitates Huang Tingjian has been virtually ignored by literary historians, and, perhaps, it deserves to be, because much of it consists of social poetry, dutifully composed as part of Fan's obligations to his friends and relatives, for the most part comprising works in which Fan follows the rhyme scheme of verses written by his friends or fellow officials.

Yet one may rightly ask why a poet so accomplished as Fan would be willing to work in two seemingly contradictory styles. We have already mentioned the social pressures that compelled Fan to write in the Jiangxi style, particularly when he was serving as a lowly official in Huizhou trying to curry favor with his superiors and cement friendships with other intellectuals of his rank. However, social pressures would hardly explain why he continued to write such poetry into his old age, and even if Fan did not entrust his most intimate thoughts to his Jiangxi-style verse, his more formal works modeled on Huang Tingjian must not have displeased him. The answer to this question lies in the fact that there were more points in common between Fan's better-known verse and his Jiangxi-style poetry than many Chinese literary historians have been willing to admit, and, as we shall see in Chapter 3, Fan Chengda's mature style, which did not suddenly arise ex nihilo but was slowly developing long before he arrived in Huizhou, is firmly based upon the late Northern Song dynasty tradition of the Jiangxi school.

3
Jiangxi wit and Fan Chengda

Wit

Earlier we suggested that Huang Tingjian's extensive use of allusion in his poem on the orangutan fur writing-brush was much less important for the formation of Fan Chengda's mature style than the general approach to writing that underlies Huang's allusions. Critics have properly paid much attention to allusion in Jiangxi-style poetry, but they have overlooked something that would seem to be even more fundamental to the creations of Huang Tingjian and his followers, namely, the central position of wit in their writing. Of course, various critics have mentioned the importance of humor in Song poetry, and Yoshikawa has stressed the intellectual qualities of Song verse, but no one seems to have explored the connections between Song humor and intellectuality to elucidate the central importance of wit in the work of many of the major poets.[1] Although it does not lie within our scope to recapitulate the history of Song dynasty verse, it would seem that a neglect of the wit of Song poetry has tended to obscure some of the important unities that underlie more than two centuries of Song literature.

Most Chinese critics draw a clear line between the work of Su Shi and Huang Tingjian, and yet if we examine Su's poetry more carefully, we discover that he shares many traits with Huang.[2] Su was not just witty in the sense that he had a good sense of humor (Yoshikawa also speaks of his "transcendence of sorrow"), for his diction and figures of speech display a striving for cleverness quite equal to Huang Tingjian.[3] Otherwise, how could one explain the ingenious extended metaphor with which Su begins his famous poem "New Year's Eve" in which he compares the passing of the old year (and by extension human life) to a "a snake slithering to its burrow / Its long scales already half down the hole. / Who could stop it from leaving? / Even if you grab it by the tail, / You know your efforts are in vain,"[4] or the equally striking metaphor in a poem to his brother Su Zhe 蘇轍 (1039–1112) in which Su Shi compares human life to "a swan that treads on the snowy mud. / If by chance he leaves his footprints behind, / What does he care after he flies off?"[5] Even though Huang Tingjian rarely employs the extended metaphor, there is much in common between Su's metaphors and Huang's more condensed and complex figures of speech (see the discussion later in the chapter) for they all surprise and then delight the reader with their originality and cleverness. Thus, the wit of both Su Shi's and Huang Tingjian's poetry is manifested not only in their rich sense of humor but at all levels of their poetic creation, including the most fundamental verbal level.[6]

Although we shall see that Fan Chengda's poetry differs from that of the Northern Song masters in many respects, his witty approach to writing clearly demonstrates the debt that he owes to Huang Tingjian and other authors of the Northern Song. Even during his early years, when he was still imitating Tang authors, he was already writing witty poetry clearly under Northern Song influence:

On the river

The hues of the sky are heartlessly pale;
The din of the river is relentless and never ends.
Men of antiquity couldn't use up all the world's sadness,
So they left plenty of sadness behind, just for us, their posterity![7]

The idea behind this poem is clever, namely, that the past's legacy of sadness can be "bequeathed" to posterity and that our forefathers would have been perverse enough to leave us such a "legacy." On this level alone, the poem is a witty response to a theme that was already hackneyed by Tang times, that is, the landscape's evocation of sad thoughts in the traveler who is separated from his family and traveling on some government mission or into exile. Of course, Fan Chengda does not completely overturn this old theme, but he softens its melancholy with his wit, which derives from his complaint against the "ancients" and, hence, tradition.

Nonetheless, the poem's success is not only a result of the clever idea that lies behind it but also arises from its verbal wit. First, Fan creates a clever contrast between the word *chou* 愁 (sad) in the third and fourth lines, by using it as a verb in the Chinese original of line three (literally, "Men of antiquity could not finish off being sad") and as a noun in line four, as well as placing it in the critical "eye" (third syllable) of the third line, as opposed to the even more important final rhyming syllable of the fourth line. Second, the expression "heartlessly pale," or *wuqing dan*

無情淡 (literally, without feeling, pale) is quite ingenious, because in Chinese the word *dan*, or "pale," can refer to both pale colors and calm or indifferent emotions, and in the first line it can be taken as a description of the sky's "hues" as well as nature's "lack of emotions."

Such a poem is only one of the first in a long line of witty works that Fan Chengda produced during his life, and although his wit is certainly connected to the optimism inspired by his Buddhist faith, it involves much more than a healthy outlook on life and an undeniably good sense of humor, for at all levels his poetry is a product of a keenly perceptive mind striving to express itself cleverly and aptly.

Diction

A poet who values wit will inevitably be concerned with the clever use of language, and Huang Tingjian's concern for diction (*yongzi* 用字), which has elicited so much comment from traditional Chinese critics, served as an important model to Fan Chengda in the formation of his mature style before his arrival in Huizhou. Huang Tingjian made many pronouncements about the importance of selecting exactly the right word for a particular line, and in a poem addressed to Gao He 高荷, a minor member of the Jiangxi school, he praises Du Fu's poetry by saying that "there are *eyes* 眼 in the lines of Du Fu's verse," the word "eyes" referring to the particularly forceful or clever use of words at critical junctures (normally the third syllable of a pentasyllabic line and the fifth syllable of a heptasyllabic line).[8] This observation is paralleled by another statement in a colophon to Gao He's poetry to the effect that "the placing of one word is like a key to the gate of a pass"[9] and the dictum (in a colophon on Ouyang Xiu's 歐陽修 [1007–1072] poetry) that one must "place words forcefully."[10]

The main thrust of these pronouncements on diction is that Huang Tingjian maintained that the clever use of individual words was critical for the success of a poetic line or even an entire poem. Huang Tingjian's use of diction is too complex to consider in detail here, but one can obtain an idea of what it entails from a couplet on a frosty, moonlit evening in which he writes: "The Lunar Lady walks hand in hand with the Black Frost Maiden / Their smile, flashing across ten thousand tiles," where the word *can* 粲 (translated inadequately by the English word "flash") is particularly effective in the "eye" or third syllable of the second line, because it contains both the idea of smiling and shining in addition to providing a clever description of the reflection of moonbeams on the frost-covered tiles.[11]

Although Fan Chengda never perfected his diction to the heights (and one might argue, the extremes) of Huang Tingjian, even in the early poems written long before he assumed his post in Huizhou, Fan exercises great care in the selection of words and frequently employs them in an unusual or lively manner. For example, much of the beauty of an early quatrain (translated on pp. 99–100) arises from the clever use of the word *juan* (rolls up) in the concluding line, "for it [the spring tide] rolls up Xixing's rain and delivers it to me!", where the idea of the spring tide "rolling up" the rain startles the reader with its freshness, and the wit of the conceit contrasts pleasantly with the poem's predominantly dreary atmosphere.

Another interesting example appears in an early quatrain (translated on p. 100), which starts with the attractive line "Insects' thousand-foot gossamer would tug the spring season back," where the word "tug" (*wan* 挽) occurs in the critical "eye" or fifth syllable of the heptasyllabic line, creating the striking image of the spiders' and insects' silk strands (here exaggerated into "thousand-foot gossamer") actually pulling the departing spring season back to the world willy-nilly. That the line echoes and improves upon one by Huang Tingjian, who himself was probably echoing a line by Han Yu, further exemplifies Fan's indebtedness to Huang.

Fan Chengda's imaginative diction creates a highly original effect in a quatrain included in one of the first series of nature poems that he ever wrote:

Xukou

My small boat slaps against the waves, going east or west as it wishes;
Where will this thousand-mile wind carry my lone sail now?
As soon as the weather clears, the trees are liberated from the mist;
Two mountains split apart before me and the river's water is *glued* to the sky![12]

The first and second lines of the work are conventional, but in the third line, Fan employs the word *fang* 放, or "liberated," in an ingenious description of how the clouds and mists lift from the trees and make them visible again, while the poem reaches its climax in the fourth line, where the unexpectedly violent image of the mountains "splitting apart" combines with the lively use of the word "glue" to represent the illusion of the river before him seeming to flow between the mountains up into the sky.

A number of traditional Chinese critics have commented on particularly apt uses of individual words in Fan Chengda's poetry, but the Song scholar Sun Yi 孫亦 was the only one who examined this aspect of Fan's work in the overall context of Northern Song poetry:

Mei Yaochen 梅堯臣 [1002–1060] wrote: "Birds from the southern mountain range pass the northern range crying; / Water from the upper fields enters the lower fields flowing,"[13] and Huang Tingjian wrote: "The wastelands waters increase on their own, the fields' water fills; / Turtledoves in the sunshine sing, while those in the rain return home." The ideas behind these two poems are similar, but Huang Tingjian's diction is more skilled and superior to Mei Yaochen's. I said to Master Luxi: Minzhan's [identification uncertain][14] poem "My Prayers for Rain Were Answered" reads: "The clouds above the eastern mountain range are obscured, those above the west range are blackened; / The water of the upper fields penetrates to the lower fields," while Fan Chengda's "Dian River County" reads: "The old rain invites the new rain to come; / The upper fields' water enters the lower fields singing." Although these poems imitate the two gentlemen [Mei Yaochen and Huang Tingjian], they are superior in their language. [Sun then quotes two more poems by the Song author Wang Anshi and the Tang author Bai Juyi] . . . If one looks at all six poems together, Fan's single word "invites" is superior to all.[15]

Although Sun does not analyze his examples, we can see how they demonstrate the evolution of one poetic idea from the early Northern Song master Mei Yaochen through Huang Tingjian down to the time of Fan Chengda. Huang's couplet is considerably more sophisticated than Mei's, avoiding its more obvious structure in which the fifth and six words (*beiling* 北嶺, "northern range," and *ditian* 低田, "low fields") of each line serve as the object for the respective verb (*guo* 過, "pass," and *ru* 入, "enter") that precedes it before the caesura, and employing the expressions *qingjiu* 晴鳩 (literally, sunny turtledoves) and *yujiu* 雨鳩 (literally, rainy turtledoves), which, in spite of the difficulties they present the translator, make the second line highly compact and more complex than the second line of Mei's couplet. Fan Chengda, on the other hand, reverts to Mei Yaochen's simpler syntax, but creates the most satisfying couplet of all the authors by means of the skillful use of the single word *zhao* (invites).

In spite of the examples we have given above and the critical comments of Sun Yi and others, one of the principal differences between Fan's post-Huizhou poetry and that of Huang Tingjian appears to be that Fan rarely falls into what many critics regard as Huang's excessive concern with diction. Although Fan was already striving to emulate Huang Tingjian's search for exactly the right word in the early verse that he wrote before his arrival at Huizhou and the success of much of his later poetry derives from his skillful diction, he seems to have had an innate feeling for the limits to which the classical Chinese language could be pushed without creating an impression of forced contrivance.

Syntax

Huang Tingjian's diction exercised a great influence upon Fan Chengda's search for clever effects in his poetry, but he was also attracted by the witty and complex effects that Huang achieved through his careful attention to the syntax of his antithetical couplets (the traditional critical term is *jufa* 句法, "line rules"). Huang Tingjian's fascination with unusual syntax appears in many of his famous poems, and the following couplet, extracted from a poem written by Huang to Wang Gong, a friend of Su Shi, was later commended by the critic Wu Rulun 吳汝綸 (1840–1903) as typical of the best in Huang's poetry:[16]

> Blizzard snow, piled on a platter: minced fish maws;
> Glistening pearls, measured in pecks: boiled cocks' heads.[17]
>
> 飛雪堆盤鱠魚腹
> 明珠論斗煮鷄頭

Translated literally into English, this description of the feast Huang is proposing to Wang Gong is difficult to comprehend, because the couplet's syntax is so unusual and complex. The actual sense is that the minced fish maws (really the air bladders of fish, still considered a delicacy in China) are as white as "blizzard snow" and piled high on the platters, while the boiled chicken heads (or lotus seeds) shine like bright pearls and are plentiful enough to be measured in pecks. Huang creates a striking effect in the original Chinese by reversing the usual grammatical order, placing the objects to which the foods are compared first in the line and following these metaphors with the location ("platters") or measure ("pecks") of the foods. By arranging his lines this way, Huang stresses the metaphors themselves rather than the real physical objects (the fish maws and cocks' heads) they describe, with the result that the poet violates common sense, since we do not normally think of blizzards on platters or precious pearls measured by the peck. When read in the original, such a couplet is highly enjoyable because of the intellectual surprise it provides, but the complexity of the grammatical structure obviously demands more of a reader than more conventional poetry. In short, one of the most striking features of Huang Tingjian's poetic line is that it frequently departs from the normal word order of earlier poetry and thus resembles a path that twists and turns when one least expects it, constantly delighting the attentive reader.

Poems written in Fan Chengda's mature style rarely employ the contrived syntax that mars some of Huang Tingjian's verse, but many of Fan's pre-Huizhou works are characterized by quite complex lines that must have been modeled on Huang Tingjian or other Jiangxi poets. We encounter almost the same structure we have just observed in Huang Tingjian's couplet in one of Fan Chengda's early couplets (translated more literally here than in lines three and four of "Walking outside the City on the First Day of Spring" on p. 105):

> Yeast powder, about to darken: the drooping, drooping willows;
> The wine's surface, just brightening: the shallow, shallow waves.[18]

> 麴塵欲暗垂垂柳
> 醅面初明淺淺波

Here, as in Huang's poem, Fan has reversed the normal word order, placing the metaphors in each line ("yeast powder" and "wine's surface") before the objects to which they refer ("the drooping, drooping willows" and "the shallow, shallow waves"). By doing this he complicates the two lines, so that only a careful reading reveals the couplet's sense, namely, that the poet is comparing the color of the freshly sprouted willow leaves, about to darken into late spring's green, to the yellowish-green tinge of the yeast powder, and the brightness of the waves to fermenting wine that has just clarified.

The references to time in both lines are also quite complex, and the present light green color of the leaves (and yeast powder) is juxtaposed with the darker green of the near future (the delay in the process nicely echoed by the "drooping, drooping" of the willows), this delayed time contrasting with the immediacy of the just brightened waves, which are appropriately "shallow." Even more remarkable is the way in which the second and third words of each line in the Chinese original (translated by "about to darken" and "just brightening") can be read with either the first and second words ("yeast powder" and "the wine's surface" in English) or the fourth, fifth, and sixth words ("the drooping, drooping willows" and "the shallow, shallow waves"). Hence, although we "know" that the poet is describing the darkening of the willow's leaves, our first reading almost inevitably suggests that the darkening refers to the fermenting yeast, because of the normal caesura after the fourth syllable in the Chinese original, and although we also "know" that it is the waves that have brightened, again, on first reading, the normal caesura makes us understand that it is the fermenting wine that has brightened (clarified), and not the waves. Such difficult couplets are considerably less common than in Huang Tingjian's poetry, but the syntactical complexity in such an early poem by Fan suggests that he was already consciously imitating the line structure of Huang's verse long before the development of his pure Jiangxi poetry at Huizhou.[19]

A number of later critics admired Fan's mastery of syntax in his couplets. Although the well-known Yuan dynasty critic Fang Hui (1227–1307) did not analyze any of Fan's poems in detail, he frequently praises individual lines and admires the cleverly constructed parallelism of Fan's couplets,[20] while the Qing dynasty scholar Zhou Zhilin 周之麟 uses the terms *gongzhi* 工緻 (skilled and delicate) and *jingxi* 精細 (refined and meticulous) to describe two finely wrought couplets that he particularly enjoyed.[21] In spite of the praise Fan Chengda's syntax has received from traditional critics, after his Huizhou period it underwent a most peculiar development, in that the syntax of his purely Jiangxi-style poetry eventually became even more complex than it was in Huizhou (recall the late poem to Yang Wanli discussed in Chapter 2), while the syntax of his better-known poetry gradually became simplified until most signs of its earlier contact with the Jiangxi school disappeared almost entirely. This simplification of Fan's syntax is, of course, one of the main differences between Fan Chengda's later verse and the poetry of Huang Tingjian, but we should never forget that its final development came about only after Fan had imitated Huang's works for a long period of time and that, even when the complex Jiangxi syntax disappeared from Fan's more "typical" later works, he was still writing much poetry in a pure Jiangxi mode. One is tempted to suggest that once Fan proved to himself that he could master the complexities of Jiangxi poetry in his social verse, he saw no reason to cultivate it further in his more personal creations.

Figures of speech

Chinese critics, whether friendly or hostile to Huang Tingjian, constantly refer to the unusual (*qi* 奇) quality of his verse. In Chinese critical language the word *qi* has a wide range of meaning, varying from something like "miraculous" or "prodigious," when used in praise, to "weird" or "grotesque," when negative in connotation. Thus, in an encomium of Huang Tingjian's poetry, Cai Zhengsun 蔡正孫 (thirteenth century) wrote that "the diction of his poems is especially exalted, the power of his writing-brush is unrestrained, and his poems are truly miraculous [*qi*] creations; since the beginning of the Song dynasty, he has been in a class by himself."[22] Less charitably, the Southern Song critic Zhang Jie 張戒 (twelfth century) wrote, "Huang Tingjian only knew how to make poetry from strange [*qi*] language, but he did not understand that common language is also poetic."[23] Most of these traditional critics only focused upon the strangeness of Huang Tingjian's diction, but, in fact, his "strangeness" derives from a number of interrelated qualities of his verse, all of which are products of a fertile imagination, which both unconsciously and by design functioned in a way quite different from that of earlier poets.

One of the most striking features of Huang's imagination is the often startling way in which he employs metaphor and simile, which can be observed in the following two couplets from different poems:

> On the mat by my curved table I listen to the water simmer,
> Until it boils into the rumble of cart wheels on a twisting path.[24]

And:

> Literature is of no use for ruling the world:
> It's like a strand of spider's web strung with beads of dew![25]

Both of these tropes are apparently without precedent in Chinese verse, since Huang seems to have taken special pains to invent completely original figures of speech and rarely uses the stock metaphors and similes that even the major Tang and Song poets employ. Each of the two tropes is successful in its own peculiar way – the first, because it draws our attention to two sounds that we would not ordinarily associate but that, in fact, do resemble one another closely, and the second, because it suggests the "futility" of literary endeavors, when viewed from a worldly perspective (the frailty of the web), but the world of beauty they create in spite of their "uselessness" (the shining dew on the web).

In his comments on Huang Tingjian, Yoshikawa Kôjirô refers to Huang's "introversion," a character trait that led Huang to a "dislike for the commonplace" and the avoiding of "both the diction and the modes of expression of earlier poets, and to seek to discover poetry in the minor happenings of the everyday world."[26] Huang's use of simile and metaphor is certainly one aspect of his introversion and "dislike of the commonplace," but perhaps it would be more appropriate to say that one reason why much of Huang's poetry concentrates on the "minor happenings of the everyday world" is that only through a witty reexamination of the everyday world could an author discover those metaphorical relationships that would revitalize his poetry.

One more example will suffice to show how Huang Tingjian created a delightfully fresh poem by means of his original metaphors and creative reexamination of the immediate world around him:

Two poems on playing chess presented to Ren Gongjian (first poem)

By chance we've no government business and the guests have retired;
We armchair strategists compare our wits in a game of chess.
Our minds are spider webs floating through the empyrean's void,
Our bodies, moulted cicada shells, cast off on a withered branch.[27]
"One-eyed" like the King of Xiangdong, we willingly perish in battle;[28]
Our chess "empire" is divided in two, and we can both hold out forever.
Who says that we humans always worry about time's onslaught?
We don't even know Orion is dipping and the moon set long ago![29]

Such a poem is successful for a number of reasons. On the strictly verbal level, the metaphors in the third and fourth lines are highly memorable; the comparison of the players' concentration to a spider web floating in the sky is completely original to Huang Tingjian, and the comparison of the players' bodies to moulted cicada shells cast off on a withered branch is a clever reworking of a passage from the philosophical text *Zhuangzi* 莊子 (369–286 B.C.?), which Huang has brilliantly rearranged so that he has made it his own. The "introverted" quality of the poem is obvious in its exclusion of the world of politics and guests, but probably the most striking feature of the poem is the way it produces poetry from a "minor happening," both on the strictly verbal level – through the clever and original use of metaphor and allusion – but also through a witty but serious statement about human beings' anxieties over the brevity and futility of life and how they frequently manage to cope with these anxieties in such nobly civilized ways as the game of chess, or, as one might be tempted to say, the "game" of literature.

We have already seen how much of Fan Chengda's earlier poetry is a poetry of "minor happenings," and we shall have much more to say about his "introverted" verse, particularly his poems that treat the themes of sleep and sickness (see Chapter 4), but in its use of metaphor and other tropes much of Fan's pre-Huizhou poetry already displays the same striving to emulate the wit of Huang Tingjian. Thus, in one early poem Fan compares the rain falling from a cloud to "inverted chopsticks," a clever metaphor for the appearance of a rainstorm seen from a distance, and Fan Chengda begins another early quatrain (see translation on p. 107) with a couplet that contains two ingenious tropes:[30]

A raven's evening silhouette in the window resembles a drunkard's sketch;
A vine climbing the wall is a green serpent slithering off.

Both of these tropes possess the originality that Huang Tingjian valued, and the second one is endowed with the element of surprise found in

Huang Tingjian's poetry, because in spite of the obvious resemblance between a vine and a serpent, we normally think of a vine as something stationary and hardly capable of "slithering away." Although, as we shall see later in the chapter, Fan Chengda gradually began to use tropes in a way that creates a different effect from Huang Tingjian's poetry, the inspiration for the clever similes and metaphors that he created before he arrived in Huizhou was the poetry of Huang Tingjian, and he, too, was already employing his wit to carry out a similar "introverted" reevaluation of the seemingly "minor happenings" of the world around him.

The pathetic fallacy

At the outset of this chapter we discussed the ingenious language of the expression "heartlessly pale" (*wuqingdan*) from Fan Chengda's poem "On the River," but this phrase is even more important as an example of one of the most highly developed witty conceits in Fan Chengda's poetry, the pathetic fallacy. The pathetic fallacy was nothing new to Chinese literature, and is already used humorously in such an early work as Kong Zhigui's 孔稚珪 (447–501) parallel prose piece, "Proclamation on North Mountain" (*Beishan yiwen*).[31] Although the pathetic fallacy is less common in Huang Tingjian's verse, Huang's "teacher," Su Shi, employed it effectively.[32] However, Southern Song poets such as Fan Chengda used the pathetic fallacy in their poetry more consistently than any authors before their time.

It is interesting to trace the development of this device in Fan's work, because he is the only one of the three early Southern Song masters whose early poems survive in any quantity. In one of his earliest extant poems (see "The Cotton-Rose in Front of My Window," translated on p. 99), he already follows the tradition established by Han Yu and other Tang poets by ascribing human emotions to flowers.[33] However, most of Fan's early verse employs the pathetic fallacy in a more negative way, as in the poem "On the River," just translated, where he complains about nature's *lack* of human emotions (*wuqing*), or as in the conclusion to an early poem entitled "Red Plums on the Mountains," where he writes: "The flowers are unable to speak and this traveler is speechless; / The sun sets and we create a pure sorrow in each other," suggesting a rather vague sympathetic relation between poet and flowers.[34]

As the years pass, Fan increasingly sees nature's personal qualities in a more positive light, as in the line, "I sit for a long time, and the face of heaven turns warm and beautiful," but it is not until much later (1180) that he develops the full potential of the pathetic fallacy as a vehicle for wit:[35]

The windstorm

In Siming they also have typhoons.

Madame Typhoon, venerable scion of Ocean's Clan,
You send sand flying through the blue sky and over the white land.
We beg you to rid us of this late summer heat –
But please don't get too wild and hurt the rice paddy's blossoms![36]

Fan frequently uses Chinese mythology to personify the forces of nature as he does here, and although this need not imply belief in the myths themselves, the popular tradition enables Fan to develop the pathetic fallacy more cleverly by exploiting the humor of human relations, in this case, the "human" relation between the goddess Madame Typhoon, the "superior," and Fan Chengda, the "petitioner."

Fan employs the pathetic fallacy in ways that are quite different from poets before Southern Song times. First, the range of natural objects that Fan personifies is much broader than before his own age, when flowers were by far the most popular subjects of such poetry. Second, Fan does not usually use personification to make some moral or ethical point, as most earlier authors did. Kong Zhigui's parallel prose work "Proclamation on North Mountain," which is a witty satire on a man who has abandoned his life as a hermit for a position in court, is an example of this ancient tendency, but even in the Northern Song dynasty, Su Shi discussed the conflict between the ideals of political service and reclusion by means of a "talking" stork,[37] and in another poem on a painting he wrote: "Slender bamboos are like hermits; / Secluded flowers are like virtuous maidens,"[38] with quite obvious references to the ideals of Confucian eremitism.

Some of Su Shi's poems that employ the pathetic fallacy are free from this didactic element and can be seen as precursors to the Southern Song approach:

The pink plum

Fearing spring melancholy, this sleepyhead alone opens late,
Apprehensive that her icy countenance will not fit the season's mode.
She purposely dyes her tiny, pink blossoms the hue of peach and apricot,
With a hint of snow and frost in their solitary frailty.
Her cold heart refuses to comply with spring's manner,
And the blush of wine suffuses her pale, jade complexion.

> The old poet Shi Manqing didn't know this side of Plum's personality:
> He only observed her green leaves and verdant branches![39]

Author's note: Shi Manqing's poem on the pink plum said: "You can take it to be a peach but for its lack of green leaves, / But you can distinguish it from an apricot by its verdant branches."[40]

Although Su Shih's poem is a masterpiece in its own right, its use of personification seems somewhat less successful than that of many Southern Song authors. First, the "character traits" that Su Shi ascribes to the plum are more stereotyped than what one encounters in Fan's creations, drawing from the work of Han Yu, among others.[41] Second, Su's personification of the flower is also more strictly "literary," functioning as a device for "responding" cleverly to a poet from the previous generation. In fact, Su Shi's riposte to Shi Yannian 石延年 (Manqing) (994–1041) in the last two lines compromises the consistency in his personification of the flower by shifting from the personification itself to the author's "real intent" – his witty disagreement with the work of an earlier author.

Su Shi's influence can be observed most clearly in Fan Chengda's "At Night I Walk to Shangsha and See a Plum Tree . . . ," his best early poem that exploits the device of personification (see translation on p. 102). Fan's poem refers directly to Su Shi, and, like Su's work, personifies the flower as a somewhat coquettish female. However, it is interesting that, although Fan's early work is written skillfully, its dominant tone can hardly be described as witty, for unlike Su, Fan does not make fun of tradition but instead expresses his admiration for Su Shi's literary genius. Furthermore, the rather depressing conclusion to the work gives it a more deeply personal feeling.

In light of the later development of the pathetic fallacy in Fan's writings, the most significant difference between his poem and Su Shi's is that he does not violate the illusion of the pathetic fallacy until the end of his work. When Fan eventually began using personification to write witty verse, he almost always followed this practice and normally maintained his personification of natural objects throughout an entire work, as in the quatrain "The Windstorm," above.

Fan Chengda was hardly the only Southern Song poet who used the pathetic fallacy as a vehicle for wit, and one could say that his friend Yang Wanli had even greater success with this device. Yang Wanli wrote all of his best works making use of personification after his poetic enlightenment, and he was quite possibly inspired by Fan Chengda's example in this regard, but since Yang's contributions in this area have been examined before, one of his quatrains will suffice to demonstrate how he built on the example that Fan Chengda provided:[42]

My boat passes Anren

I fell in love with the painted scroll you presented me, distant mountains,
But you rolled it up so suddenly, it's dim as if it never had existed.
Don't try to fool my old eyes; my sight is still sharp –
Even with all your mist and clouds, I still can count you![43]

In such poetry Yang Wanli breaks loose from the earlier tradition of personification to create a witty work totally free from didactic concerns.

The art of nature and the nature of art

The wide use of the pathetic fallacy in Southern Song poetry is closely related to a general fascination with the problem of the ambiguity between nature and art. Interest in this ambiguity is universal among human beings, and Huang Tingjian's poems on painting frequently explore this question:

Inscribed on an album of paintings owned by Zheng Fang

Geese fly home through Huichong's clouds and mist;
I stand by the Xiao and Xiang Rivers on Lake Dongting's shore.
I just get ready to call a boat to take me back home,
But my dear friend informs me that it's only a painting![44]

The first two lines of this poem contain a rather conventional description of a rural landscape near one of China's famous beauty spots, which leads to the idea of homecoming and the associated idea of reclusion in the third line, but the final line suddenly destroys the reader's reverie with the sudden revelation that the "real" landscape he has been contemplating is, in fact, only a painting. The appeal of the work derives almost entirely from the wit of the fourth line, which could be interpreted as merely a clever observation of the painter's skill, but certainly hints at the whole philosophical question of the nature of reality and the aesthetic problem of how art reflects the world around us.

Fan Chengda's treatment of this theme of the relation between the arts and nature certainly owes something to Huang Tingjian but is more complex than what we find in Huang's works, and it behooves us to say something about its development in his writing. Fan's earliest verse did not concern itself so much with the ambiguity between art and nature as with the more ancient but related idea of nature's inspiration of the poet, which happens to be the theme of one of Fan's earliest extant poems:

A summer night

I lovingly cherish this wondrous night,
And transform its pure coolness into a grand song.
If I do not pen any poems this night,
How shall I face the refulgent moon?
A dewy vapor weighs down the flowers with its mist,
And the sighing of the wind invades the forest.
But before I can relish the night's unsullied pleasure,
The image of the lunar cassia dips beneath the river's waves.[45]

This work is unusually archaic for Southern Song poetry with such expressions as *haoge* (grand song), the proselike diction of the fourth line, and the clumsy closure, which harks back almost a thousand years before Fan's age to the poetry of the Three Kingdoms period (220–263).[46]

Although this early imitative poem is almost devoid of literary merit, we can compare it with profit to one of the first works in which Fan employs the same theme in a witty fashion:

Rainy and cool, two poems shown to Zongwei (second of two poems)

Unexpected thunder rumbles over the earth and sends a cool breeze;
I rise and dance, then watch the mountains, beside myself with joy.
People say that a poet has got to always be on his toes –
A mere wisp of clouds provokes rain, and rain provokes poems![47]

The basic idea of the two poems is identical: nature's wonders move the poet to write, but one could hardly imagine two more different works. There is a hint of the personification of nature in the second poem, but the wit of the work largely derives from the clever use of the word *cui* 催 (provoke), for although it is a commonplace to say that the beauties of nature inspire us to write poems, it is unexpectedly witty to suggest that rain "provokes" poems. Of course, Fan has already abandoned the clumsy archaism of the earlier poem, and he fills this quatrain with his typical joie de vivre.

The theme of the relationship between nature's phenomena and the poet's creation underwent many permutations in Fan Chengda's later verse, but one more example will suffice for what was a richly developed theme in his mature poetry:

On the twenty-second day of the eighth month I spend the night at Upright Jade Hall, and after a rainfall, it suddenly cools

The rain intentionally steams up clouds to obscure the setting sun;
A dense perfume pervades the courtyard – the fragrance of fallen blossoms.
Sporting with my brush, I write this poem beside my north window:
An effort that will suffice to reward this cool weather![48]

The wit of this poem derives from a reversal of the normal relationship between the poet and nature, for now nature has lost her primacy, and the poet is "rewarding" nature for the cool weather, rather than viewing his work as her gift.

We have already seen how Huang Tingjian blurs the distinction between nature and art in the poem we translated at the beginning of this section, but Huang's poems on this theme are largely restricted to such obvious topics as painting, whereas in the work by Fan Chengda we just examined, the dichotomy between nature and art is reduced even more, and in fact, one of the most appealing features of Fan's writing is the close fusion of the external world of nature with the internal world of art. The resulting nature in Fan's poetry is, for obvious reasons, less "natural" than nature in the raw, for in line with his Jiangxi background, Fan creates a poetry that relies upon the use of clever language and tropes. But in spite of the artificiality of Fan's nature, it is adorned so skillfully that it takes on a life of its own, that is, it is both artificial and natural.

Decorative language is one of the principal tools that Fan Chengda uses to make nature more artistic and, hence, narrow the distance between nature and art. Fan Chengda's earliest works abound with color words, a practice in which he varies completely from Huang Tingjian, whose poems resemble monochromatic ink painting in their avoidance of color.[49] One of Fan's earliest surviving poems starts with the couplet: "Emerald rushes and green willows don't suit the frost, / So it dyes them yellow-brown to make a belt for the river" (see the full translation on p. 99) in which we encounter three color words, "emerald" (*bi*, actually a blue-green color), "green" (here *qing*, a word of broad application, ranging from green to blue and even black, and "yellow-brown" (*huang*, another color word with a broader range than in English) in a mere fourteen syllables, not to speak of the verb "dye" and, of course, the implied contrast between all these colors and the white of the frost together with the blue of the river.

Fan's Huizhou-period poetry already displays a penchant for combining color perception with the sense of smell, as in the following concluding couplet from a quatrain: "After a rainfall, the green shade turns as black as a woman's mascara; / When the wind arrives from nowhere with its freight of a myriad odors."[50] Here the colors are not as superficially decorative as in the previous work, and the interplay of vision and smell creates a more complex effect typical of Fan's mature verse. The rainy weather darkens the "green shade" until it becomes almost as black as mascara, but Fan suddenly lightens the almost oppressive atmosphere and complicates our sensory perception by introducing a mixture of subtle fragrances carried by the wind from some unknown place.

The first line of this couplet not only contains color words typical of Fan Chengda's verse but also provides an example of another of the commonest types of decorative language that Fan uses to create his artificial nature, that is, tropes that employ objects from the human world to describe natural objects (in this case "mascara" as a trope for dark shade). Of course, this device occurs in practically all nature poetry, but Fan Chengda and other early Southern Song poets developed it to a higher degree than any Chinese poets before their time. Huang Tingjian had already displayed great ingenuity in this area; in one particularly memorable poem about the lotus, he compares the embryonic lotuses inside their seeds to the "fists of a small baby's hands,"[51] and in another work he writes: "I lean against the railing, wind and rain fill the river; / Mount Jun is tied up like the twelve buns on Princess Xiang's hair,"[52] but not even Huang develops this particular form of decorative language to the extent that Fan Chengda does.

As Fan's poetic art progressed, his use of this device increased, and, thus, even in two earlier poems he compares the sun to a "golden gong"[53] and icicles to "silver bamboo shoots."[54] In Fan's later verse, rice plants heavy with morning dew are "an emerald net studded with shining pearls,"[55] the moon is a "red copper platter" that rises from "the lake's silver surface,"[56] and a twisting path resembles "reflections in multiple mirrors."[57]

Although some of the tropes in Fan Chengda's nature poetry are not completely original to him, they have interesting origins, which confirm his debt to Jiangxi verse and Northern Song poetry in general. In an earlier poem Huang Tingjian had written: "After snow, frozen silver bamboos [i.e., icicles] are arranged in a row on my eaves,"[58] from which line Fan may have derived the idea of comparing the icicles to "silver bamboo shoots," which, in any case, is an even more appropriate metaphor than "silver bamboos," because of the greater similarity of bamboo shoots to icicles. The figure of speech "golden gong" for the sun has an even more complex origin. In one poem Su Shi wrote: "The morning sun suspends its golden gong at treetop,"[59] a line that probably inspired Huang Tingjian's line "The golden gong [i.e., sun] is half revealed on the eastern wall."[60] In Su's poem, the referent ("sun") of the metaphor "golden gong" is present in the poetic line, but Huang Tingjian is already using the trope in much the same way as Fan does; that is, in his line the trope replaces the word "sun," functioning rather like a kenning. Nonetheless, the fact that some of Fan Chengda's tropes derive from Northern Song verse does not detract from his originality, because he used this device much more frequently and with greater ingenuity than any poet before his own age.

One is particularly struck by the great quantity of mineral and metallic metaphors that Fan Chengda employs (even in the small sampling above), and his landscapes frequently scintillate like subtly crafted works of the jeweler's art. There really is no exact precursor for this side of Fan Chengda's style, for although earlier poets such as Li He and Li Shangyin wrote richly decorated poetry during Tang times and were imitated by the Xikun 西崑 poets during the first decades of the Song dynasty, their tropes do not impress one as being particularly witty, and, in any case, the lushness of their verse is even more the product of complex allusions and recherché vocabulary, something that Fan by and large avoided.[61] In fact, in addition to the Jiangxi poets, the only other model available to Fan would have been the bejeweled landscapes encountered in Chinese translations of Indian Buddhist sûtras, and although these are also quite remote from Fan Chengda both in spirit and style, we cannot completely dismiss their influence, because, as we shall see, Buddhism was a decisive factor in Fan's artistic and spiritual life.[62]

In any case, Fan's blurring of the boundary between the worlds of art and nature by means of decorative language was the main characteristic of his style, which influenced traditional Chinese evaluations of his poetry. Although in his preface to Fan's works, Yang Wanli had described Fan's style as multifaceted,[63] another friend of Fan Chengda, Jiang Kui, characterized Fan's verse as "mild and rich,"[64] an idea that the Ming critic Song Lian echoed when he used the terms "vast and beautiful" to describe Fan's poetry.[65] Although Jiang obviously meant to praise Fan Chengda, the word *li*, or "beautiful," employed by Song Lian suggests a kind of decorative beauty verging on preciosity, a quality that the early Qing dynasty critic and poet Zhu Yizun 朱彝尊 (1629–1709), who generally opposed Song verse, uncharitably labeled "weakness."[66]

Although one must agree with Zhu Yizun that some of Fan's less successful works suffer from a weakness that arises from excessively decorative language, Fan's wit usually rescues his poetry from such a charge. Critics like Zhu Yizun also failed to understand the basic premises about art and nature that underlie Fan's verse, namely, that art and nature are so inextricably interconnected that they are really one and the same thing. Early in his poetic career Fan had already expressed this idea in a couplet from a long poem describing a snowstorm:

> The Lord of Heaven is marvelously skilled at decoration,
> Applying his art to the river covered with snow![67]

For an almost identical idea, see Fan's later poem, "Returning to Huangtan," translated on p. 117.

Whether or not we agree with the adverse evaluations of Fan Chengda's more florid creations, we must admit that the traditional critics' impressionistic descriptions of his style suggest one of the principal ways in which his poetry differs from Huang Tingjian and his Jiangxi school. Although Huang was interested in the ambiguity between nature and art, he never fused nature and art together in the way that Fan Chengda did in his mature work. Fan's highly creative use of decorative tropes created a style that was his own.

Conclusion

At this point it would be useful to return to the comments of the Qing dynasty scholar Ji Yun that we used as a starting point for our discussion of the influence of Huang Tingjian on the formation of Fan Chengda's mature style. We recall that following his examination of some of Fan's early imitations of Tang poets, Ji commented that "after Fan took on his post of Clerk of Xin'an [Huizhou], his poetry gained gradually in vigor, because he revived the poetic practices handed down by . . . Huang Tingjian, which he controlled by means of his 'mildness', so that . . . he attained his own style," and in this chapter we have seen how almost every aspect of Fan Chengda's poetic craft is a product of his reaction to the literary practices of Huang Tingjian and of other Northern Song authors such as Su Shi, and that, by examining Fan's reactions to the Jiangxi style, we can provide a satisfactory description of practically all the main characteristics of his mature style. It is true that Fan Chengda greatly transformed the Jiangxi tradition through his use of decorative language and the development of the Northern Song tradition of personification and that his "mildness" led him to reject Jiangxi allusiveness and avoid the extremes of Jiangxi diction and syntax in most of his verse, but Ji Yun is fundamentally correct in seeing Fan Chengda's poetry as a compromise between the Jiangxi school and his own unique personality. Although Fan Chengda is certainly one of the most original authors of his age, his originality is firmly based upon the literature of the generation that preceded him.

4

Buddhism and the dharma of sleep

Fan's Buddhism

We generally tend to regard the Song period as part of a post-Buddhist period, when neo-Confucian philosophy rose to its later position of dominance and Buddhism was relegated to a cult of the unwashed masses. Although it is true that the creative vitality of Chinese Buddhism greatly declined after its golden age during the Tang dynasty, Buddhism still played a major role in the intellectual life of the Song period. Our most important source for Chan (Japanese, Zen) Buddhist history, the *Jingde chuandeng lu* 景德傳燈錄 (*The Record of the Transmission of the Lamp of the Jingde Era*), was compiled about 1004,[1] and the most extensive *gongan* 公案 (Japanese, *kôan*) collection, the *Biyan lu* 碧巖錄 (*Records of the Green Cliff*) was written in 1125.[2] The collected sayings of the Chan masters frequently did not receive their final form until Song times and were heavily edited by Song writers.[3]

Throughout the Song dynasty, Buddhism continued to serve as one of the primary sources of inspiration to Chinese poets. A Buddhist-influenced worldview underlies much of the poetry of Su Shi, generally considered the greatest author of the Northern Song,[4] and even a neo-Legalist such as Wang An-shi wrote imitations of the Tang Buddhist poet Han Shan 寒山 (probably seventh century A.D.).[5] Buddhist concepts formed the basis of much of the critical examination of Chinese poetry during Song times; Wu Ke 吳可 (ca. 1126) wrote, "Studying poetry is entirely like studying Chan"[6] and Yan Yu 嚴羽 (fl. 1180–1235), the most influential critic of the Southern Song, divided poets into a Great and Small Vehicle and a North and South Sect in line with current Chan Buddhist doctrine, maintaining that "the Way of poetry lies in miraculous enlightenment (*miao wu* 妙悟)."[7] Perhaps even more significant for our own study is the fact that Fan Chengda's close friend,

Yang Wanli, couched practically all of his critical remarks in Buddhist-inspired language.[8]

However, Buddhism seems to have influenced Fan Chengda more strongly than any of the other major poets of his period, so that an understanding of his verse is impossible without some reference to the central philosophy of his life. Fan's Buddhism was known to his contemporaries, and a friend Zhang Zi 張鎡 (b. 1153) wrote to Fan: "In the morning you burn Buddhist incense and then engage in meditation,"[9] while another contemporary, Lou Yue 樓鑰 (1137–1213), wrote a colophon in which he discussed the Buddhist symbolism behind the poems Fan wrote on his pilgrimage to Mount Emei in Sichuan.[10] In spite of the obvious importance of Buddhism for Fan, post-Song critics rarely mention his Buddhism, and the only scholar to have written much of significance on Fan in contemporary China, Zhou Ruchang, seems to have almost gone out of his way to omit Buddhist poems from his anthology of Fan's verse and is critical of Fan's Buddhism, heaping particular scorn on his *gâthâ* poems, works written in imitation of Chinese translations of Buddhist Sanskrit verse.[11]

In one of his earliest surviving poems, Fan already complains that the fragrance of some daphne flowers "disturbs my secluded meditation (*nao you chan*)," and one of the best sets of quatrains that he wrote before assuming his first official position is entitled "The Shrine of Meditation" (see p. 101), after a shrine that Fan had constructed specially for his own Buddhist exercises.[12] From such works we can conclude that Buddhist meditation formed a regular part of Fan's life from his earliest years, but after 1177 when, at the age of fifty-one, Fan made a pilgrimage to the Buddhist holy sites of Mount Emei in modern Sichuan province, his Buddhist poetry increased greatly in quantity and quality, and from that time until his death, he filled every chapter of his collected works with many poems that refer directly to Buddhist ideas.

Fan's specifically Buddhist poems leave us with the general impression that, although he was certainly versed in Buddhism's philosophical side, his Buddhism was less intellectual than other Song authors, and piety and faith played a more important role in his religious life. While serving in his first official post, Fan composed a poem about prayers offered to the Fifth Arhat for rain in which he writes that "the spiritual powers and compassionate vows [of the Arhat] are infinite,"[13] and not long after, he wrote another poem about a visit to a Buddhist monastery, in which he records the various pious legends associated with the holy site.[14]

Throughout his life Fan was fascinated by religious miracles; in the preface to a poem about a Buddhist monastery near the West Lake at

Hangzhou, Fan writes: "The gate of the monastery is enclosed by rock walls. Three immortals named Yan Yu, Li Jia, and Xiao Yun wrote poems on the rocks, and just as they were wielding their brushes, an arm stretched out more than three meters. The startled gate-keeper reported this to the head monk, but when everyone returned to see it, the arm had already disappeared."[15] Similarly, when on the way to his pilgrimage to Mount Emei, Fan writes in the preface to a poem about the holy places near Middle Peak (Zhongyen) in Sichuan: "It is said that a monk of Mount Tiantai [modern Zhejiang province] once met a sick monk who gave him a wooden key and said, 'In the future when you travel to Middle Peak in Meizhou, knock this against a stalagmite, and I will immediately reappear.' Later it actually happened as he said."[16]

The most moving religious experience of Fan's life was unquestionably his ascent of the main peak of Mount Emei in 1177 when he saw the "Buddha light" (*foguang*), believed to be a manifestation of the Bodhisattva Samântabhadra (Chinese, Puxian), who is especially revered at Mount Emei. Fan was so overwhelmed by his experience that he had the long poem that he wrote on the occasion engraved on the mountain so that it could serve as a "lesson for meditation [*gongan*]." At the climax of this poem Fan writes:

> A giant round form suddenly wells forth from the mountain before me;
> The sun is circled by a halo like the moon and floats in the blue sky.
> All the forests, streams, and plants are wrapped within
> What people call the radiance of Samântabhadra, the Wise.
> A vocabulary vast as the ocean would not suffice to describe
> The golden bridge that lies athwart the mountain's northern peak.[17]

From this time until Fan's death, Buddhism was the faith that sustained him through the illnesses and other adversities of his later years. Even in 1176 before he made his pilgrimage to Emei, Fan had composed a poem to comfort his friend Chao Zixi 晁子西, who had written Fan about the many deaths in his family, reminding Chao that, according to Buddhist teachings, both life and death are unreal (*wu sheng yi wu wang*).[18] In common with other Chinese poets such as Wang Wei in the Tang dynasty and Fan's friend Yang Wanli, Fan Chengda enjoyed comparing himself to the Indian sage Vimalakîrti, the most famous Buddhist layman of all time, and even on one occasion to Bodhidharma, the Chan sect's legendary founder.[19]

Fan's Buddhism was unusual for a Song intellectual in the closeness that he felt to the Buddha, as he wrote on his return from Mount Emei to Chengdu:

Late in the day I gaze from the Pavilion for Praying to the Buddha toward the dozens of peaks of the Snow Mountains, which resemble molten silver glowing in the summer light

Their bright snow illuminates the sky's western corner;
Sunrays float continuously high above the rain.
Their summits never experience the months of summer;
I imagine the dusty world below has bid farewell to high autumn.
It seems that the Buddha wants to keep me from leaving –
Even by evening he does not remove his gold bridge that arches over the wastes.[20]

Such poetry suggests that Fan did not regard the Buddha as some remote deity, but rather as an amicable being with whom he was on intimate terms. Fan's work may be far from the devotional Christian verse so common in European literatures, but it certainly proves that for Fan Buddhism was more than an abstract philosophy or a discipline of meditative practices.

Before we leave the topic of Fan Chengda's specifically Buddhist poetry, we must briefly examine his *jiyu* 偈語 or *gâthâ* verses. As we have mentioned above, the contemporary scholar Zhou Ruchang severely condemns Fan Chengda *gâthâs*, but, in fact, other illustrious poets wrote similar verse. The Chinese *gâthâ* developed from Chinese translations of Indian Buddhist sutras, which generally consist of prose passages alternating with sections in poetic form (*gâthâs*, or "songs"). The literary quality of the Chinese translations of these poetic passages is, for the most part, mediocre, aiming more for literal accuracy than literary grace, and they did not exercise any major influence on the basically aristocratic verse of the Period of Division, during which many of the most widely used translations were completed. However, such popular forms of literature as the Tang dynasty *bianwen* 變文, or "miracle texts," seem to have been inspired by translations of Indian Buddhist sutras,[21] and by early Tang times popular poets such as Hanshan created a substantial amount of verse that displays the mark of the *gâthâ*.[22] Even renowned High Tang authors such as Wang Wei did not disdain writing verse that resembles *gâthâ*, and, as we have seen, the form remained popular into Northern Song times.[23]

However, no major Southern Song poet seems to have been as interested in the *gâthâ* as Fan Chengda. He was already composing poems like *gâthâ* long before he obtained his first official position, although the first work that actually uses the word *gâthâ* in its title was not written until around 1155.[24] Three quatrains that Fan wrote in 1185 when he was sixty years old are typical of this sort of verse:

The disciples of Buddha and our defiled bodies
Are pervaded by the same marvelous fragrance.

In the past, it came here to lead me astray,
But now I'm going to fool it myself!

A method to calm your mind does exist,
And everyone should practice it without respite.
Just busy yourself with today's concerns,
And finish your life, as it was fated.

Outside my window lie the world's dust-defiled affairs;
Inside my window, my body exists in a dream.
Now that I know that my body is a dream,
I can dismiss the world for the defilement that it is![25]

Admittedly such poems, with their unabashed didacticism and clumsy language taken from Indian Buddhist sutras (e.g., *shengwen*, Sanskrit *srâvakas* or "disciples of the Buddha"), do not rise to the level of Fan's better verse. However, even in these poems, we observe the flash of Fan's wit (particularly in the first poem with the playful conceit of revenge against the illusions of past experience), and Fan's *gâthâs* hardly deserve Zhou Ruchang's censure. Fan probably did not take such poetry too seriously or else he would have preserved many more *gâthâs* in his complete works, but his *gâthâs* comprise a significant record of his spiritual development.

Sleep and sickness

In the last of the three quatrains just translated, Fan refers to his "body that exists in a dream," and this brings us to two of the commonest and most successful Buddhist themes of his poetry, sleep and sickness. At first sight we might be tempted to ignore the connections between these two themes and Fan Chengda's Buddhist faith, for we have seen that he was frequently ill, and one would expect that a poet who wrote so much about everyday experience would treat the subject of sleep.

In fact, Fan's early sleep poems do not display any philosophical pretensions:

Setting out in the morning: The courier station at Guantang

Couriers holding hooded lanterns call us to set off;
The Milky Way's stars fade just before the fifth watch.
On horseback I am startled from my thousand-mile dreams –
A small cart rumbles past me, just below Rock Ridge.[26]

This work lacks obvious Buddhist symbolism about the dreamlike nature of human existence, but it still is a remarkable evocation of the twilight realm between the "unreal" world of dreams and the world of "reality," the hooded lanterns and the setting Milky Way reflecting Fan's still unawakened mind, which is startled from its physically impossible dream by the rumble of a cart located specifically "just below Rock Ridge." Although the poem describes the transition from dream to waking, it also suggests that the "dream" world and "real" world are both mysteriously interconnected and at the same time mutually exclusive.

Early in his literary career, however, Fan begins associating sleep with the Buddhist's detachment from the world, especially the world of the scholar official. In the early set of four poems about his Buddhist meditations (see translations on p. 101), he already contrasts his sleep with the materialistically motivated activities of the officials [who] "await the emperor's water clock with frost-covered boots." By opposing his sleep to the world of officialdom, Fan is continuing the tradition of mystically inspired poetry, originated by Tao Qian, who frequently contrasted his *xian* 閑 (idleness or leisure) with the worldly bustle of vulgar people.[27]

It was not until middle age that Fan fully defined the connection between the world of sleep and his Buddhist faith in his poetry:

In bed at the Nuoxing shrine

I awake terrified by a nightmare on my cold bed at dawn;
The dim lamp still shines by my herbal stove's side.
Light plays across the window's paper like a hazy moon;
I have completed one more night's sleep in my drifting life.[28]

Here Fan interprets the waking-sleeping dichotomy in purely Buddhist terms, describing how he awakes from the illusory nightmare world of sleep to the equally hazy and illusory world of reality. However, such a work is much more appealing than the purely didactic *gâthâs*, skillfully capturing the evanescence of "real" life through the images of the cold bed, the dim lamp, and the comparison of morning sunlight to hazy moonlight, a trope that is not only strikingly original but that also underscores the illusory nature of time.

The theme of sickness also occurs at the very beginning of Fan Chengda's surviving verse, where Fan already sees the close connection between sickness and sleep:

After I sit up sick at night I show this to Tang Zhiyuan

Like fog, like smoke, the night's vapors swirl around me;
A stork's cry scares away my dreams; I sit up and scratch my head.
Shadows of wind-tossed bamboos faintly retain the moonlight;

Chants of rain-soaked crickets complain bitterly of the autumn.
Mind empty of the world's affairs, I grow accustomed to my dullness,
The year grows late for my body, assailed by disease on all sides.
Of course, I should walk to the West Hills and gather medicinal herbs,
But my gait is halting, and I fear the long journey![29]

Here Fan's illness only heightens the sense of the world's insubstantiality, which he experiences upon awakening from the realm of dreams. A fog swirls around him, and his mind has difficulty focusing on the "real" objects in his surroundings. However, the poem is not entirely negative, for although Fan's disease seems incurable, he has been able to empty his mind of worldly affairs, and even manages to close his work with some of his typical wit.

The connection between Fan Chengda's description of his recurrent illnesses and his Buddhist faith would have been obvious to Fan and his contemporaries. The Prince Siddhârtha's first experience of "old age, sickness, and death" (*lao, bing, si*) was the direct inspiration for his renunciation of the world and the beginning of the quest that led to his enlightenment as the Buddha. Fan's early poetry on his sickness frequently refers to meditative practices, and at the conclusion of a poem written in 1176 he says: "Weary from disease, this mortal frame is no longer Me; / All I think of now is the meditation board and mat."[30]

In the examples cited so far we have seen how Fan uses sleep and sickness as a metaphor for the illusory nature of the material universe, but later in his life he gave an imaginative twist to a theme that already had a long history in China by stressing the more positive side of sleep and sickness. We have already noted that in his old age Fan identified more and more closely with the sage Vimalakîrti, who was supposedly more enlightened than Buddha's disciples although he did not leave the world to enter a monastery, and Fan repeatedly stresses this particular element of the Vimalakîrti ideal in such lines as: "By chance my worldly home is just like a monastery,"[31] from which it was not a long step to conclude that his life of sleep and recuperation from his illnesses resembled the life of a monk, or, as Fan put it in 1185, when he was sixty years old: "Old and lazy I live at home like a monk who has taken his vows."[32] Similarly, Fan could view the sickroom not just as a symbol for mankind's brief life in an insubstantial world, but also, more positively, as a place of Buddhist meditation: "My sickroom's window is withdrawn and hidden like a meditation hall; / Half-bathed in light all day, unbroken clouds of incense curling upward."[33] or "Under a lone lamp's light herbs boil in my cauldron, / And I kneel on my meditation cushion like a sick, old monk."[34]

Although Fan's poems on sleep and sickness are a remarkable record of his spiritual development and commitment to his Buddhist faith, their strongest appeal to the reader lies in values that transcend their philosophical and religious content. By limiting so much of his later verse to his sickroom, Fan Chengda not only saw the immediate world about him with special clarity but also heightened his perception of the world outside, experiencing it almost entirely through hearing or smelling with a sensitivity unusual for "healthy" individuals.

An excellent example of Fan's heightened sensitivity is a group of four quatrains he wrote about the sounds of the street activities outside his sickroom and how he used them to regulate his own life (see translations on p. 158), of which the following is the second:

> When the vegetable vendors start shouting, my window is bright;
> When the cake seller hawks his wares, I've finished boiling medicine.
> I stay idly at home and have no reason to go out;
> I hear only the opening of doors and the swish of brooms.[35]

In these poems Fan would seem to have withdrawn completely from the world, living "idly" like some Buddhist monk in a monastery, his "devotions" centered on the daily ritual of boiling his medicinal herbs, but, in fact, his awareness of the world has been intensified by his isolation from it, and even the slightest auditory sensations do not escape him. We have already referred to Yoshikawa's characterization of Huang Tingjian's verse as "introverted," but such poetry is the logical development and perfection of Huang's "introversion," which, by downplaying the intricacies of Jiangxi-style verse, distills the very essence of ordinary human experience.

5
The mountains and rivers

Human nature

It is customary to divide Chinese nature poetry into two genres, bucolic poetry (*tianyuan shi* 田園詩, literally "poetry of fields and gardens"), which describes the cultivated countryside, and landscape poetry (*shanshui shi* 山水詩, literally "poetry of mountains and rivers,"), which celebrates untamed nature. Fan Chengda is much more famous for his bucolic verse (particularly the works written after his retirement), but, in fact, Fan created much fine landscape poetry before he reached old age.

Before we examine the development of Fan Chengda's landscape poetry we should note that it is sometimes difficult to distinguish between it and his bucolic verse, because of changes that he and other Southern Song authors brought about in their treatment of nature, changes that seem to have been influenced by a fundamental alteration in the way intellectuals viewed nature during Southern Song times. We have already examined the pathetic fallacy as a witty conceit in Fan Chengda's poetry, but, in fact, Fan's frequent personification of nature should also be viewed in relation to the general tendency of Southern Song poets and painters to humanize nature. Just as the painters of the so-called Ma-Xia school (named after the two painters Ma Yuan 馬遠 [fl. 1190–1230] and Xia Gui 夏珪 [fl. 1190–1230]) replaced the overpowering, almost forbidding mountains and rivers of Northern Song artists with their tranquil and more accessible visions of the Chinese landscape, Fan Chengda and his contemporaries created their serene vision of a landscape that was more approachable for human beings in place of the Northern Song fascination with the wilder aspects of the landscape.[1]

In Fan Chengda's case at least, this transformation seems to be connected with his religious views. We have already seen how Fan believed that he could enjoy an intimate relationship with the Buddha himself, and such a belief would logically lead to the view that nature is fundamentally benevolent. Thus, in one poem Fan tells us that "the face of heaven is warm and beautiful," and in another long landscape poem, he interprets a rare snowstorm sent to subtropical Guilin as a sign of the Lord of Heaven's solicitude for him:[2]

> The Lord of Heaven was afraid Guilin's miasmas would depress me
> And let the wind howl for ten days until the rocks split open.
> Only then could snow clouds cross over the steep passes
> And crags of white jade loom around me after a single night.[3]

In other works the relation between poet and nature is so intimate that nature constantly plays tricks on Fan and jokes with him like some kindly uncle, as in a poem on some rapids that Fan passed, in which he writes: "The clear stream is terrifying and delightful, too; / The Creator is always playing his pranks on us humans!"[4]

Of course, it is difficult to determine the boundary between literary conceit and true convictions about the fundamental nature of the universe in such works, but the quiet, subdued landscape poetry that results from Fan's view of a basically benign world exemplifies the blurring of distinctions between landscape and bucolic verse in much of his early poetry:

Fragrant Mountain

Where the King of Wu planted fragrant flowers.[5]

My magnolia-decked boat enters the path where they once picked fragrant flowers;
Now I chew the blossoms and exhale their perfume, as I drift through them, dazzled.
Setting sun and green mountains are both just where they belong;
White buckwheat among the mulberries overflows the redolent isles.[6]

Just as in a Ma Yuan painting, the realm of untamed nature (the mountains and flowers) merges harmoniously with the world of man, represented by the buckwheat and mulberries growing in the peasants' fields. Although this poem approaches bucolic verse more closely than others in the same series (see, for example, the more purely landscape poem "Xukou" from the series translated on p. 44), all the poems in the series assume the same tranquil vision of a world in which everything seems to have been designed expressly for the enjoyment of the human poet, who drifts at ease through its brilliant colors and subtle perfumes.

The Yangzi Gorges poems

Fan continued to write landscape poetry in this mode well into his forties, and produced similar works even in his old age, but the voyage that he undertook through the Yangzi Gorges during the year 1175 on the way to his official post in Sichuan substantially modified his landscape poetry. Signs of future developments are already apparent in the descriptive passages of a long poem he wrote about Mount Heng, the Chinese holy mountain of the south, which he visited in 1173 on his first journey outside the gentle landscapes of Jiangsu and Zhejiang provinces:

> There are so many mountains along the Xiang River,
> Stationed on either side like a thousand war horses.
> They slant and slope but don't dare climb too high,
> Out of polite deference to lofty Mount Heng.
> At morning I rest at the Cloud-Gazing Pavilion,
> Which is hemmed in by a palisade of crowded foothills.
> Dense mists suddenly drift all over Mount Heng,
> And layers of turquoise float on the tips of its clouds.
> Mount Heng's Pillar of Heaven climbs up precipitously,
> But its frigid peak of Zhurong towers even higher.
> The Violet Shroud soars gloomily in their middle;
> With slopes that hurtle forward like crashing waves. . . .[7]

Here Fan does not abandon the devices of his earlier verse, cleverly comparing the mountains on both sides of the Xiang River to "war horses" that have been tethered there, commenting wittily how its foothills resemble humans in their "deference" to Mount Heng, and painting the mountains with his usual rich palette of colors, but his description of Mount Heng's four peaks in the last four lines is suffused with a vitality never encountered in his earlier landscape poetry. Unfortunately, this poem does not live up to the promise of the opening lines we have translated, largely because its later sections are poorly organized, a fault that mars much of Fan Chengda's nature verse of the Guilin period. We have already suggested that the deficiencies in Fan's Guilin poetry may have arisen from his depression over reverses in his official career, but it is also possible that he was experiencing difficulties in overcoming the aesthetic problems of describing a landscape so different from the part of China where he had lived before his journey to the south.

In any case, Fan Chengda eventually surmounted his emotional and literary problems to create his finest landscape poetry about the wild and sometimes frightening mountain scenery of the Yangzi Gorges, which, as we have seen, was already admired by his contemporaries in Sichuan and was to be praised highly by later critics such as Fang Hui during the Yuan dynasty.[8] Fan was not the first Chinese poet to be deeply stirred by the Yangzi Gorges' spectacular vistas, for in the Tang dynasty both Li Bai and Du Fu created some of their most powerful works about their travels in this region, and Fan Chengda's friend, Lu You, who traveled to Sichuan before him, celebrated the marvels of the Gorges in both poetry and prose.[9]

Although the obvious physical differences between the Yangzi Gorges and the lowlands of Fan's native place are partly responsible for the contrast between Fan's Sichuan poems and his earlier works, stylistic concerns are of at least equal importance. Fan had composed most of his previous landscape poetry in the eight-line regulated style (or the closely related quatrain), a form of verse which, with its antithetical couplets and tightly controlled rhyme schemes and tonal patterns, was a perfect vehicle for the detailed miniatures of his early years. Fan obviously found the regulated form unsuitable for describing the Yangzi Gorges or the holy mountains of Sichuan, and, perhaps under the influence of Li Bai, he adopted the much freer "ancient" form (*gushi* 古詩), which is as different from regulated poetry as a long silk scroll is from a painting inscribed on a fan.[10]

At the same time, Fan's Sichuan Gorge poems do display certain traits in common with his other verse. We note a tendency to see nature at least partly in human terms, the most striking example of which occurs in the conclusion to "The Maelstroms" (translated on p. 138), where Fan personifies the Yangzi River as the River God, a deity who is expected to bow before the Chinese emperor's authority. Original and striking figures of speech also abound. In "Where Snakes Slide Back" (p. 135), the cliff in front of Fan "rises sheer as if pared by a knife" and Fan's ascent up the mountain is "like shinnying up a thin bamboo pole," while in "The Forty-Eight Bends" (p. 137) the path Fan traverses "twists and curves, going nowhere, like an inept official." Fan must have experienced problems in adapting to the greater freedom of ancient-style verse, for many of the poems exhibit a verbal and syntactic complexity (largely diluted by our English translation), which is certainly more suitable for the regulated poetry that he had favored earlier for his landscape verse.

Even after noting some of the congruences between the Sichuan poems and Fan's earlier works, however, we cannot avoid being struck by the great contrasts between these poems and the type of poetry for which Fan is best known. For example, although some of the poems do employ the pathetic fallacy, the River God does not appear until the conclusion of the poem on maelstroms, where Fan atypically reverts to the political and moral symbolism of pre-Southern Song literature, the River God representing the wild forces of nature that are supposed to submit to the emperor's civilizing influence. In another poem, "The White Dog Gorges" (p. 137), Fan describes the river boulders as if they were evil bandits with "hard, steely faces," who "eye one another in treacherous conspiracy; / They crouch on the banks, evil thoughts in their minds, / Or lurk in midriver with hideous grins." Here the pathetic fallacy produces an effect exactly opposite that of his earlier nature poetry, for now the landscape is "dismal and bleak," "so dark and gloomy, no human voices can be heard"; that is, it is no longer Fan's benign, human landscape, but rather a landscape that is hostile to all human life.

The other conceits of Fan Chengda's ealier poetry also create quite unexpected effects in his poetry on the Yangzi Gorges. When his poem on the maelstroms says that the Yangzi's water is "smooth as ironed gauze" or rolls like "agitated silk," we imagine that we are still in Fan's world of artificial nature, but when his boat descends into a "cauldron" of "bubbling and seething water," whirling like a "millstone grinding tea" amid waves "spewn from a hidden leviathan's jaws," we are less impressed by the cleverness of the tropes than by their incredible energy. In fact, although Fan does not banish wit from his Yangzi Gorges poems, the vital force of these poems is what remains with the reader longest. Fan's experiences in the Yangzi Gorges clearly opened his mind to new possibilities for landscape poetry, and although after his arrival in Sichuan he returned to a somewhat quieter mode, there is a strong spiritual undercurrent to most of the landscape poetry he wrote there (see, for example, his poem composed on the summit of Mount Fengding, p. 141), which reached a new climax in the Buddhist nature poetry arising from his pilgrimage to Mount Emei's holy sites at the end of his stay in Sichuan.

To a large degree, however, Fan Chengda's Sichuan poetry constitutes a departure from the general direction of his poetic development, for although the new spiritual insights he gained in Sichuan strongly influenced his later religious and literary life, he never again wrote landscape poetry with the uninhibited vigor of his Sichuan period. In a sense, Sichuan is not just geographically isolated from Fan Chengda's homeland in Jiangsu but also represents a literary realm, which is divorced from the normal world that his poetry inhabits. Passing out of the Yangzi Gorges on his return voyage to his home at Stone Lake (Shihu), Fan Chengda writes:

In midstream at Jiangling I look back toward Witch Mountain, but I cannot see it at all, and I compose the following short poem in jest

Traveling among the Yangzi Gorges' thousands of mountains,
You can't believe there's a level spot in the entire world,
But when you gaze back from Jiangling, water merges with sky,
And you suspect there never were any mountains to begin with!
The mountains and rivers that once greeted me wave farewell now,
They vanish in an eye's twinkling, just as in a dream.
Today I've covered a third of my thousand-mile journey home;
I'm ready to dream I've arrived at the shore of Stone Lake![11]

This poem is both a farewell to Sichuan and an anticipation of Fan's return to his native village, but it is much more than a record of leaving one part of China for another, for the poem constitutes a literary leave-taking of one style and a return to the more typical style that he had neglected during his service in Sichuan. Now Fan departs from Sichuan's awesome landscapes, and Sichuan's mountains and water vanish "just as in a dream" so that the poet suspects "there never were any mountains to begin with." Not only does Fan leave the mountains physically to return to the plains of the Yangtze Basin, but he also returns to the "broad plains" of his mature poetic style, creating a poem "in jest" (i.e., a witty poem) in his favorite form, eight-lined regulated verse, in which he employs one of his standard devices, the pathetic fallacy. Yet Fan is not only bidding Sichuan's mountains farewell; he is also bidding farewell to landscape poetry in general, for although he continued to write interesting landscape poetry for the rest of his life, he became increasingly involved in the second genre of Chinese nature poetry, the bucolic poetry of fields and gardens, the genre for which he has been most widely admired by Chinese readers over the last seven centuries.

6
The fields and gardens

Early bucolic poetry

Bucolic poetry, in its broadest sense, has a long history in China, for already in the *Classic of Poetry*, or *Shijing* 詩經 (twelfth century B.C.–fifth century B.C.), poems such as "Seventh Month" give detailed accounts of agricultural activities and rural life.[1] However, the *Shijing* poems of this sort did not achieve a particularly high level of inspiration. Most Chinese literary historians consider true bucolic poetry to have originated with the work of Tao Qian (365–427) from whose series of poems, "On Returning to My Garden and Field" (*Gui tianyuan ju*), the Chinese term for bucolic poetry (*tianyuan*, "fields and gardens") derives.[2]

Tao Qian's bucolic poetry was different from the work of Western bucolic poets such as Theocritus and Virgil, because Tao used the backdrop of the countryside and peasant life to discuss his philosophical and social concerns (of course, social concerns are not completely lacking from the Greek and Latin bucolic poets). The resulting poetry is underpinned by neo-Daoist, eremitic Confucian, and possibly even Buddhist ideals, and the "return to nature" (*fan ziran* 返自然) is a metaphor for the poet's return to his originally pure nature (*xing* 性), and the "purity" of the peasants' lives is opposed to the "dusty," materialistic world of official life.[3]

Religio-philosophical poetry dominated the genre for many centuries, but an alternative approach to bucolic poetry appeared in Tang times with the work of Bai Juyi (772–846) and the poets associated with him.[4] Bai and his followers created their poems under the influence of renascent Confucian ideals, expressed particularly aptly in Bai's preface to his *Xin yuefu shi* 新樂府詩 (*New Music Bureau poems*), in which he restates the old Confucian dictum of the political and social purposes of literature.[5] Although Bai's poems are not usually classified as bucolic poetry in China, since they focus on the exploitation of the peasants and generally exclude a wider treatment of the countryside, they had a strong influence on later bucolic poetry.

It is obvious that neither the Buddho-Daoist tradition initiated by Tao Qian nor the neo-Confucian work of Bai Juyi was interested in the rural landscape or the peasants' life per se, for in both traditions, the beauties of countryside and peasant folkways were largely incidental to the authors' "larger" purposes, and although Fan Chengda's verse displays the influence of both approaches, one of his greatest contributions to bucolic poetry was the liberation of the tradition from its earlier intellectual burdens. In the following discussion we are not going to treat Fan's poetry on rural scenery, because, as we have seen, in his pre-Sichuan verse, the boundary between landscape (*shanshui*) poetry and bucolic (*tianyuan*) poetry is difficult to define, and what we have already said about the stylistic evolution of his pre-Sichuan landscape poetry is applicable to most of the bucolic poetry he wrote before he entered the Yangzi Gorges. Instead we are going to focus on his treatment of peasant life in his bucolic verse, because it is easier to see his originality in this sphere.

The "Bamboo Branch Songs," or *Zhuzhi ci* 竹枝詞, originally of folk origin and first imitated by the Tang poet Liu Yuxi 劉禹錫 (772–842), would seem to constitute an exception to the philosophically and politically inspired bucolic verse written before Song times. The possible influence of these works on Fan Chengda must be examined in more detail. According to his own account, written about 821 when he was serving in an official position in Sichuan, Liu Yuxi composed his first "Bamboo Branch Songs" after witnessing a performance of folk songs sung by male villagers to the accompaniment of flute and drum music.[6] Although there is some variety in Liu's works, the following poem is fairly representative:

> Mountain peach flowers fill the high places with red;
> Spring water of Sichuan rivers dash against the hills.
> The red blossoms wither easily like your love for me,
> And the water flows without end – the same as my sorrow![7]

The simple diction and colloquialisms such as *shangtou* ("above," translated as "high places" here) betray the folk origins of the poem, and the theme of the deserted lover was already conventional in Chinese folk poetry many centuries before Liu wrote.

Even in Liu Yuxi's "Bamboo Branch Songs," however, the concerns of the scholar official frequently intrude into the folk form:

> Before the west city gate stands the Yanyu Rock,
> Which the waves have not destroyed through countless years.
> How it rankles me that men's hearts are not as firm as this stone,
> For they veer east a short time, and then swerve back west again![8]

Although one could interpret Liu's poem as another imitation of the peasant's complaint against an unfaithful lover, it is much more likely that he is attacking his "unprincipled" enemies in the court, who brought about his downfall after the failure of the Yongzhen Reform.[9] In conclusion, one can say that although Liu Yuxi was unusual in his interest in and imitation of folk poetry, the folk element is frequently subordinated to his own concerns, and even when he does treat rural life, his poetry is largely confined to stereotypes present in the older folk tradition.

In our discussion of Fan's imitative period, we mentioned his interest in the poetry of the Tang author Wang Jian (metropolitan graduate degree in 775). Although Wang was not predominantly a bucolic poet, and we must be cautious about making too much out of Fan writing a total of four poems in imitation of Wang, there are some interesting resemblances between Wang's original poems and Fan's later bucolic poetry. According to Fan Chengda, his work "Peasants Entertain a Guest" (see the translation of Fan's work on p. 106) was modeled on Wang Jian's work by the same name:

Peasants entertain a guest

> "It's a shame so few people stay overnight in our cottage:
> You'll eat our fresh rice gruel, and we'll feed your horse grain.
> Your servants must be tired and hungry after such a long walk;
> My new daughter-in-law in the kitchen is almost finished cooking dinner.
> I hope our run-down cottage doesn't offend you:
> We just plastered the silkworm shed to keep the wind and dust out.
> Dear guest, drink your fill and don't worry about our poor life;
> Your honor must be exhausted after such a hard journey."
> The peasant turned his head and commanded his wife
> "Don't let the children cry tonight and bother our guest."
> "A pair of tomb mounds," he continued, "marks the path to the highway.
> I'll tell my eldest son to guide you there tomorrow morning."[10]

Although the peasant host's extensive speech in Wang's poem creates a rather different effect from the third-person narrative of Fan's imitation, the similarities between the two poems are obvious, and unlike so much bucolic poetry of Tang and earlier times, neither poet advances any particular philosophical or political viewpoint but merely provides a vivid and appealing portrait of the Chinese peasant's hospitality toward travelers. Two other poems Fan wrote in imitation of Wang Jian resemble Bai Juyi's New Music Bureau verse, but Fan's first poem of the series of four, like Wang's original, provides a highly original picture of peasant religious customs (see p. 106), a topic that most Tang authors avoided.

However, we should not fall into the trap of overemphasizing Wang Jian's impact on Fan Chengda, because Fan's early imitations of Wang's work did not lead to any immediate change in the themes or style of his poetry, and whatever inspiration Fan derived from Wang lay dormant many years, for in spite of the prominence of bucolic poetry in Fan Chengda's later verse, poetry on peasant life is not extremely common in his earlier years. Nevertheless, a few of the bucolic poems Fan wrote before he went to Sichuan are free of both the New Music Bureau poets' political concerns and the Buddho-Daoist approach of authors such as Tao Qian:

Transplanting rice seedlings

First planted close, now apart, they resemble a level, green carpet;
Cool, shallow water ripples like brocade between the rows.
Who could guess that among these slender, green plants
Is concealed the sound of clappers celebrating the rich harvest to come?[11]

This early poem already displays many of the stylistic characteristics of Fan's mature verse: the decorative tropes (rice paddies like "a level, green carpet," water like "brocade"), and the unexpected wit of the conclusion, namely, that the beat of clappers could be "concealed" among the tender, green leaves of the rice seedlings. At the same time, Fan's interest in peasant life itself is still embryonic, for the poem focuses on the rice paddy rather than the peasants' activities, although at the end of the poem we can sense the excitement with which the peasants observe the growth of the rice seedlings and can anticipate the jubilation of their harvest celebration in the future.

Although peasant life is largely peripheral to the rural scenes Fan creates in most of his early bucolic poetry, a few poems deal directly with the livelihood of the farmers and rural proletariat:

Beneath the bamboos

Under pines and firs, the morning air chills;
Under mulberry trees, the shade turns sparse.
Gilded rice tassles prepare to droop;
The rose of Sharon stays red, unprepared to fall.

In autumn the oriole still acts coy and coquettish;
This late in the year butterflies glide and flutter about.
My stupid dog chases a horse and its cart,
Scaring the chickens so badly they swoop against the fence.
On the road I meet an itinerant peddler and ask:
"How many pairs of shoes have you worn out in your life?"
"My carrying pole," he answers, "has rubbed my shoulder red in my travels;
I work to feed my family and don't worry about my feet.
I earn just enough to keep the wolf from the door,
But I haven't been able to put any money away."
"I, too, slave for a few bushels of rice," I replied,
"And for three years I've been away from the hills of my home.
Both of us have lost what's most important in life –[12]
No sense in bothering about who's better off than the other!"[13]

It is not impossible that Fan Chengda had Bai Juyi's New Music Bureau ballads in the back of his mind when he created this work, but this poem is remote from Bai Juyi's Confucian-inspired critiques of Chinese society. First of all, the languorous early autumn atmosphere evoked in the first eight lines contrasts markedly with the typical bleak late autumn or winter scenes that form the backdrop for so much of Bai Juyi's critical poetry, and Fan dilutes his political message even further by comparing his own plight to that of the peddler.[14] Nonetheless, one could argue that by underscoring the common humanity between the peddler and himself, Fan creates a richer and more complex poem than one usually finds in Bai Juyi's political verse, for although both Fan and the peddler suffer from material deprivation, the main point is that they have lost "what is most important in life," suggesting spiritual dimensions never explored in Bai Juyi's Music Bureau poems.

Thus, we can conclude that certain elements of Fan's treatment of peasant life in his bucolic verse are present in his early work, but just as Fan Chengda's voyage to Sichuan spurred the development of his landscape poetry, the same voyage comprised a turning point in the development of his bucolic verse. As in the case of Liu Yuxi three centuries earlier, Sichuan folk poetry seems to have been one influence, and Fan Chengda composed two sets of "Bamboo Branch Songs" during his stay in Sichuan:

Women with goitres rush downtown to be on time for the market,
Racing in dozens along the south street, where goods are for sale.
Gentlemen, please don't make fun of these ugly ladies;
Just see how their young boyfriends buy them silver hairpins![15]

However, such a poem is a bamboo branch song only in its adherence to the form of the folk poems and its description of peasant life, for it lacks the conventional love interest of the original "Bamboo Branch Songs" or Liu Yuxi's allegorical extension of such romantic themes. Fan Chengda's "Bamboo Branch Songs" (see translations on p. 140 and a similar work, "The Great Fork Narrows," on p. 136) provide a realistic portrait of Sichuan peasant life, which transcends the earlier philosophical or political conventions of most Tang dynasty verse. Of course, Fan does not attempt to cover up the peasants' poverty, and the huge goitres that hang from the peasant women's necks in this poem might suggest to the "gentlemen" that they are inferior to other humans, but Fan counters that, just like other people, they love self-adornment, and their beauty is appreciated by their lovers. Although Fan manages to conclude his poem wittily, his wit is directed against those who would look down upon the lower classes and only serves to strengthen the strong sense of humanity that underlies all his poetry on the Chinese peasant from this Sichuan period until his death.

The four seasons

Without a doubt, Fan Chengda's most famous group of bucolic poems is his *Impromptu Verses on the Four Seasons of the Countryside* (*Sishi tianyuan zaxing* 四時田園雜興), a sequence of sixty heptasyllabic quatrains translated in its entirety into rhyming English verse by Gerald Bullett (1946) as *The Golden Year of Fan Ch'eng-ta.*[16] As one can see from the title, this series of poems is a sequence of bucolic poems arranged in order according to the seasons of the year (actually five seasons are represented – early spring, late spring, summer, autumn, and winter). Therefore, one might be tempted to view the sequence as an organic whole, but Fan's short preface warns us not to adopt this approach:

> In the *bingwu* year of the Chunxi reign period [1186], my illness became less serious, and once again I could go to my old place of reclusion at Stone Lake. Whenever I found inspiration in the fields, I immediately wrote down a quatrain, and by the end of the year I had obtained sixty quatrains, which I entitled *Impromptu Verses on the Four Seasons of the Countryside.*[17]

Although Fan's series does not lack all plan (for example, there are exactly twelve quatrains in each of the five seasonal subdivisions), and the use of the heptasyllabic quatrain for the entire series provides an undeniable sense of stylistic unity, the series includes such a wide variety of verse that any attempt to discover some grand design is futile, and

Fan's preface suggesting the improvisational nature of his creations should be taken at face value.

The variety of themes is, in fact, so great, that certain themes that are relatively rare in Fan Chengda's post-Sichuan bucolic verse reappear. For example, although most of the poems on peasant life avoid social commentary in the tradition of Bai Juyi, criticism of the peasants' plight is present in some works:

> The water chestnut pickers' labor is hard, with no plow or hoe to help;
> Red blood flows from their fingers, their bodies are thin like ghosts.
> They have no money to buy fields on land and farm the water instead,
> But lately landlords force them to pay rent for lake water – too![18]

Nor is Tao Qian's Daoist-inspired idea that the life of the recluse is superior to that of city dwellers and officials completely absent:

> The sun by the eaves toasts my back like a stove's fire;
> I am intoxicated by its warmth and drowsy with sleep.
> What official is this who gallops past my gate on horseback,
> Hat aslant, hands stuffed in sleeves, at war with the north wind?[19]

Of course, Fan's treatment of these two conventional themes is quite different from what we expect from either Bai Juyi or Tao Qian, for both of these poems succeed largely because of their wit and not so much because of their evocation of earlier traditions. The poet's vivid sketch of the water chestnut picker's difficult life naturally excites our sympathy, but the last line works so well, because Fan's clever use of the word *yi* 亦 (too), heightens our shock at the absurdity and unfairness of renting out lake surfaces to landless peasants. In the same way, the second poem transcends its conventional theme by means of its comical portrait of the worldly official in the last line, which derives its energy from the clever conceit of his being "at war" (*zhan* 戰) with the north wind.

The fact that we find Fan's wit at work in two rather atypical poems in the series would prompt us to look further in the series for the other poetical devices that dominate most of his mature verse. However, we are surprised to discover that these devices are really quite rare in the series as a whole. Unlike most of Fan's poetry before and after his composition of the *Impromptu Verses*, few of the poems are humorous, and the wit, when present, is usually subdued.[20] The pathetic fallacy figures importantly in only one poem,[21] and Fan Chengda's typical decorated language and clever tropes are few.[22]

That Fan frequently employed these devices both before and after the composition of this series and that the devices appear only occasionally in the series' poems suggests that Fan was exercising self-restraint on his more natural literary inclinations in the *Impromptu Verses* and that he must have viewed these poems in a somewhat different light from his other creations of the same period. Critics employ the Chinese critical term *dan* 淡, or "bland," to praise Fan's poems, a term that they also use to characterize the plain, unadorned style of the ancestor of Chinese bucolic verse, Tao Qian.[23] It is possible that Fan Chengda was consciously repressing his normal style to fit in with the mainstream of the tradition of bucolic poetry represented by Tao.

Unfortunately, it is impossible to prove this theory, because Fan's preface to the series is so uninformative, but it is interesting to note that Fan Chengda's account of his informal approach to the composition of the series resembles Tao Qian's preface to his famous group of twenty poems on drinking wine:

I was living idly at home with few pleasures at a time when the nights were becoming longer. By chance I happened to have some vintage wine, and I drank every evening, emptying my bottle in the company of my shadow, suddenly finding myself drunk once again. As soon as I was drunk, I would write down several verses for my own entertainment. As time passed, the number of pages grew, but without any particular order to what I had written. I requested a friend to make a copy of everything in order to give people a good laugh.[24]

Tao, too, claims that there is no underlying plan to his poems, all of which have been created in a spontaneous and natural manner. Of course, a careful reading of Tao's poems reveals a clear philosophical message in his wine poems, something that Fan Chengda largely eschews in his *Impromptu Verses*, but it is reasonable to suppose that Fan's cultivation of a different syle in the series arises from his desire to conform more closely to the pre-Song poetic tradition represented by Tao.[25]

In spite of Fan's deemphasis of his normal style, the use of surprise in the closure of many of the more successful poems of *Impromptu Verses* is closely related to his more typical wit:

The soil begins to quicken, urged on by the rain;
Thousands of flowers burst open in a single instant.
Even the fallow plot behind my house is green with life,
Bamboo shoots from my neighbor's yard pop up from under our wall![26]

Although the rain urges on the process of renewal in the early spring, and even the fallow land behind the poet's house is flourishing, the reader is not prepared for the bamboo shoots to pop up from under the wall, and his surprise is akin to the pleasurable reaction he experiences upon reading Fan Chengda's more obviously witty poetry.

Related to such poems of surprise are what might be termed poems of revelation, in which the poet first produces suspense, which he relieves by a revelation in the closing line, frequently introduced by a word such as *zhi* 知 (know):

> I set off by boat and watch the sky clear above snowy peaks;
> The wind calms and the unseasonal cold intensifies at evening.
> I listen to my oars crackle like shattering jade in the water;
> Only then I know; the lake's surface was frozen already![27]

The first two lines of the quatrain create an atmosphere of unhindered space and tranquility, suddenly interrupted in the third line by the auditory sensation of the oars breaking the water, which abruptly makes us aware of the water's changed state.

Unlike the poems of surprise in the series, most of these poems of revelation are subdued in tone, and the departure from the pervasive tranquility is only momentary:

> Pair by pair, butterflies enter the rapeseed blossoms;
> No guests arrive at our cottage on this unending day.
> A hen swoops over the fence, and the dog barks in his kennel:
> I know an itinerant peddler has arrived to sell tea.[28]

Here the tension created in the third line is reduced to a minimum, so that it is only a minor interlude in the calm, drawn-out days of late spring.

The tendency to control wit and reduce surprise to the absolute minimum necessary to sustain the reader's interest leads the poet to break the rules that are assumed in most of his other poems:

> Caterpillars on the orange trees transform magically the same as silkworms;
> The cocoons they hang on branches resemble raincoats of straw.
> Suddenly they metamorphose into butterflies like flowers;
> The powder on their wings is barely dry, when they start learning to fly.[29]

Instead of leaving the surprise in the quatrain to the last line, as he and most of his contemporaries normally do, Fan describes the startling transformation of the unimpressive cocoons into flowerlike butterflies in the penultimate line, as if he is purposefully downplaying the unexpected in this poem to achieve the more traditional goal of *dan*, or "blandness."[30]

In fact, not only do most of the *Impromptu Verses* avoid overt wit, but many of them are even devoid of surprise, which we have regarded as an extension of Fan's normal wit. The reader may very well ask how Fan sustains interest in works in which nothing much seems to happen, but although many of his poems on the four seasons seem to violate the spirit of his other verse, they develop his earlier introspectiveness, which he inherited from Huang Tingjian through Chen Yuyi and further refined by means of his Buddhist meditation:

> From a lane awash in willow catkins a cock crows at noon;
> New mulberry leaves are sharp as needles, not competely green yet.
> I sit sleeping and then awake without a care in the world;
> Sunshine floods my window, and I watch the silkworms grow.[31]

Such "uneventful" bucolic poetry possesses the same narrow focus and meditative quality of Fan's later Buddhist poetry of sleep and sickness, but here the wit of Fan Chengda's more typical verse is replaced by an extremely subtle juxtaposition of action against inaction. The peaceful lane hidden in willow trees is penetrated by the crow of a cock, the needlelike quality of the new leaves seems to contradict their tenderness, and the poet's complete inactivity, which closely resembles Buddhist meditation, presents a foil to the vigorous growth of the silkworms under the brilliant sunshine.

Sometimes Fan Chengda effects this contrast between action and inaction by switching from one form of sense perception to another:

> Morning air chills the newly green gardens and groves;
> After breakfast, I go and watch them transplant rice seedlings.
> Flowers have been blown to the ground; mulberry and hemp are small;
> A breeze follows the path, bearing the asafoetida's fragrance.[32]

Our eyes observe the flourishing gardens and forests as well as the peasants' intense labor in the first and second lines, but the third line dulls our vision of nature's vitality by revealing that early spring's flowers have fallen and that the mulberries and hemp are yet too small to compensate for their loss. In the closing line, the breeze resumes nature's activity, which is perceived not through our sense of sight but rather through the more delayed and indirect sense of smell. This subtle olfactory perception confers an almost spiritual quality to the poem, which resembles the intuition of higher reality through the medium of Buddhist meditation.

The two *Impromptu Verses* dealing with peasant life that we have discussed so far are atypical of both the themes and style of the series as a whole, but most of the other poems on peasant life in the series adopt the same *dan* style that typifies the poems on rural nature that we have been analyzing:

> A horseback honor guard, horns blazing, rides west in the lanes;
> The governor's horses and wagons on spring tour raise a hubbub.
> Peasants tie up their ox not to block the path in front of the gate,
> But then they move it west of the gate, to the millstone's side.[33]

If one insists on discovering political content in the peasant poetry of the series, it is possible to interpret this quatrain as a criticism of the vulgar cacophony of the official procession. However, the beauty of this work does not derive from any political connotations but rather from the same kind of juxtaposition of action (the official procession) with inaction (the peasants' tranquil life) that is typical of many of the best poems on the rural landscape.

Although most of the poems on peasant life are in the *dan* mode and utilize the same devices as the poems on rural scenery, certain poems on peasant life can hardly be described as *dan*:

> On the newly built threshing ground flat as a mirror,
> Each family rushes to work during the cold, clear weather.
> Above their songs and laughter a faint rumble like distant thunder:
> All night flails will clatter until the sky brightens again![34]

It is true that this poem sets up contrasts similar to the *dan* poetry, for the empty threshing ground is opposed to the bustle of the peasant laborers, and their clearly perceived songs and laughter differ from the flails' muffled clatter, but the threshers' exuberant spirit is contrary to the meditative tranquility of most of the other *Impromptu Verses*. Although such peasant poems are in the minority, practically all the action of the series comes from peasant poetry of this sort.

In conclusion, the *Impromptu Verses* represent a major departure from the witty and cleverly constructed verse that Fan Chengda usually wrote. Yet it would be a mistake to see them as a rejection of his earlier stylistic innovations, because he continued to write poetry in his typical style after he finished the series, and many of the devices that make the poems successful are related to his more normal poetical practice and his Buddhist approach to the world. Although the care with which Fan composed the *Impromptu Verses* suggests that he viewed them as something special within the context of his other work, he would no doubt have been somewhat perplexed to discover that he has become best known for a series of poems that differ so greatly from his favorite style.

Village ballads

Although the *Impromptu Verses* comprise Fan Chengda's most widely appreciated collection of bucolic poetry, their success with readers has unfairly obscured the excellence of some of his other late rural verse, most notably his series *Village Ballads of the Year's End*, a group of ten longer poems about folk customs observed in his native village during the twelfth lunar month. Fan Chengda's preface to the *Village Ballads* proves that he conceived them with a greater sense of artistic unity than the *Impromptu Verses*:

> After my return to Stone Lake, I associated with the peasants, and having noted ten customs they observe at year's end, I selected suitable language to compose a poem about each of them with the intention of explaining our local traditions. I called these poems *Village Ballads*. . . .[35]

Fan's reference to "selecting suitable language" suggests a definite effort to select a proper poetic medium for the series, and in fact, he composed all the *Village Ballads* in the heptasyllabic "ancient" (*gushi*) form, which allows the author more freedom from metrical constraints and a larger scope for presenting a realistic picture of local peasant customs, as opposed to the highly compact heptasyllabic quatrain employed in the *Impromptu Verses*.

Furthermore, Fan Chengda chose to compose his works in a special form of ancient verse, classifying the entire series under the rubric of *yuefu* (ballad) poetry and entitling six of the poems *xing* 行 (lays), two terms that derive from Han dynasty folk poetry. We noted that in his youth Fan Chengda wrote quite a few *yuefu* ballads in imitation of Bao Zhao, Li Bai, and Bai Juyi, and this early apprenticeship in ballad poetry must have been useful when he returned to a poetic form so different from the regulated verse he had favored for most of his life. Fan Chengda wrote most of this earlier ballad poetry in the archaic tradition of the poet lamenting his unjust fate, which has no relation to the theme of peasant folk customs, and it is likely that his selection of the *xing* and *yuefu* forms was dictated more by a conviction that these ancient popular forms would accommodate the "suitable language" for the presentation of current popular traditions. With the exception of Liu Yuxi's Bamboo Branch Songs, about the only *yuefu* poetry before Fan's time that attempted to describe peasant life realistically was Bai Juyi's *New Music Bureau Poetry*, which, as we already have seen, emphasized social criticism, and Fan was certainly breaking new ground by utilizing *yuefu* ballad poetry to depict peasant life in such a realistic, but largely apolitical manner (only one of the ten poems is political).[36]

Since the meticulous craftsmanship of Fan's regulated verse even spilled over into the ancient style of verse that he wrote in the Yangzi Gorges, one would expect his *Village Ballads* not to stray too far from his customary practice, but they exhibit a freedom of form unusual in his other poetry. "The Lamp Market" (translated on p. 161) displays a preference for the rhyming couplets typical of popular verse, and "The Sacrifice to the Hearth God" (translated on p. 162) consists of thirteen lines, a form that is unusual even for earlier folk ballads or works written in imitation of them. The colloquial language of the poems along with the folk proverbs they incorporate lend even more support for the idea that Fan is not primarily imitating the *yuefu* verse of pre-Song poets in this series but instead is bending traditional *yuefu* as much as possible to create a poetry more in tune with the current popular tradition.

If that is the case, it is rather ironic that in some respects these "popular" poems exhibit more similarities with Fan's normal style than his more "refined" *Impromptu Verses*. Many of the ballads are witty, and we cannot help smiling at the people's attempt to bribe the Hearth God in "Sacrifice to the Hearth God," nor can we resist the clever humor of "Selling Foolishness." The wit is less restrained than in Fan's more refined poems, but this is only in keeping with the popular nature of the works.

The poems' wit is not the only carryover from Fan's mature style, for although we would not expect to encounter the adorned world of Fan's nature poetry in his *yuefu* verse, he does not suppress his love of clever and original tropes in these poems. For example, in "Lighting up the Fields and Silkworms" (p. 163), Fan says the villagers' torches resemble "stars glimmering through a broken cloud" or "fireflies fluttering in a fresh breeze," and in "A Song on Sharing the Harvest" (p. 164), he compares the sweets and tarts arranged on platters to "cells in a beehive." The detailed descriptions of the foods offered to the Hearth God and of the lamps in "The Lamp Market" are also typical of Fan Chengda's more ordinary style. In all these cases, Fan exercises the restraint necessary to prevent the occasional trope from destroying the overall effect of a poetry closer to the popular tradition.

However, the stylistic innovations of Fan's *Village Poems* do not really account for their charm, which arises mostly from their vivid portraits of local peasant life. This realism is a product of Fan's strong pride in the distinctive folk customs of his region, as opposed to the more homogeneous culture of the upper classes. In his preface to the collection, Fan takes considerable pains to explain these regional traditions for Chinese not from his area (see the relevant sections that have been translated with each poem), commenting, for example, that the people of his village shoot off firecrackers on the twenty-fifth of the twelfth lunar month (see the fifth poem of the series) and not on New Year's Eve, as in other parts of China, or noting with pride that the custom of "beating dust," preserved only in his native land (see the last poem of the series), can be traced back to a story preserved in a fourth-century collection of legends, the *Soushenji* 搜神記. It is probably no coincidence that at about this time Fan Chengda was busy compiling his most important work of scholarship, the *Wujunzhi* or *Monograph on Wu Prefecture*, a detailed history and gazetteer of his region with one chapter on the area's folklore and several chapters on local religious traditions.[37]

In conclusion, we can say that our examination of the *Impromptu Verses* and the *Village Poems* suggests that there is a much greater stylistic diversity in Fan Chengda's bucolic poetry than most earlier Chinese critics (with the exception of Yang Wanli) would allow. From the prefaces to both series we can determine that Fan wrote the two series with different purposes in mind, and we have seen how he adapted his literary art to accommodate these different purposes. Both of these styles differed greatly from his typical mature verse and the less well-known imitative Jiangxi poetry that he continued to write, and we are rightly amazed at Fan Chengda's incredible flexibility as a writer.

Before we conclude this examination of Fan's bucolic poetry, we should discuss a charge made against it by Yoshikawa Kôjirô, who stated that "perhaps, because of his high official position, Fan Chengda's attitude toward the life of the farmers is more detached than that of Lu You and lacking in Lu You's warmth."[38] One really wonders how carefully Yoshikawa read Fan's bucolic verse, since it is difficult not to be moved by the warm humanity of Fan's poetry on peasant life, especially the ten village poems just discussed, but it is conceivable that Yoshikawa's opinion was formed by his reaction to Fan Chengda's and Lu You's distinct styles. Although Fan wrote in a number of different styles, it is fair to say that the quintessence of his mature verse is his witty use of language and figures of speech, an approach that inevitably involves a certain artistic distance, as opposed to the simpler and more straightforward approach to writing taken by Lu You. We have already demonstrated that Fan's introverted approach to poetry developed in response to Jiangxi school verse over an extended period of time, commencing long before he attained a high position. Although it is difficult to prove what other personal factors determined Fan's individual response to the Jiangxi school, as opposed to Lu You's, it seems likely that his delicate nature and poor health played a more decisive role than any political positions he ever held. Fan Chengda's typical style is less dynamic than Lu You's, but his deep love of the peasantry is obvious in everything that he wrote.

7
The poetry of patriotism

Living in a period when the existence of China was threatened, Southern Song poets made a particularly significant contribution to poetry on political themes, particularly "patriotic poetry" (*aiguoshi*), a term coined by modern Chinese critics. Patriotism is a concept open to varying interpretations in any age, and one discovers that even among the friends of Fan Chengda, love of country was expressed in different ways. According to his official biography in the *Song History* (*Songshi*), Fan's friend, the poet Yang Wanli, who supported a forward policy toward the Jin throughout his political career, died of anger in 1207 when he learned that Han Tuozhou 韓侂胄 had carried out an invasion of the north,[1] while Fan's companion during his stay in Sichuan, the poet Lu You, an equally ardent proponent of north China's reconquest, supported Han.[2]

The issue of patriotism in Southern Song poetry has become even more confused by the polemics of some contemporary Marxist literary critics in China, who, to put it somewhat crudely, seem to value a poem if it is either critical of the old social order or is patriotic. One result of this approach is an all too common tendency to exaggerate the importance of patriotic verse in the literature of the time, with the result that one anthology of Lu You's poetry selects his patriotic poems to the almost total exclusion of the many other types of poetry he wrote.[3] One Western scholar has already noticed the unbalanced picture that such an approach to Lu You's poetry produces,[4] and the same problem arises in the limited studies of Yang Wanli and Fan Chengda in Chinese published so far, which have certainly overemphasized their patriotic poetry.

Fan Chengda's patriotic poems comprise only a small part of his work, but it is, nonetheless, an impressive part. Zhou Ruchang would have Fan writing patriotic verse early in his career as an author (see translation and notes on p. 99), but Zhou's attempt to read patriotic sentiments into Fan's earlier works seems rather forced. Although some of his earlier poems may hint at dissatisfaction with the government's pacifistic policy toward the Jin, Fan Chengda's first unequivocal statements in poetic form on the Jin problem were rather disappointing works presented as parting poems to Hong Mai, who, as we have seen, led an embassy to the Jin in the year 1162, at which time Fan was already serving in the capital city.[5]

It is conceivable that Fan Chengda's patriotic verse would not have developed beyond this level if he had not been sent on a mission to the Jin Tartars, which we have already discussed in his biography. The dramatic events of Fan's mission to the Jin figure prominently in the traditional accounts of his life, and Fan himself must have attached great significance to his mission, for in addition to writing a prose account of his experiences, the *Lanpei lu* (*Record of Holding the Reins*), he composed seventy-two poems about his travels, which now make up Chapter 12 of his complete works.[6] Although these poems are not as well known as Fan Chengda's *Impromptu Verses*, the early Qing master Qian Qianyi 錢謙益 (1582–1664), who also lived in an age when China had fallen under foreign control, regarded the poems highly enough to write eight works in response to them,[7] while the early nineteenth-century critic Pan Deyu 潘德輿 (1785–1839) thought that one of the poems was superior to anything Su Shi had written and equal to the best verse of Du Fu.[8]

A number of the poems in this series are scathing indictments of the political weakness and treachery that, in the view of the pro-war party, had caused the collapse of the Northern Song dynasty and the failure of Yue Fei's counteroffensive against the Jin:

The Double Shrine

This is located outside the north gate of Nanjing and is a shrine to Zhang Xun and Xu Yuan. Most people call it the Double Shrine, but the people of Nanjing call it the Shrine of the Two Kings.[9]

> Their fortress was isolated on a plain and besieged by rebels,
> Yet they knew how to drive off the enemy's vicious attacks.
> *Our* capital was impregnable, sheltered by the Yellow River's might,
> So who caused the loss of our nation's sacred soil?[10]

As in most earlier political verse, Fan alludes to historical events long before his own age in order to criticize the policies that caused the loss of north China, contrasting the bravery of two Tang generals, Zhang Xun and Xu Yuan, who, in spite of unfavorable geographical conditions, were able to hold out against rebel armies during the An Lushan Rebellion, with the cowardice and incompetence of the Song dynasty's leaders. It is interesting that Fan did not feel obliged to cloak his obvious attack on the last emperor of the Northern Song, Huizong, and the first Southern Song emperor, Gaozong, in the ambiguous allegorical language so popular with Chinese critics of the government, since at the time he was writing the imperial court was entering a new anti-Jin phase.

In addition to poems criticizing past errors in China's foreign policy, we encounter works that depict the Jin government's cruel treatment of its Chinese subjects (the most moving is Fan's poem on a slave girl, Qingyuandian, p. 127) and a number of poems that describe the desolation and decay of north China's cities caused by Jin misgovernment. If one evaluates Fan's series of poems only according to patriotic criteria, however, the praise that a Marxist critic such as Zhou Ruchang has lavished on them does not seem completely justified, because in some of the poems, Fan's criticism of the Song dynasty's blunders is quite muted and is frequently limited to the expression of nostalgia for "the good old days" before the Chinese court had been forced to flee the northern capital of Kaifeng for the south (see "The Market Streets" on p. 124).[11]

One searches Fan's series of poems in vain for the seething indignation and explosive violence of Lu You's celebrated patriotic poems, and at times it seems Fan momentarily forgets he is traveling in enemy territory:

Linming town

It is thirty miles from Mingzhou, and since the wine of Ming is famous, the enemy's attendant ambassador presented several pots along with a freshly killed hare.

> The day-long cold finally raises its siege at dusk;
> Summery mulberry trees are dyed red by the sunset.
> The Tartars try their best to make me drink Linming wine,
> They claim the falconer has just returned with a freshly killed hare.[12]

Fan could easily have written this poem in response to some entertainment provided him by officials of his own government, and in fact, a fair number of poems that Fan wrote during his mission suggest that he bore no personal animosity toward his hosts (even before his arrival in Jin territory Fan had written, "You say that our enemy does not value loyalty and trust? / Just watch them dismount from their horses and walk past his [Lei Wanchun's] tomb in respect!").[13]

One factor that accounts for the difference between Fan Chengda's poems and Lu You's patriotic verse is the form that the two poets employed, for Fan Chengda's entire series is written in finely crafted heptasyllabic quatrains, while much of Lu You's best patriotic verse is composed in the unrestrained ancient style, which was the only suitable vehicle for the strong emotions of

> His beard bristles like a porcupine's quills;
> His eyes flash with the rays of purple amethyst –
> The hero leaves his home, thinking nothing of a thousand-mile journey . . .
> He sleeps outside beneath the moon of Kokonor, in pursuit of his enemy,
> And treads the Yellow River's ice at night to seize their cities.
> The rain murmurs and sighs as his steel armor crosses the sands.
> His war drums climb ridges, roaring like thunder.
> At midnight the defeated enemy offers surrender;
> At dawn their armor is piled up high as a hill . . .
> The dark hosts lie prostrate;
> The brilliant sun soars!
> The barbarians are vanquished;
> The Song rises again!
> If a hero can repay his ruler this way,
> He will laugh at the white-haired scholar reading books by lamplight![14]

Nonetheless, we have already seen that Fan Chengda composed ballads in the ancient style long before he became an official and went on to create powerful ancient-style landscape verse during his journey through the Yangzi Gorges, so there is no reason why he could not have employed the form if he had wanted to express emotions similar to Lu You's celebration of the military life. Although we cannot be sure why Fan did choose the more restricted heptasyllabic quatrain, it is possible that he was writing with a court audience in mind, in contrast to Lu You, who as a low official, was creating verse for himself and his small circle of friends, a hypothesis that becomes even more plausible when we keep in mind the many parallels between Fan's prose travel diary, which was certainly penned for public consumption, and the poems themselves.[15]

Once Fan Chengda made a choice of the heptasyllabic quatrain, it was nearly inevitable that the poems created would reflect his previous endeavors in the form, but anyone who encounters the series after reading Fan Chengda's complete works from the beginning cannot help being surprised by its generally solemn tone and the overall austerity of its art. This solemnity is certainly a product of the series' public nature, and the austerity of style, which arises from a careful control of Fan's normal poetic devices, was demanded by Fan Chengda's higher purpose in writing the series. Hence, we do not encounter the pathetic fallacy in the series and Fan suppresses most clever tropes, the comparison of the Taihang Mountains (p. 123) to "mist-shrouded conchs" and Fan's description of the courier station at Fanyang (p. 126) as "a man dressed in furs crouching in a dirt hole" being two notable exceptions to this rule.

Nonetheless, the connections between these poems and Fan's other works are clear. We immediately recognize the flash of wit in the concluding line of Fan's poem on the dilapidated Xiangguo Temple (p. 124), when he writes, "Sheepskin coats and wolf fur caps scurry after the latest fashions," a line full of irony that both pokes fun at the Jin dynasty's low cultural level and comments upon the sad state of a temple that was once patronized by the Northern Song emperors before their ignominious defeat. In fact, it is quite appropriate that unlike most of Fan's other poems, the wit of these politically inspired poems is largely ironic, as when in the conclusion to his poem on the slave girl at Qingyuandian, who has had the word "escapee" tattooed on her cheeks, Fan comments: "A large tattoo on her face is really light punishment, after all."[16]

Finally, despite the limited use of tropes in these poems, Fan's sense of color seems to make up for the missing figures of speech, although just as in the case of wit, his use of color imagery differs from his more typical verse. Since Fan must have desired to present a portrait of a wasted, bleak land under enemy occupation to his audience in the Southern Song court, one would expect somber colors to dominate these poems, and, generally speaking, most of the poems conform to our expectations, creating a mood best characterized by the conclusion to Fan's poem "Lüancheng": "How desolate is the scenery in the county of Lüancheng!"[17]

In spite of this somber mood, words depicting bright colors do occur frequently in the series, but Fan almost always juxtaposes them against gloomy scenes. For example, in a poem about the nearly deserted town of Dingxing (p. 127), Fan contrasts the desolation of the countryside to the image of a dyer peddling his wares ("Light red, deep blue, they dangle from a long bamboo pole"), and when he describes the Xiangguo Temple just mentioned, Fan writes, "Old dust obscures the Buddhist temple's gold and blue tiles," a fitting metaphor for the way the Jin government has obscured the Song dynasty's glory. Of course, such a subtle use of words of bright color only serves to strengthen the overall impression of desolation that permeates the works.

Patriotism is a rare theme in Fan Chengda's later verse, even during his close association with Lu You in Sichuan, when Lu was writing some of his most renowned patriotic poetry. However, Fan Chengda did compose one poem that refers to his experiences among the Jin, when he was serving in Guilin after he had been forced out of the central government because of his opposition to the emperor appointing one of his in-laws to a powerful military position:

The painter Li Youzhi painted two pictures, Frozen Sky *and* Cassia Sea, *for me, the* Frozen Sky *about my crossing the Yellow River on my mission to the northern enemy and* Cassia Sea *about my journey on the road near Buddha Cliff. I inscribed the following poem on them in jest.*[18]

Though I vainly whipped on my horse in a failed mission to serve my country,[19]
Heaven did allow me to savour the delights of Han's mountains and rivers.
Now southern tribesmen dance as I drink, and flowers incline toward my cap,
But I dream of Tartar horns and my riding saddle blanketed with snow.[20]
I cannot put the times back in joint, for I'm already too old,[21]
And drift around this world like duckweed, my mind in a fog.
Tomorrow morning I'll submit my resignation to the court again:
Can I escape a thousand-mile journey to Sichuan's Min River?[22]

In this poem, written just before Fan was forced to travel from Guilin to his new post in Sichuan, the poet relives his earlier commitment to sacrifice his life on his mission to the Jin Tartars, but now his recollections of the mission mingle with his more recent experiences in the deep south at Guilin and are recalled only in a drunken old man's dream, inspired through the artifice of a friend's painting, which Fan commemorates with a poem "written in jest."

One scholar has observed that much of Lu You's later patriotic verse is confined to the realm of dreams, presumably because Lu finally realized that his ambition to assist in north China's reconquest was hopeless, and the same sense of futility dominates the dream scene in Fan Chengda's work.[23] But Fan Chengda's later patriotic verse is even more negative than Lu You's, for unlike Lu You's later dream verse, in which Lu fantasizes about military encounters against the Jin, Fan's later work is devoid of even a hint of action.

It is fair to say that with the notable exception of Fan's series of seventy-two poems on his mission to the Jin, patriotic verse does not comprise a significant part of Fan Chengda's works. This does not mean that Fan was unpatriotic, for his daring in the Jin court aroused the admiration of his contemporaries and later Chinese historians, and although the loss of most of his prose works renders it difficult to know what he thought about the threat of the Jin Tartars, he must have retained his strong feelings on the issue, because, as we have seen, during his service in Sichuan he expended much effort in studying the military problems of that area. In this respect Fan Chengda resembled his friend Yang Wanli more than Lu You, for although Yan Wanli always supported anti-Jin policies in his official career, the theme of patriotism plays only a minor role in his poetry.[24] Although Fan's poems on his embassy to the north still make highly enjoyable reading, we do not relish them for the strong emotions and noble sentiments of Lu You's verse so much as for their subtle artistry and the vivid portraits they provide of life in north China under Jin rule.

Part II
Translations

Early verse (ca. 1150–1155)

An autumn day (one quatrain of two)

Emerald rushes and green willows don't suit the frost,
So it dyes them yellow-brown to make a belt for the river.
Don't brag about south China to exiles from the north;
Our cold clouds and frigid streams are even bleaker than up there![1]

(5, 3)

The cotton-rose in front of my window

My lone cotton-rose braves the year's first cold with such great effort,
His flowers ought to be as depressed as a traveler far from home.
But instead he invites Lady Frost[2] to stay as long as she wishes,
Just so no one will dare compare him to melancholy blossoms of spring!

(5, 3)

A small jetty by the river Zhe on a spring day

I have no one to share a wine cup with on my journey;
Who do the peach trees and plums bloom for back home now?

1 After the Jin occupied north China, many northern Chinese moved south to the Yangzi Valley to escape foreign rule, and since the weather there is much milder than in the north, southerners bragged about the superior climate of the south to their northern compatriots. Zhou Ruchang would make this poem into a political satire. Although he quotes another work by a Southern Song author to support his contention, it is difficult to find any obvious political message in Fan's early poem. The method of citing texts is the same in these translations as in the notes to Chapters 1–7. The first number refers to FSHJ, the second to FCDSX. If only one number occurs, it refers to FSHJ. See page 168 for abbreviations.

2 Qingnü, the goddess of frost.

The vernal tide doesn't care about the sorrow of men in faraway places,
For it rolls up Xixing's evening rain and delivers it to me! (10, 7)

A description of a walk outside the town on the Cold Food Festival[1] *(second poem of two)*

Field wheat rejoices and turns green again,
Mountain peaches redden in lonely silence.
A fishing weir ripples at my boatside in the water;
A tavern's banner flutters in the breeze above the treetops.
I follow the fragrant grasses wherever my feet lead me,
Get lost on the paths, and ask a little boy for directions.
A joyful heart fills my legs with such energy,
I shout out to the ferry to take me east of the stream! (11, 10)

Early summer (second of two poems)

Insects' thousand-foot gossamer would tug the spring season back,
But the shrike is mute and swallows are too busy to help.
Days lengthen, and the scholar-tree's shade thickens around my house;
Fanned by a gentle breeze, wheat tassels perfume the air. (11, 11)

On the way to Nanjing

At evening, brown goats follow the sun down the mountains;
Homebound white calves frisk in the wind under a frigid sky.
Dismal dust swirls along the road that heads to Nanjing;[2]
With a smile I dream of my skiff flying across my home's sandy lakes!
(13, 13)

Spending the night at Yilin Temple

The night air is gloomier than during a downpour;
The hall for meditation freezes like ice.
But then the moon rises from the east ridge's bamboos
To the top of the pines – a lamp for the temple.
A startled hawk soars around the pagoda;

1 The day before the Grave-Sweeping Festival (Qingming, approximately April 5), when only cold food was eaten.
2 Literally, Xizhou, a town close to Nanjing, used here to denote the area near that city.

Early verse

Trembling fireflies brush the Jade Rope's[1] stars.
Tomorrow morning, I'm going to give my legs a real workout:
By night I'll chop a path through the vines, right up the cliff! (14, 16)

At White Heron Pavilion

Though weary from travel, I can't stand the inn's idle life,
Where every day the pure river watches me lean against the railing.
So I'll wait until the west wind blows the rain clouds away,
Then go gaze at the Huai mountains, where the river splits in two.
(15, 17)

Rouge Well (one poem of three)[2]

Chen's last emperor raised luxurious towers beneath Radiant Hall,
And gave up the nation's hard-won land for a cup of wine.
Spring's hues have already vanished from his gilded well,
And the moon's rays climb his fort's rocks, for no purpose at all. (15, 18)

Reading history (one poem of three)

After scheming a lifetime for victory over others,
They ended up feasting the ravens and worms.
I adjust my flickering lampwick to read more clearly,
My eyes blur trying to decide, who was right, who was wrong. (17, 20)

At the Shrine of Serene Meditation (four quatrains)

My oil lamp grows dim but suddenly flares;
My stone pot is nearly dry but still hisses with steam.[3]
A patched quilt covers my head, and I stuff my hands in my sleeves:
There's no space for fame or fortune on my broken-down bed!

1 The Jade Rope lies near the Big Dipper.
2 Chen Houzhou, the last emperor of the Chen dynasty (reg. 557–589), was notorious for his extravagant life-style that supposedly brought about the fall of his dynasty. When the Sui armies entered his capital, he hid with his favorite concubines in this well but was captured by the enemy.
3 Fan's poetry frequently mentions the stone pot in which he boiled herbs for the relief of his frequent illnesses. Richer people used pots of bronze but Fan used one of stone, the material favored by the poor.

At fifth watch the wind rustles the bamboos outside my window,
But I confuse them with waves murmuring beneath a riverboat's bed.
I turn over on my pillow and resume broken dreams,
Just as friends await the emperor's waterclock in frost-covered boots.[1]

After the monks' breakfast rattle, morning drums boom out,
But I lie listening to a hungry mouse climb my lamp at dawn.
A patch of slanting sunrays flashes on my bed canopy,
Suddenly I realize – a sparrow has broken through the paper window!

Eyes drooping in meditation, I enter Nonbeing's Realm;
In the tranquility of my trance I hear only the sparrows' chirps.
A worldly man raps on my door to ask for advice,[2]
Troubling this lay Buddhist to rise and pull on his boots. (17, 21)

At night I walk to Shangsha and see a plum tree and remember Su Shi's lines about summoning the soul of the imperial consort Yang[3]

The imperial consort Yang was banished to the earth as a plum tree,
To stand in this village on the purling stream's bank.
Heaven's wind puffs at her exquisite blossoms,
Which flutter and then perish on this deserted shore.
In her fragrant heart she laments her unfair fate;
Her jade countenance is pained by the grime of the road.
Her beloved emperor does not come for his tryst,
In the twilight, red sunset clouds turn dark blue again.[4]

1 That is, they are waiting for the morning levee, which took place at dawn.
2 Literally, "ask about a character," an allusion to the Han scholar Yang Xiong (53 B.C.–A.D. 18), who was so noted for his knowledge of rare Chinese characters that he was constantly bothered by people asking him questions about difficult texts.
3 Su Shi is the famous Northern Song poet, whom Huang Tingjian regarded as his "teacher," while the imperial consort Yang is Yang Guifei 楊貴妃, the favorite of the Tang emperor Xuanzong 玄宗 (reg. 713–756). Xuanzong's infatuation with Yang Guifei is traditionally considered to have been a factor in his failure to take action against the An Lushan Rebellion, which brought about his abdication from the throne and Yang Guifei's death. Later their tragic love was the subject of many poems and dramas. Su's original poem refers to the popular tradition that Yang Guifei became a fairy after her death, but Fan's poem does not emphasize the connection between the plum and Yang.
4 Allusion to Jiang Yan's lines: "The day is late and the dark blue clouds gather; / The fair one still does not arrive," where the "dark blue clouds" describe the appearance of the sky after the red colors of the sunset have disappeared and night approaches. Jiang Yan 江淹, *Jiang Wentong ji* 江文通集, *Wanyu wenku huiyao* (Taipei, 1965), 4–40.

The brook's voice chokes in grief at her lot;
The moon, too, shines down with knitted brow.
Suddenly Lady Plum meets me, exhausted from my travels,
But she does not begrudge me one of her smiles.
We stare at each other, inquisitive, yet speechless;
She stands so erect, her feelings seem all the more genuine.
She begs me to compose verses of ice and pure snow,
To summon her lonely soul back to paradise.[1]
Immortal Su Shi is already a guest of high heaven,
And his sublime thoughts lie beyond my powers of expression.
The Big Dipper's jeweled handle is now declining too rapidly,
And morning mists darken the depressing green of the mountains.

(19, 23)

Late spring (one poem of three)

Guests leave, and I recite a short poem by the sculpted window;
Floating gossamer entangles the sky, willow blossoms are meager.
All day long a gentle breeze blows on the fragrant grass;
Butterflies fly pair by pair – hugging the ground. (21)

At the height of summer my boat traveled to Mount Han when a rainstorm suddenly blew up, and I was frightened by the thunder and the clouds shaped like dragons hanging from the sky

Lowering clouds blacken the storm's vanguard;
The thunder's kettledrums rumble at its rear.
Lofty ridges vanish with its violent onslaught;
Dark turmoil envelops the ancient county.
A white dragon rears from his obscure den,
Murky mist abetting his mystic transformations.
The sudden deluge deafens my ears,
And the unexpected darkness dizzies my eyes.
Sails are puffed into bulging bellies;
Drenched oars slap the water with vigor.
The rain ripples in circular halos across the river;
Droplets of water scurry all over its surface.
Lone mandarin ducks grieve for missing mates;

1 Reference to ancient shamanistic practices that play an important role in the second oldest anthology of Chinese poetry, the *Chuci* or *Songs of Chu* (earliest parts from the third century B.C.), in which, according to the differing interpretations, the souls of poets, kings, and even gods are summoned by the shaman authors.

Violent gusts blow hungry swallows sideways.
Ripe, old wheat lies on a pillow of water;
Young rice seedlings do combat with the wind.
Cows' hoofprints crumble like mud walls;
The downpour deluges the tunnels of ants.
Peasants dash to put their water wheels to work –
Never are they free from the burden of farming.
The springs of the wheels creak and grind,
And their linked chains clatter and rattle as they turn.
Women and children work shoulder to shoulder;
From every hut, relatives and friends lend support.
The east field is still dry, but the west field floods;
A small plot is saved from drought, a large one, submerged.
But still, I do not think I'm wiser than these people,
For there's no real difference between the farmers and me.
I've grown accustomed to wind and dew in my boat,
Ranging for half my life over lakes and rivers.
I do not know how to care for the land's crops,
And I'm only expert at stuffing my own belly.
From afar I still pity the peasants' bitter existence;
How dare I complain of the exhausting life of a traveler? (22, 27)

On the sixth day of the seventh month I get up at night and sit by a side hall to enjoy the coolness

Suffering from the heat, I rise at midnight,
And go outside to the moon's pure dew.
The Milky Way reclines above me, sparkling and glittering,
While the Jade Rope's[1] scattered stars sink into obscurity.
The temple's carved windows enclose a miraculous fragrance;
An ancient lamp perches in its pavilion of stone.
Suddenly a breeze arises from nowhere at all,
Slightly cooling the monastery's halls and galleries.
Yet the dignified cassia trees[2] do not even stir,
And the sculpted ceilings loom even higher in majesty.
The entire temple bristles with rafters and beams,
All locked together like demons in combat.
A monk's iron staff clatters loud in the night
And wakes roosting swallows that chatter in fear.

1 See note, p. 101.
2 Literally, "cassia banners," a term used to refer to magical banners in Chu shamanistic poetry of the Zhou dynasty, but probably referring to the tree itself in this case.

Vulgar people do not appreciate what I now witness,
Their snores rumbling forth like a spring storm's thunder.
The Morning Star suddenly dispatches dawn back to our earth,
And all the temple's windows glimmer with a hazy light.
The pure breath of Heaven has cleansed my mortal body,
And revitalized my spirit, so I feel ready to sprout wings.
I would ride the wind to my abode in the sky,
Straddle a phoenix to the azure paradise above.
I'm only afraid the fairy Fangping[1] will learn of my scheme,
And for no reason at all, I'll get a false reputation for cunning! (23, 29)

Walking outside the city on the first day of spring

Bamboos crowd the stream's bridge, wheat decks the hillside;
Piping and singing follow the spring ox[2] everywhere it goes.
Drooping willows turn yellow-green, like yeast about to ferment;
Tender ripples play over the water, bright as newly clarified wine.
Sunshine fills the entire county; spring markets assemble;
The tide is level with the inlet; sails increase toward evening.
Spring is here, but I don't drink and can't think up any good poems:
Hardly a way to do justice to my glittering New Year's pendants![3]
(26, 31)

A single oar

A single oar dips in the green water, east and west of the inlet;
Snow-like fluff inundates the river; the geese don't fly up.
The sky clears from last night's rain, and the wind shifts again –
Impossible for my tiny patch of sail to make it home on time! (27)

1 Fangping is the courtesy name of Wang Yuan 王遠, an immortal who was the elder brother of the immortal Magu (Auntie Hemp). According to a story in the *Shenxianzhuan*, Magu asked for some rice, which she spread on the ground and transformed into pearls, whereupon her brother Wang Yuan laughed and said, "Magu is still definitely young, while I am old, for I do not perform such cunning magic tricks any more." Fan is obviously alluding to this story here. See Ge Hong 葛洪 (284–364), *Shenxian zhuan* 神仙傳, BBCSJC, 2-8a.
2 In ancient times it was the custom to make a clay ox that was whipped and paraded through the countryside at the time of the spring equinox in order to prepare the peasants for spring planting.
3 This refers to the custom of cutting colorful paper pendants to hang from the head or from the branches of flowering trees at the beginning of the spring season.

Blue tiles

Blue tiles crown the house concealed behind embroidered curtains;
A green stream slants away, beyond a red-railed bridge.
No breeze, but poplars and willows flood the sky with fluff;
No rain, but crabapples and pears litter the ground with petals. (27, 32)

On the road to Hangzhou

Blossoms fall into the current, dyeing the depths and shallows red:
All day long sailboats fly among these embroidered waves.
Mulberry leaves, like tiny squinting eyes, suffer from the drought;
The wheat's whiskers, long buffeted, can withstand any wind now.
Cow and sheep paths blur and merge with a thousand mountain peaks;
A single road stretches to this village where cocks and dogs hide.
It wouldn't take much space to plant five willow trees[1] for yourself here,
So why bother dashing about on your nonstop journeys? (28, 34)

A song to please a god

The four poems below [only three poems translated] were written in imitation of Wang Jian.[2]

Pigs' trotters fill the platters, wine fills the cups;
A cool breeze sighs, when the god approaches.
They hope the god will come cheerfully and leave cheerfully, too;
Young boys bow low to welcome him, little girls dance.
Old men brandish incense sticks, smiling as they talk:
"This year farmers' lives will definitely be better than last.
Last year we had to sell our clothes to pay the rent and taxes;
But this year we'll have plenty of clothes to wear for the autumn thanksgiving!"

Peasants entertain a guest

Traveling gentleman, do not disdain the peasants' tiny house;
Its doors and windows may be low, but they must be washed and swept.

1 Allusion to the poet Tao Qian (365–427), who wrote a "Biography of Mr. Five Willows," which is a thinly veiled autobiography about a recluse who plants five willow trees in front of his house. Tao Qian also used the name Mr. Five Willows, and in later times this name became synonymous with the ideals of the recluse.
2 See the discussion of Wang Jian and Fan Chengda in Chapter 6.

Early verse

Their eldest son ties your donkey, at the side of the mulberry tree;
The youngest son brushes the floor mats, softer than finest felt.
They husk rice, white as snowflakes, in a wooden mortar,
Then hurry to steam it fragrant to feed their honored guest.
"Whenever a good man like you enters our home, everything turns out well:
This year we won't have to worry about the silk and wheat harvests coming late!"

Pressing the peasants for taxes

Though they have a tax receipt, officials press them for more taxes:
The village head staggers to their hut and pounds on the door.
When they hold out the document he is both annoyed and relieved:
"I've only come for a little drink and then I'll be on my way."
At the head of the bed there's a money jar big as a fist,
And they smash it open to get three hundred cash:
"We're sorry it's not enough to get your lordship really drunk,
But at least it'll pay for the wear and tear on your shoes." (30, 36–8)

Spending the night at East Monastery (second poem of two)

With one cry a brown goose flies home, deep in the night;
Nesting sparrows chirp in fright, knocking against the hall's door.
The Big Dipper hangs halfway down, outside the pavilion;
Wind-buffeted banners seem ready to fly up into the clouds. (32, 40)

The Jin Clan's shrine

The shrine was unoccupied and in ruins.

A raven's evening silhouette in its window resembles a drunkard's sketch;
A vine climbing the wall is a green serpent slithering off.
In late spring a swallow skims by a butterfly in flight;
With evening's onset, no one sweeps the scattered blossoms away. (37, 41)

White Lotus Hall

Ancient trees soaring to heaven guard the emerald pool;
Tender lotus leaves, like green coins, tremble on the water's ripples.
The hard-pressed traveler always rushes, rushes away, in his haste,
And never sees a cold breeze shake the lotuses, under the moon's frigid light.
(38, 43)

Sitting up sick at night, shown to Zongwei

The night air floats in the sky, like fog, or like smoke;
A heron's shriek wakes me up, and I rise, scratching my head.
The bamboos' shadows, full of wind, retain the moon only dimly;
The cries of crickets, cloaked by rain, bitterly mourn for the autumn.
Mind empty of all concerns, I am dull by habit;
At year's end, sickness assails every joint in my body.
I ought to travel to the western hills and search for medicinal herbs,
But my legs are far too wobbly, and distant journeys scare me! (40)

Going home at night

My bamboo litter creaks and groans as we race through the street;
The cold wind grazes my face and retrieves me from drunken dreams.
The winding alleys lie silent, the gates are all shut;
One lamp still shines – yes, the wine shop is open! (41, 43)

Peasant huts

One shout and the peasants arrive carrying hoes;
Then everyone busily tends to the rice-threshing ground.
Their children doze among the fallen leaves,
And sparrows wrangle under the sun's slanting rays.
Hearth smoke curls up, village sounds seem distant;
The woods are lush, the country air, fragrant.
Oh, what a joy is the harvest this year –
Ripe rice stretches to the horizon like clouds of gold! (41, 44)

Composed in bed on the morning of the twelfth day of the eleventh month

The bamboos rustle and the wind comes in gusts;
My window brightens, and flowers of snow swirl down.
A freezing dog whines by my brushwood gate;
A hungry raven pecks at my paper window.
Last night's wine combats the power of the cold;
A new poem dispenses with the change in season.
The sun is high, and I am still embracing my blanket,
Ashamed my neighbors ate their breakfasts[1] long ago. (43, 45)

1 Literally, "breakfasts in bed." It was the custom for peasants and other people who had to rise early in the morning to prepare food the night before and eat it in bed.

In bed

The bright moon silently floods the rafters of my room with moonlight;
Dreams fade, and a sliver of her reflection climbs my bed.
The White Lunar Lady wistfully gazes down, depressed and lonely;
She delegates the wind chimes to speak her grief – all night long. (45)

Written during my illness (one quatrain of eight)

The stone cauldron hisses as I boil medicine at night;
I toss in sesame with the atractylodes and let the herbs fight it out.[1]
I wonder what the Creator had in mind conjuring up a man like me –
Maybe so somebody could try out all of the world's prescriptions! (46, 46)

There is a light snow after the spring equinox but the sky clears in one night

We've changed seasons again with glittering pendants and gilded banners;
The sky hangs lower and lower, touching earth by evening.
Prince Spring[2] hasn't let the vernal flower buds burst,
When Snow Lady[3] scatters her white blossoms, snipped from water.
The howling whirlwind pursues them through the downspouts at night;
The morning changes them to drizzle that drips from jutting eaves.
The morning sun causes the snow clouds even more hardship,
Steaming them into a thousand wisps of pink mist that cram the blue sky.
(49, 47)

After it stops snowing, I climb South Tower alone

Snow stops, the wind strengthens, and water freezes at evening;
On top the tower, the unexpected cold shocks my sickly body.
Sparrows peck at empty eaves; bamboo-shaped icicles crash down;
Ravens whirl in treetops; snow cascades like jade dust.

1 Literally, "I toss in sesame with the atractylodes (*zhu*) and let them fight over 'warmth' or 'coolness.'" Both sesame and *zhu* (genus *Atractylodes*) are common Chinese medicinal herbs. "Warmth" and "coolness" do not refer to the actual temperature of the herbs but to the traditional belief that certain herbs are endowed with a "warm" property that has to be balanced with the "coolness" of other herbs.
2 Literally, "East Prince," a name for the spring god.
3 Qingnü, the snow goddess.

A green curtain flashes and sparkles; a thousand houses lie silent;
A lone mast[1] stands erect; a single river stretches in front.
I sit a long time; heaven's face turns warm and lovely;
The new moon's arc rises opposite the bright Evening Star. (49, 48)

Returning at night from Mount Lofty

My bamboo litter creaks and groans as we traverse dewy grass;
The night is cool, the moon's dim – we race among rugged peaks.
Suddenly we meet a banked stream, bright as a mirror,
Reflecting, from deep within it, Mount Lofty – upside down! (50)

Written at South Pool on a winter evening in answer to a poem

I toast myself by blazing beanstalks, at the night-enshrouded window:
From time to time friends' new poems demand answers from me.
Some say poetry must be written in a blizzard on the Ba River Bridge,[2]
But a blazing fire in a peasant hut is far better inspiration!
My cold lamp grows dim, yet I'm hard at work writing;
I can barely move my freezing brush, but my calligraphy strengthens.
People laugh at my obsession with the boring life of a poet,
But at least I'm not always fretting about how much money's left at year's end!
(53, 51)

On the way to Fox Ford on the Grave-Sweeping Festival[3]

Drizzling rain soaks kerchiefs;
Gusts blow hats askew.
Flowers blaze in the mountains;
Willows recline by gurgling streams.
Carved stone horses stand by the road;[4]

1 Literally, "a yellow hat," which originally meant a boatman, since boatmen traditionally wore yellow hats. In later times the term became synonymous with the word "boat."
2 Allusion to a minor Tang poet Zheng Qi 鄭綮, who when asked if he had composed any poetry lately is supposed to have replied that he had not, because the only proper inspiration for poetry was when he rode on a donkey across the Ba River Bridge (near modern Xian, the Tang capital of Changan) in a snowstorm. Huang Che 黃徹, *Gongxi shihua* 䂬溪詩話, BBCS, 1-7a.
3 At the time of the Qingming Festival, which is celebrated about April 5, the Chinese sweep the graves of their ancestors and present offerings to them.
4 These are statues near a larger tomb.

Early verse

Paper kites hum in mid-sky.
People sweep graves and leave;
Ravens swoop on offerings, east, west. (54, 53)

On the way to Gaochun

The road enters Gaochun, and the wheat seems thicker;
Though grass and soil are soggy, my horse gallops on.
Rain returns to mountaintops, where clouds thicken like mascara;
Sunlight leaks through at midpeak and soaks the rock in its gold.
An old willow, unequal to the spring, is still inundated with catkins;
By an ancient shrine without walls, a tree gives useless shade.
Of course, I'll buy a lunch basket at the village shop ahead,
Where the kitchen smoke billows up from the bamboo grove. (55, 55)

In Huizhou (1156–1160)

Walking in the evening in West Garden

The slight chill intensifies in the evening's darkness;
Flowers fall in the courtyard, resenting spring's end.
The wind opens red and blue flowers and blows them down later;
Although the same spring wind, he's definitely of two minds! (59)

In the morning I set off from Zhuxia

We tie up our baggage in the morning, then brave the early cold;
I sit astride my horse's saddle, to relieve my weariness a bit.
After a while we encounter a sparse, light fog,
Which sometimes permits a glance at layer after layer of mountains.
Green catkins, blown by mist, hover above straight trees;
Green ripples appear on the creek's water under a curving bridge.
Clear-throated birds sing over and over as if to welcome this guest,
Just when my mind is somewhere – between emotion and thought. (59)

A further ballad on collecting taxes

An old peasant's fields lie fallow in the autumn rain;
Formerly on a high bank, they're covered by river water now.
A tenant farmer like him is always starving,
And he knows all too well he can't pay rent or taxes.
Ever since the latest governor arrived at his post,
Tax remissions have been canceled and new bills press payment.
The peasant sold his family's clothes to make good his debts;
Though his sickly family froze, he avoided trouble a while.
Last year the clothes were gone, and he started selling his children;
He parted with his eldest daughter first, there, at the crossroads.

In Huizhou

This year his second daughter was engaged to be married,
When he had to sell her off, too, for a few bushels of rice.
Still his youngest daughter remains, living with him at home,
He needn't fear tax collectors for another year – at least. (60, 57)

In the morning I left Ancient Cliff: shown to Zongwei and Ziwen

The wind at morning chills everything slightly;
Mountain mists moisten my cap and my sandals.
Overnight clouds bury the trees in blackness;
An impetuous brook circles the mountain irately.
A glittering radiance shakes the east,
And the sun shoots forth, a dazzling gong of gold.
A thousand giant peaks vanish and reappear;
The agitated air swirls around me.
All my life I've been obsessed with the search for the hidden,
And by chance I experience something new to me.
No one would guess my rice steamer is loaded only with dust,
That from breakfast to lunchtime I've had nothing to eat.
I'm not ashamed of my hunger-etched face
And continue my quest along Ancient Cliff's road.
For rice and sorghum are easy to obtain,
But my craving for clouds and mist is hard to cure.
There's only one way to soothe my grumbling stomach –
Yes, even from my shriveled belly, I can summon forth poems!
(61, 59)

The next day when it rains and cools off I write two poems in the same rhyme as before (one poem of two)

Rain splashes tiles, pours off eaves, and breaks into a myriad strands;
A wild gale buffets the young bamboos so hard they can barely stand up.
I'm grateful for the heat's end, but how can I pay nature back?
Quick – write the very first poem about the cool weather! (64, 61)

In the same rhyme as Wenbo's poem on mosquitoes

The mosquitoes buzz around me in hunger all night;
Driven off by my incense, they escape out the window.
Little insects, you and I have exactly the same problem:
An empty belly forces us to fly around, without rest, all the time!
(67, 64)

At dawn I leave Old-Wall Mountain

The setting moon plummets through the vaguely lit sky,
Where the remaining stars pale in blurred, hazy air.
My bamboo sedan chair roils up mud in a pure stream,
And, with its canopy open, enters mist-filtered light.
Morning fog dampens the pines and junipers;
Mulberries and hemp perfume wind and dew.
Turquoise clouds drip on my dust-polluted hatstrings –
No need to wash them in Canglang River as ancient men did![1]
Mountain folk have also risen early from bed,
To take advantage of the cool dawn air.
I hear no sounds of men deep in the forest,
But above the treetops I can see gray smoke from stove fires.
Fruits droop heavily in this land of melon and taro;
Jujubes and chestnuts rise in solemn ranks in the fields.
From ancient times men have claimed country life is a joy,
But this scene only makes me more homesick than ever.
Suddenly a crowd of peasants throng to a country market,
Their bamboo baskets hurrying around the mountain road's bends.
Government business drags me back to my journey;
My path twists and turns under the morning sun's rays. (67, 65)

After it snows, the plums at Shouzhi's house still have not bloomed, and I show this poem to Zongwei

My tile eaves troughs freeze up with left-over snow;
My downspouts are glued tight by a light coating of ice.
A sun just above the horizon breaks the cold spell,
And spring is reborn, in accordance with man's wishes.
Yet, leaf-sized snowflakes have whitened the earth several times,
And the plum's south branch still coyly conceals its blossoms.
I'm absolutely positive the Governess of Flowers
Still hasn't agreed to marry off her graceful charges.
Life in my official residence is both uncomfortable and boring;
I smile about as often as the Yellow River runs clear![2]
Leafless trees stand in relief against the barren hills;
A frigid stream circles the lonely wall of our city.
About all I ever see from morning to night

1 Allusion to an ancient song: "The water of the Canglang River is pure; / I can wash my hatstring with it." The reference to washing his hatstrings means that Fan wishes to cleanse himself of the vulgar world's pollution.
2 According to a Chinese proverb, "The Yellow River clears once every thousand years."

Are the hungry hawks that shriek high above the brown clouds.
If the spring wind doesn't make up its mind what to do soon,
My sad eyes will never shine with joy again.
My neighbor to the north has a small plum complete with shade –[1]
Just perfect to lay out a mat for a chat on mossy ground.
I'm counting on you, Zongwei, to rush news of its flowers to me;
Have a drink, shake its branches, and make it bloom – quick! (72, 66)

Inscribed on the Zhuhu Pavilion on the sixteenth day of the fourth month

At noon I hear the cock crow; the days are getting long;
This small pavilion, three yards square, collects all the sky's light.
After a rainfall, the verdant shade turns as black as mascara,
And the wind arrives from nowhere with a hundred fragrances. (77, 67)

The Qingyi River

I was born long ago in a land of fishermen,
Where I used to drift all day on rivers and lakes.
I tapped my boat's gunwales and washed myself in the water,[2]
Singing about how small the world I lived in then was.
Ever since, I've been racing around in carts and on horseback,
So depressed, that all my poetic inspiration has left me.
Yellow dust from the road cakes my brow,
And I drive myself on as if I owed a debt to the world.
I hold my starving nag tightly at rein,
When we pass wild dogs that bay at us fiercely.
Thoughts of home entered my sleep last night,
And I dreamt of a small boat that tossed with the surf.
In the morning I rose to pass through the next town,
Where, to my joy, I found fish and shrimp for sale.
Suddenly I saw the pure river before me,
Swollen into a torrent by all of the rain.
I rolled up my robe and called a small skiff over,

1 Literally, "My north neighbor has a little 'horizontal slanting,'" in which "horizontal slanting" is a trope for the plum tree, the idea originating in the Northern Song poet Lin Bu's "Poem on the Small Plum in the Mountain Garden" (first poem of two) in which he writes: "Its meager shadow lies horizontal and slants, the water is pure and shallow." Lin Bu 林逋, Lin Hejing xiansheng shiji 林和靖先生詩集, SBCK, 2-14a.
2 Literally, "washed in the Canglang River." See note on p. 114.

Though it pitched so badly it couldn't carry a load.
I'm not going to worry about the dangers of crossing this river;
Oh what a thrill – to play in the water again! (81, 71)

The Xin Mountains

My skinny horse jostles me awake from my torpor;
A cock crows bleakly from the vast, barren wilds.
Silken spiderwebs snare the morning dew –
Nets strung with a thousand dewdrops enmesh a fence.
Slumbering clouds brush over the treetops;
Flying waterfalls cleave the mountain with a roar.
An old mulberry tree is coiled like a hiding dragon;
Weird vines dangle as if they were slithering pythons.
Now I have journeyed so deep into these mountains,
That the air's purple mist drips from my bridle and halter.
The endless rain and cold weather breed melancholy in me,
But the morning sun breaks loose to banish my depression.
The dawn sky unfurls its vermilion banner;
The solar orb climbs resplendent, a round gong of gold.
All creation stirs; grass and flowers waft their fragrance;
Everthing is pure and mild, the wild birds sing.
My servant, too, has some good words to say:
The sand is level, the road is flat as the palm of his hand.
Still I'm worried that we can't cross the Three Creeks –
The bridges are broken and the mountain streams swollen! (82, 72)

Fuyang

It's been exactly five years since I've seen rivers or lakes:
My residence was surrounded constantly by the green of Mount Xi.
Now the ford of Fuchun lies clearly before my eyes –
A lone boat at sunset, waves slapping the sky. (85, 73)

Cutting the mulberries

The axes have left only a thousand dry stumps,
Squatting, dense and jagged, by the darkening road.
First they fed the spring silkworms, whose cocoons have been gathered,
Now what's left over they give to the firewood gatherers. (86, 75)

In Huizhou

Gazing at evening from Zhuhu Pavilion

Although each of the forest's springs is pure and cool,
Mountains that surround the pavilion's railings keep me busy.
It's not raining, but rainbows swoop down to drink the streams,
While cicadas crowd the high willows, flooded by the sunset. (89, 77)

The Milky Rapids

Between Huizhou and Yanzhou, there are as many rapids as joints on a bamboo, but the Milky Rapids are the most dangerous.

The clear river is terrifying but delightful, too:
Such are the cruel jokes the Creator plays on men.
The rapids thunder and swirl, graying my hair;
I've come to try my luck, but I risk life and limb.
There's nothing more hazardous than these Milky Rapids;
My boat rolls like a stone down a high mountain peak.
The painted halls of the rich overlook the twilight rain;
Do they know anything at all about the hardships of river travel? (89)

Returning to Huangtan

Vermilion maple leaves wither then drop;
Black as mascara, the cypress stands lonely.
Paddy rice glints with yellow in the evening;
Hillside grass grows verdant once more in autumn.
The horizon stretches before me on a long painted scroll,
Revealing to my drunken eyes an infinite panorama.
Sails float downward on the gold and turquoise of the river;
A horse whinnies in a valley embroidered with flowers.
The world we live in is adorned and embellished,
By a creator untainted by a hint of vulgarity.
If I had not traveled on my distant journey to this land,
Never, never, would I have witnessed this miraculous scene! (92, 79)

In and out of the capital (1160–1172)

Following the rhymes of Bian Gongbian

The Heavenly Banner's[1] scattered stars net the tops of the bamboos;
My wood hut overlooks the river, its brushwood gate, tightly shut.
The spring wind puffs the dawn, the moon's jade toad[2] totters;
Thick dew washes the sky, the Milky Way looms high.
Two magpies circle a branch, weary for good reason;[3]
A lone cricket chirps by the wall, sounding bold enough.
The new autumn is just right for inspiring poetry,
I mustn't copy Pan Yue, sighing over two little white hairs on his head![4]

(98, 84)

Water is released at Cold Spring Pavilion

A staff helps me climb a flagstone path slippery with ancient moss,
While waves crash and roar beneath me, ready to fly into the air.
Walking wearily along the capital's streets, you can't see such a sight;
Let the river's snowy foam splash the dust from my traveling clothes!

(104, 88)

1 The twenty-first constellation of the Chinese zodiac that makes up part of Orion.
2 Reference to the popular belief that there was a toad on the moon.
3 Allusion to the lines of the Three Kingdom's period ruler Cao Cao: "The magpie flies south, / Circles the tree three times, / And finds no branch to rest on," which in later times became a symbol for a hopeless future. Cao Cao, *Cao Cao ji* 曹操集 (Beijing, 1962), p. 5.
4 Allusion to the preface of the "Prose-Poem Inspired by Autumn" by Pan Yue: "I have reached the age of two and thirty, and I already have gray hair mixed with black." In later times Pan Yue was taken as an example of premature concern about old age. *Han Wei Liuchao baisanjia ji* 漢魏六朝百三家集, vol. 34 (1817 ed.), p. 23a.

Using the same rhymes as Li Yong's long poem on snow

At dusk the cold's so bitter, even ravens are scarce;
The snow attacks head on, like sand or gravel in a duststorm.
My cotton quilt is cold as iron and soaked through and through;
I dream of the spring wind arriving to lift winter's siege.
But I never could have imagined the strange thing that happened:
At midnight my paper windows started to glow in the dark!
Outside the Buddha had conjured up a jewel-spangled world of cotton;[1]
Even Dark Winter[2] did not begrudge his treasure of jade snow.
I opened the door and leant on my staff, dazzled by its pure whiteness;
I seemed to stand at a distance, free of the empty world's support.
Then I vaguely recalled how I once enjoyed myself as a boy,
On paths I wore through crystal forests lined with pearly trees.
My hound was proud, my falcon, dauntless, my horse galloped swiftly:
So many foxes and hares in their burrows, just waiting to be hunted!
But my spirit of adventure and my boldness left me long ago;
I barely remember how my arrow once shrieked like a hungry hawk.
My neighbor to the north leads an uneventful life, too,
And he insists I brave the cold to compose this poem for him.
My hands are chapped; my brush grows bald and is too cold to hold,
My ink is freezing here and there, and ice glazes my robe. (107, 90)

Presented to Li Yong after it stopped snowing

There's no place for snow clouds to moor in this azure sky;
Sunlight invades the desolate garden, where sparrows are tame.
A light wind blows the pool's icy surface, which seems to quiver;
A strong sun warms the snow, and my roof tiles fume.
I've long had the dusty face and rough features of a wanderer;
Once more cold buds and sparse branches get ready for spring.
I hope my poems will produce just a bit of warmth in this world,
Will overcome the cold, and force you, neighbor, to write something for me!
(111, 94)

1 Fan Chengda uses a Chinese transcription (*doulou*) of the Sanskrit word for cotton (*tûla*).
2 The original name for the Winter God was Xuanming, but Fan has changed this to Mingling here to avoid the Song dynasty taboo on the word *xuan*.

On the fourteenth of the first month I return home at night in the rain with Zhengfu and Pengyuan after a small party

The lamp market[1] is cold and deserted, the lamps' flames, dull.
Caps soaked, hats blown crooked, we laugh about our late return.
The moon must be shining high above the thick heaps of clouds;
We're so drunk we don't know when our horses slip in the mud.
As I grow older, I see flowers hidden in a mist when I drink;[2]
Spring comes, but my temples turn gray from writing poetry.
In this floating life, there's no end to either my joy or my sorrow:
Better not tell the partying youngsters about this – they just won't understand!
(113, 96)

On the second day of the seventh month we float near Shangsha at night

I lean wearily on the boat's window and watch the Big Dipper turn;
When I rise, wind and dew blanket the world's remotest corners.
A roosting heron flashes white among wild rice leaves;
A cold firefly enters the blooming paddy, sparkling and shimmering.
A wisp of clouds under moonlight – it will rain tonight;
At mountain's foot, a torch flickers – somebody's house.
There's no limit to such scenes along the rivers and lakes,
But I've spent half my life in the world's grime, just to get old! (127, 98)

Li Cishan painted two pictures, the first of a servant girl playing a flute in the bow of a boat floating on a lake beneath mountains, the other of a rider crossing a small bridge on a donkey into a deep valley. I wrote a quatrain for each of the paintings.

Moon overhead, she sits at the bow, her return home all forgotten,
Unworried by the wind messing her hair or the dew soaking her clothes.
With three notes from her flute waves swell in the lake;
From the mountain in front, magpies soar up, startled.

1 For more information on the Lantern Festival, celebrated on the fifteenth day of the first lunar month, see the translation of Fan's poem on this festival, pp. 161–2.
2 Allusion to a line by Du Fu: "As I get older, I seem to see flowers in a fog." *A Concordance to the Poems of Tu Fu*, Harvard-Yenching Sinological Index Series, (Taipei, 1966), 562/20/4. Although Fan means that his eyesight is growing worse, the word "flowers" can be used to refer to the singing girls who would normally entertain at such a party.

In and out of the capital

He has just awoken from the dream life of an official,[1]
And vanishes with his donkey into the foothills' purple mists.
Now he can really get to know the myriad mountains' true faces,
How he wasted his time looking at them while he served at court![2] (128, 99)

The king of Changsha Sun Ce's tomb outside Heaven Gate[3]

Our hero came to naught like the river that always flows east in vain,
His hundred victories buried with him in a lump of cold clay.
The buckwheat is boundless, its flowers like snow,
A herding boy trills a flute as he mounts Sun Ce's tomb mound!

(131, 101)

When I am on duty at the Academy of Scholars the emperor sends me a cup of wine as a gift

Returning ravens swoop on the palace's scholar-trees, one by one;
At evening, boudoirs' curtains hang down here and there.
A light drizzle delivers the autumn season to me,
And a wind from afar carries market noises hither.
Near heaven, I can see the seven stars of the Big Dipper's handle,
But West Mountain's green peaks still loom in my dreams of home.
I am embarrassed when His Majesty's gift arrives at the first watch;
The imperial eunuch urges me to drink from the glittering gold cup.

(136, 103)

For Vice-Director Zhou Zichong, who spent the night with me at Stone Lake

Hidden fragrances perfume the orchid-patterned bed curtain,
Where unsullied dreams are tranquil and auspicious.

1 Allusion to the popular story "Dream of Handan" about a man who dreamed that he married a beautiful woman, attained high position, and died at the age of eighty. When he woke up he discovered that the millet he was cooking for dinner was not yet done.

2 Literally, "In the past he leaned on his tally and looked at the mountains in vain," a reference to a story about Wang Huizhi of the Jin dynasty, who served under Huan Chong. When Huan suggested that he was going to promote Wang to a higher position, Wang supposedly paid no attention and supporting his face with his official's tally, looked at the nearby mountains and commented on how beautiful the scenery was. This was generally taken as an example of Wang Huizhi's lack of worldly ambition, but Fan is saying that only after one quits court life can beautiful scenery really be enjoyed. *Jinshu* 晉書 (Beijing, 1974), 50–2103.

3 Sun Ce was the elder brother of Sun Quan, one of the three rulers of the Three Kingdoms period (220–265) and a major figure of the period himself.

The vine-entangeled moon sets in the hazy dawn,
And the wind sighs mysteriously in the midst of the pines.
At sunrise the birds peck and then start to sing,
Calling me to get up, wash my face, and comb my hair.
The sculpted window admits the billowing clouds,
Which rinse and bathe the newly born sun.
As soon as its golden gong soars up into the sky,
The sun's inverted image totters on my bookcase.
This fair, cloudless day sets us new tasks –
Well-dried seeds urge the planting of millet.
From now on we won't have a moment of leisure;
The eastern marsh's grass already stands knee-high! (138)

Ballad on mowing wheat

I planted my wheat in the season of plum flowers,
And it started to turn green, as the peach petals took flight.
But last week I was too ill to go out of doors –
Already the eastern slope is changed to a cloud of gold.
Now I sickle ripe wheat while the weather's still clear;
Lest tomorrow's rain sully my wheat with mud.
Then after the rains I'll plow the field and plant late rice;
At morning I'll transplant rice seedlings and snack on roasted wheat in the evening! (139, 104)

At dawn on the sixteenth day of the seventh month I write this on the way back to Stone Lake after an informal party

In my white hemp robe and black hat, I look like an old peasant,
As I stroll in the waterwheel's breeze, north and south of the stream.
Tips of rice plants flash white from heavy morning dew –
I step into an emerald net studded with shining pearls! (140, 105)

I walk home through the fields after a party

I completely forgot who helped me climb downstairs;
My cap was upside down, and wine stained my robe.
I was so greedy to see moonlight fill the streets with snow
That I didn't get in my sedan chair, but returned home – on foot! (142)

Picking lotuses (two poems of three)

Dressed in thin clothes, they shudder at the river's brisk wind,
But the lotus pickers seem to fly when their oars mount the waves;
They pick the duckweed flowers together with a pair of leaves,
And their disheveled hair carries the fragrance home with them.

I love to linger in the depths of the lotus flowers;
But, alas, I am pressed to attend some banquet.
I won't forget the dew on South Jing Creek's wild rice leaves –
When the moon's bright, and the breeze is warm, I'll be back again!

(144, 105)

Suzhou [First of a series of poems on Fan Chengda's mission to the Jin][1]

I left the town at the fifth watch when the ghostly flames of the will-o'-the-wisp covered the fields.

Foxes howled, ghosts shrieked in the vastness of the night –
Here lies an old battlefield of our nation's army.
The God of the Fields cannot conceal the ghastly blue-green flames;[2]
They shimmer on the ridge – here, two, there, three. (145)

Lei Wanchun's[3] tomb

It lies to the south of Nanjing and is surrounded by a wall with an inscription that reads: "The Tomb of the Faithful, Valiant Duke Lei."

Even if he died nine times, his fame would never die;
He strides the age like a collosus, alive to this day.
You say that our enemy does not value loyalty and good faith?
Just watch them dismount and walk past his tomb in respect!

(145, 107)

1 For a description of Fan's mission to the Jin, see his biography, and for a discussion of the special place these poems occupy among Fan's works, see Chapter 7.

2 As befits a poem about a battlefield, this poem is full of ghost imagery. The "blue-green flames" are those of the will-o'-the-wisp, the eerie light of which was regarded as evidence of ghostly activity. The "God of the Fields" is the local tutelary deity, who normally protects his region from infernal spirits.

3 Lei Wanchun was a general who served on the Tang government's side during the An Lushan Rebellion. When the enemy besieged the city in which he was stationed and he mounted the city wall to answer a communication from them, they suddenly shot at him with crossbows, and he was hit by six arrows. In spite of his injury he stood so motionless that the enemy thought he was a sculpture of wood, but when they learned he was the Tang commander, they were startled by his bravery.

The Xiangguo Temple[1]

On a tablet in the temple there is still an inscription by our Emperor Huizong. The goods sold in the temple are the sorts of things that would appeal to the Tartars.

> Eaves sag, roof decorations decay, but the imperial inscription remains;
> Old dust obscures the Buddhist temple's gold and blue tiles.
> They announced the temple market is open for business this morning,
> Sheepskin coats and wolf fur caps[2] scurry after the latest fashions!
>
> (147, 109)

The Prefectural Bridge

From here one can gaze south to the Vermilion Sparrow Gate and north to the Pavilion for Proclaiming Virtue,[3] along the old imperial boulevards.

> North and south of the Prefectural Bridge lie the celestial boulevards,
> Where year after year old men await the imperial chariot's return.
> Holding back tears, with hoarse voices, they ask the ambassador:
> "When will the Emperor's Six Armies really come home?" (147, 109)

The market streets

The markets of the capital were deserted and only being used as residential areas.

> The Comb Market is in disarray, the Horse Market, ruined;
> The Medicine Market is desolate, the Local Market, cold.
> I mourn the fragrant dust that once perfumed these luxurious quarters;
> Now only yellow sand, fine as raindrops, pelts the traveler's saddle.
>
> (148, 110)

1 This was and still is one of the principal temples in the capital city Kaifeng (then called Bianjing) and was patronized by the imperial family.
2 Typical non-Chinese dress of the Jin.
3 The Vermilion Sparrow Gate was the main south gate of Bianjing, and the Pavilion for Proclaiming Virtue was built atop the south gate to the imperial palace.

In and out of the capital

Kingfisher Pavilion

It is north of Qin Pavilion, and both upstairs and downstairs people were drinking.

Shoulder to shoulder they welcome the Chinese ambassador;
Everyone buys wine at Kingfisher Pavilion and the whole city rejoices.
White-haired men and women help each other to bow down before me:
"We're so old, we won't have many chances to see this again." (150, 112)

The ancient wall of the state of Zhao

It stretches on for ten or twenty li to the south of Handan County.[1]

Once Zhao was unrivalled for its wealth and fine music;
Now only weasels and squirrels, pigweed and pulse, live and die on its site.
An old gardener loves the ancient wall, because its soil is so warm;
At dawn he hoes its frosty clay to plant his late vegetables! (151, 112)

The road to Handan

This was where the poor scholar dreamt that he had become a high official in the time it took his millet to cook.[2]

Near evening the frost assails the ambassador's coach;
Handan's hill is so steep we drive on slowly.
Overcome by exhaustion, I have my own millet dream,
But I don't dream of a noble title, I dream of Stone Lake![3] (151)

The courier station at Xingtai

This is the courier station of Xinde Prefecture that is closest to the Taihang Mountains. Outside the wall there is a lotus pond and a willow dike, really quite beautiful, and very unlike other areas north of the Yellow River.

Taihang's eastern foothills shine down on Xingzhou;
A thousand purple and green layers float, like mist-covered conchs.
No one knows enough to climb on high and appreciate this scenery –
Withered lotuses and decrepit willows feel dejected for me. (152, 115)

1 Fan is now traveling north and has reached modern Hebei province. Handan was the capital of the state of Zhao during the Warring States period.
2 See the note on p. 121.
3 The name of Fan's villa.

Lüancheng

This county is run quite carelessly, and the Jin host ambassador was so furious about the meal being poorly prepared that he was about to beat the prefect, who bowed down and pleaded with him until he was forgiven.

Collapsed walls and dilapidated houses sprawl by the town's wall;
The guesthouse is dreary and cold, no fire burning in its oven.
In spite of his ivory tally and red robe, the prefect almost got caned;
How desolate is the scenery in the county of Lüancheng! (154, 115)

The Ansu military district

Among the three towns of Liangmen only one is inhabited now, and the marshes have all dried up.

From ancient times, Bronze Gate's forts kept the north in check;
Hearth smoke rises from the north town, the south one is barren.
High officials argued violently about the old marshes' strategic value;[1]
My eyes are filled by autumn wasteland – fit frame for a setting sun.
(155, 117)

The courier station at Fanyang

Outside the wall of the courier station near Zhuozhou there is a nunnery with two iron pagodas sitting astride the road like snowbanks from the tops of which you can look down into the courier station.

The courier station is so cramped in this winter season,
You feel like a man dressed in furs crouching in a dirt hole.
I am startled awake from dreams of my emperor's vermilion pavilions,
Above my room the white pagodas clang with wind-buffeted bells.
(156, 119)

1 Fan has reached the region in Hebei north of modern Baoding. This area is now characterized by its many small lakes, but in Northern Song times it was still marshland and formed the boundary with the Liao before they were conquered by the Jin and Song. During the Northern Song dynasty court officials debated whether it would be wiser to fill in the marshes to increase the area of arable land or leave them to form a natural defense against Liao incursions.

Dingxing

Formerly called Huangcun, it was changed into a county seat by the enemy, but the town is still unfinished.

The site of a new town, Dingxing is still sparsely settled,
In the middle of mulberry groves, the field paths freeze.
Now a dyer comes along, peddling his wares,
Light red, deep blue, they dangle from a long bamboo pole.

(156, 119)

Qingyuandian

In front of the traveler's lodge in Dingxing County I saw a bond-servant girl who had the word "escapee" tattooed on her cheeks. She said that her master had cut the word on her himself, and even if he had killed her, the enemy government would not have stopped him.

A sweat-drenched servant girl runs behind a carriage with felt curtains;
People say her father and brothers live in a village down south.[1]
The Jin government does not care if servants and slaves are murdered;
A large tattoo on her face is really light punishment – after all. (156, 120)

Soot Cave

Between the north of Zhuo and the south of Yan, high ridges rise on both sides of the road, and although no wind blows, the road is extremely narrow, and so much dust is piled up that you cannot distinguish people or other objects from even a few feet away.

Northern frontier sandstorms weigh down my hat brim with dust;
And when the road passes Soot Cave, the filth increases tenfold.
I just lean on my saddle and refuse to speak of the grime:
My horse's ears are so fuzzy, I can't see their tips! (156)

1 Literally, "a village by the Huai River." The Huai River area was the scene of many battles between the Southern Song and the Jin, and many Chinese captives were enslaved by Jin.

The bridge at Dragon Ford[1]

Xuanyang Gate at Swallow Hill is made of marble, and water from the West Hills is used to irrigate the land below it.

> Balustrades of marble resemble stacks of jade;
> Willow ponds, north and south, embrace the wall in arcs.
> From the West Hills, men release Dragon Ford's excess water,
> To quench the imperial army's horses when they return some day!

(158, 121)

1 Fan has now reached the vicinity of modern Beijing.

To the Deep South and Far West: Guilin and Sichuan (1172–1177)

I moor my boat at the southern river shore at Yuzhang (one poem of two)

Sculpted railings overlook the river's azure waves;
Fang-like masts jut up from sandbars at evening.
Shore clouds sink in front of a lone goose on the wing,
River rain enters a flock of ravens at dusk.
The sky lies close to earth in this wild, desolate place,
And the spring has been so cold, the year has barely begun.
Tomorrow morning the wind will puff up my sails,
And I'll float with my house, wherever it takes me! (161, 122)

I see flowers on the mountains for the first time this year

Three days of clear weather, but boots still stick in mud;
I've passed most of the New Year's season in wind and rain.
In the second month at Xiangdong, spring's just arrived –
What luck! One mountain cherry, inundated with blossoms!
(165, 123)

The Brown Bear Mountains

Traveling on official business is contrary to my wishes,
And on this journey I must ascend perilous mountains.
Crags loom before me in an unbroken, sheer cliff:
I imagine I gaze into a mirror made of stone.
My shouts reverberate from high in the sky,
As I climb up into the obscure, gloomy mists.
I glimpse our vanguard above the treetops;

Still just visible, but impossible to catch.
Then I crawl and clamber up a thousand twists and turns,
When all of a sudden I run into them again!
I'm unable to reach out and grasp the white clouds,
But I can feel them dampening the robe I wear.
Giant trees flaunt black scars from a forest fire;
They thrive as before and burst with new foliage.
Spring birds cannot fly to such remote heights –
We only hear the cuckoo's homesick sobs.[1]
I never imagined men could inhabit this place,
Until I actually catch sight of hoes and plows.
These mountain folk resemble mountain ogres,[2]
Soaring as on wings, first up, then down.
They know nothing at all of the flat road most men tread,
Being born and dying in these treacherous mountains.
There are no broad places to build houses here;
I fear they live in treetop nests like men of antiquity.
Oh, if I could just yank these mountains up from their roots,
The path of good government would be clear and level for all!

(170, 127)

Late spring (one poem of two)

It's so peaceful, I listen to wind chimes tinkle on my eaves;
In my indolence, I love pillow and bed curtains more and more.
Sunbeams fly through a crack in my window all day,
Shattering at sunset on my curtain's shadow.
Babbling swallows alight on branches in bloom;
Bees circle willow fluff on the return trip to their hives.
A white ramie robe just suits the tender breeze,
As the weather approaches the mild heat of early summer. (173, 128)

Following the rhyme scheme of Judge Xu Jishao's poem on a river banquet

Blue mountains and green inlets glisten among bamboos:
Just like an excursion to Tiao Creek's wonders.[3]

1 The cry of the cuckoo resembles the Chinese words for "You had better return home."
2 *Muke* were mountain spirits with a body part human, part bird.
3 Tiao Creek, which is renowned for its scenic beauty, rises in Zhejiang province and flows into Lake Tai.

To the Deep South and Far West

The south wind that soothes sorrows arrives, our old friend;[1]
The rain that provokes poetry demands a response.[2]
In peacetime, at a general's headquarters, even ravens and hawks celebrate;
Rice ripens, and on the frontier, drums rumble and flutes shrill.
I need a rich palette to capture this scene –[3]
My finished poem embodies the coolness of water and clouds! (180, 130)

Sitting alone at Loose Sash Pavilion[4]

The noon sun bakes open the buds of the cardamom's flowers;
Dust flies on my eaves: sparrows squabble over a nest.
My eyes blur from weariness, no place for them to rest;
They idly follow the censer's smoke right to the tip of the bamboo. (178)

At New Year's Eve in the Year Jiawu [1174] I am still in Guilin, and I think of my younger brother Zhiyi on a mission to the enemy. He must be spending the night at the Huitong Hall at Swallow Mountain. We brothers, one north, one south, are separated by a distance of ten thousand li, so I was moved to write this poem.

A cup of New Year's wine in hand, I still can't smile;
"The wagtail is on the plain,"[5] and we brothers are separated.
I still live among thick, inky miasmas of the south,
And you haven't returned from the land of mat-sized snowflakes.[6]
No one is spared from separation, north or south;
But a separation like ours is, indeed, rare among men! (185, 133)

1 According to tradition, the sage king Shun made a five-stringed zither and sang, "Oh how fragrant the south wind is; it can soothe the people's sorrow."
2 Allusion to the lines by Du Fu: "A patch of cloud blackens above my head; / This must be a poem to provoke rain." *A Concordance to Tu Fu*, 289/28A/8.
3 Literally, "a colorful brush." According to legend, the poet Jiang Yan dreamt that the poet Guo Pu presented him a brush of five colors, after which Jiang could write no more. Fan is implying that such a wide range of colors will not decrease his creativity. See *Nanshi* 南史 (Beijing, 1975), 49–1451.
4 This and the following two poems were written in Guilin.
5 Allusion to the *Shijing*, "The wagtail is on the plain," which occurs in what Chinese consider the archetypal poem about longing for one's brother. *Concordance to the Shih Ching*, 34/164/3.
6 The previous line alludes to the Tang poet Liu Zongyuan's parting poem to his brother: "The miasmas of Guilin's mountains come, the clouds are like ink." See Maegawa Yukio 前川幸雄, *Rû Shûgen kashi sakuin* 柳宗元歌詩索引 (Tokyo, 1980), 088.5, and this line alludes to a work by Li Bai: "The snowflakes of Mount Yan are as big as mats." Hideki Hanabusa, *Concordance to the Poems of Li Po* (Kyoto, 1957), 088, 05.

Shi Yuanguang in his illness sends a heptasyllabic poem from faraway Kunshan, to which I respond following his rhymes

Drifting all over the world, I now stay in a guesthouse –
So many clouds and water, so much wind and mist.
I'm no longer up to galloping on an unreined steed:
In vain was my loyalty, my oath to vanquish the northern enemy.[1]
West Orion and the South Well rise above my journeying horse,
While the North Dipper and the Ox[2] still hang over the hills of home.
I don't know when I'll be able to talk heart to heart with you, friend,
But when your poem reached me at earth's end, I was wild with joy!

(186, 134)

The first time I floated on the Xiao and Xiang rivers[3]

Six oars fly in unison as we zoom down the rapids;
Snow-white foam whirls on water, blue as glazed tiles.
The color of Yuelai Creek is so incredibly pure,
The only thing missing is a fishing pole on a pier! (194)

When I moor at Wanzhou at night, a great storm arises, but I am still one hundred twenty li from Hengzhou

The Fragrant Lady[4] interrupts the traveler's sleep,
Driving her thunder chariot furiously in the middle of night.
The still waters are aroused by an eerie noise,
Which seems to echo from just under my boat's keel.
The rattle of raindrops dins on my window;
The rudder groans and creaks before it blows loose.

1 Literally, "my oath to the great river," which is an allusion to Zu Di of the Jin (263–420) dynasty, who, when he was crossing the Yangzi to repel the non-Chinese invaders of the north, swore an oath to the river that he would succeed on his mission. See *Jinshi*, 62–1695.

2 The constellation Orion (see n. 1 on p. 118) was traditionally associated with the west, and the Well was associated with the south, so together these two constellations represent Fan's sojourn in southwestern China. The North Dipper and the Ox or Herd-boy (party the same as Aquila) are associated with the north, where Shi Yuanguang was.

3 The region of the Xiao and Xiang rivers in modern Hunan is renowned for its beautiful scenery and is a favorite topic of Chinese poetry and landscape painting. Fan Chengda has now left Guilin and is on his way to Sichuan.

4 The Goddess of Thunder.

To the Deep South and Far West

The sweet demon[1] of sleep scurries away from me terrified,
And the horrid din assaults my poor ears.
But in less than a minute the tempest passes,
Leaving the rapids alone to bemoan their sorrows.
Servant girls, carrying lanterns, tidy up my luggage,
And boatmen rush to trim the sails and rigging.
I fret and worry until we set off at dawn –
Just as the village's hens start to cackle and cluck. (198, 141)

Entering Mount Heng on foot

Someone ought to live on the other side of the creek,
But only a cock crows in the green shade at noon.
Pine roots, wiry as dragon sinews, choke the path;
Bamboo shoots, orderly as phoenix tails, overspread the hill.
Ink stains thick clouds that resemble miasmas;
A light shower drizzles down, insufficient to form mud.
No honor guard chases after me with riders and raucous pipes;
I indulge in my leisure and let my horse carry me where he will. (199)

On the fifteenth of the third month I watch the moon rise near the end of Lake Huarong

The wind of Liyang River dissolves the clouds;
Waters of Lake Yueyang give birth to the moon.
I don't know who pushes her red copper platter along,
But it suddenly pops out from beneath the lake's silver surface.
There the moon hesitates a moment before she soars upward,
Wobbling so crazily I fear she will crash.
But as she ascends the sky, her disk gradually steadies,
Shooting moonbeams all over the back of my sail.
The moon sparkles and glitters until the waves begin dancing,
Glistens and glows so brightly the stars start to flee.
She enmeshes all objects in cottony[2] wisps of white cloud,
And reveals the universe to its uttermost limits.
My official residence imprisons me behind courtyards and gates,
And my vision is blurred by an illusory film on my eyes.[3]

1 Chinese Buddhists thought of sleep as a "demon" because it interfered with meditation. Fan calls sleep a "sweet" demon, so he is not adopting the typical Buddhist attitude here.
2 A Buddhist expression. See n. 1 on p. 119.
3 Another Buddhist expression. In Buddhist texts, the clearing of a film away from the eye is commonly used as a metaphor for enlightenment.

If I had never journeyed into the middle of this vast wasteland,
I never would have witnessed these incomparable marvels.
I waste my time fretting over promotions in office,
When nothing equals a life spent traveling freely.
My wife and children shout with joy over the scenery,
But what in the devil do they really understand?! (200, 142)

At Lipu

The reedy shore is straight and flat as a wall of turquoise;
River boats hug the banks, straining against the wind.
Green duckweed and white angelica are haggard and pale;
Only the white wormwood seems full of life now. (201, 143)

On the dike at Thorn Islet

The fields on the plain are lush and luxuriant,
Though water flows without pattern over flatland wastes.
Only a few people walk by the side of Great Dike:
So who takes care of all the millet that thrives here?
A single tree, approaching the end of its first century,
Stands staunch and steadfast on the bank of the river.
He has endured the conflagrations of bygone wars,
But somehow was spared from the woodman's axe.
I stroke him with my hand, keen to hear his life's story,
But, alas, he is not conversant with human tongues.
At dusk's approach we're so rushed to weigh anchor,
I can only listen to the oars splash by the sandbank's side.
(203, 145)

Setting off from Jingzhou[1]

From here you board the boat to Yiling.

Soon as I board a boat with thatch awning and bamboo hawsers,
I realize I'm an official bound for Sichuan – like it or not.
At the sandbar we buy wine to warm up at market pavilions;
At landings we purchase firewood in preparation for cold river huts.

1 Fan Chengda has now arrived in modern Hubei province and is about to enter the Yangzi Gorges. For a discussion of the special style of the following poems on the Gorges, see the discussion in Chapter 5.

To the Deep South and Far West

Even the ancients knew that Qin and Wu are far apart;[1]
Nowadays the rapids of Zigui's gorges are renowned for their hazards.
I get older and older mid thousands of mountains and rivers;
Now all I'm missing is my own version of "The Hard Road to Sichuan"![2]

(203, 146)

The Three-mile Hole through the Sky

It's not a ridge, not a mountain, certainly not a hill,
And though the swans will not cross it, we have to climb over.
My family disembarks and walks, shouting and laughing,
With hands linked together, stamping their feet in a jig.
The wind blows the sweat dry from our exhausted bodies,
When our shoes join battle with the pass's rocks.
The Three-mile Hole through the Sky seems a thousand miles long,
What in the devil will we do when we reach the Forty-eight Bends?![3]

(207, 147)

Where Snakes Slide Back

The cliff's face rises sheer as if pared by a knife,
Dropping off in back like a rock rent asunder.
The moment I clamber to the summit of the trail,
I feel like a sailor reaching shore after a great ocean voyage.
How could I imagine that the descent from the top,
Is even more treacherous than treading on thin ice in winter?
In front we clutch ropes to keep us from sliding,
But the line in back tears our clothes to shreds.
One good slip and we would plummet twenty or more feet,
So we edge down cautiously – inch by slow inch.

1 Allusion to Jiang Yan's "Prose-Poem on Parting": "Moreover, Qin and Wu are remote from each other." In Zhou times, the states of Qin and Wu were at the northwestern and southeastern corners of the Chinese world, respectively. *Han Wei Liuchao baisanjia ji*, 漢魏六朝百三家集 (1817 ed.), vol. 70, 1–1a.

2 "The Hard Road to Sichuan" was originally the title of a ballad first composed in Han times. During the Period of Division the Liang emperor Jianwen and the poet Bao Zhao, among others, composed poems on this theme, but the most famous work by this title was composed by the Tang author Li Bai. Fan is joking that it is now his turn to add to this tradition.

3 Note that most of the place names of the Yangzi Gorges used in this poem and the following ones written during Fan's trip refer to the extremely difficult terrain of the region. Although it is sometimes risky to translate Chinese place names, since we are rarely sure about their origins, many of these poems would not make sense if the place names were not translated into English.

Our ascent was like shinnying up a thin bamboo pole;
Our descent is as swift as a brass ball rolling downhill.
Not only do snakes slide thirty miles back from this place;
Even when birds see this cliff, they fly the other way.
I am already rejoicing that the path has leveled off,
When I see a thousand boulders stacked chaotically before me.
But then suddenly we encounter newly burnt fields,
Which vaguely resemble ploughed land in the plains.
I know that we are approaching human habitations;
My knitted brow smooths and my worries vanish.
The mountain folk live in huts like bundles of rushes;
Their bodies resemble demons, but they're sturdier than oxen.
Mattocks dangling from belts, they run to welcome us,
Bowing again and again and sighing as they speak:
"This is hardly a place for humans to travel,
What in the world is Your Honor doing here?
You certainly weren't driven hence by pangs of hunger,
For there's plenty of food down on the lowlands.
You must have come on official business,
Just like a horse led along by its harness!"
I can't think of anything to say in my defense,
And answer their questions with a very polite smile! (207, 148)

The Great Fork Narrows

We travel five stages in the gorges and don't see any villages,
But on horseback we suddenly meet with ploughed fields and wells.
The wheat plants are few and the bean sprouts are sparse;
The pepper leaves are pointed, and the mulberry leaves thin.
The women of the families wrap their heads in cloth turbans,
And carry babies on their backs, great goitres hanging from their necks.
Somehow, deep in the mountains they are able to make ends meet –
Two silver hairpins jut out from each woman's hair! (208, 149)

Where Even Monkeys Fear to Tread

Sheer cliffs oppress my heart, rocks bite at my feet;
Furry yaks lost their balance here and rot in the dark canyon.
Most monkeys run from this mountain, too steep to climb,
Where lone apes weep mournfully like infernal spirits.
My servants complain bitterly they can't proceed any farther,
And I entrust my own life to the hands of blind fate.
A sad wind suddenly agitates the leaves on the trees;
At sunset a tiger roars from a withered clump of bamboos. (210, 150)

The Forty-eight Bends

The path twists and curves, going nowhere, like an inept official;
Then it slants and dips, as if it had problems making connections.
But if you compare this mountain road with the road of life,
The road of life has a thousand, no, a million, more turns! (211)

At morning I set out from Zhouping courier station and pass beneath the Shrine of Purity and Ardor

This is the shrine to Qu Yuan, and in its front is the Pavilion to the Poet Who Alone Is Awake.[1]

By the scenery I know we approach man's realm,
And at morning I joyfully prepare my baggage,
The moon on the mountain makes cocks crow and dogs bark;
A wind from the fields bears the scent of hemp and wheat.
When I mount the ridge, the whole world opens before me,
And everything turns pure and cool at the forest's entrance.
I call three times to the only poet of his age who was awake;
Will Qu Yuan be willing, perhaps, to accept a libation from my cup?
(212)

The White Dog Gorges

The land route also climbs through the gorges, on the west bank of which is located the Grotto of Bejeweled Emptiness.

River eddies swirl in perfect circles then break;
Trees suddenly darken then brighten again.
Rapids follow rapids, thick as joints on a bamboo,
Surging in fury, as they careen past Yiling.
Gigantic river boulders, with hard, steely faces,

1 Qu Yuan (340?–278 B.C.), who was born in this area, is the most famous poet of the Zhou dynasty and the reputed author of several of the best-known works of the anthology *Songs of Chu* (*Chuci*). According to the traditional account of his life, he was slandered by jealous officials when he drew up a program of reform for Chu. Although he remained faithful to King Huai of Chu, his attempts to remonstrate with the king about important matters of state all failed, and after Qu was exiled from court, he committed suicide by jumping into the Mile River. After his exile, Qu is supposed to have met a fisherman to whom he said: "All men are intoxicated but I alone am awake," which is the origin of the name of the pavilion in this poem. See *Shiji* 史記 (Beijing, 1973), 84–2486.

Eye one another in treacherous conspiracy;
They crouch on the banks, evil thoughts in their minds,
Or lurk in midriver with even more hideous grins.
One bend in the gorge and the river seems ended,
But then the vicious green waters appear ahead of me again.
It's so dismal and bleak I imagine demons swarm around me,
So dark and gloomy, no human voices can be heard.
Only through hardship and danger can I find peace in the end;
Suffering has been man's lot from ancient times to the present.
When I gaze down at the river, my head whirls in a daze;
I step back from the brink, for fear of unnerving myself.
White mist billows forth from the entrance to the cliff's grotto,
Beneath which lies the Fairy Court of Bejeweled Emptiness.
There the gods and immortals sit,[1] staring out at our world,
Laughing, I am certain, at the foolish voyages of men. (212, 151)

Just before we arrived at Witch Mountain, it rained

For several days it was cool and clear, and the river fell more than a yard, which made the boatmen very happy. But then it rained, and the water began to rise.

When the water level fell in the gorges, I still worried it might rain:
All last evening a downpour drenched us, as if to spite us travelers.
White steam rose from thousands of mountains around us;
Not even on fairyland's Yangtai Peak would you find so much mist.
I've penned a prayer to the immortals behind their green fog curtain:
"I beseech you to clear the clouds with a flick of your hands.
Liberate the bright hues of Witch Mountain's twelve peaks;
Restore its grove of blue-green summits, planted high in the sky!" (214)

The maelstroms

"Maelstroms" are large whirlpools that arise when the river in the gorges is in flood, some of them as large as a room. It is said that when the water flows along the bottom of the gorges, it surges upward if it strikes a hidden boulder and immediately sinks to form a whirlpool. However, these whirlpools do not have any fixed place and since they form suddenly for no apparent reason, they are completely unpredictable. A small one can capsize a boat, while a large one can suck a boat into it. It is no wonder that they are known all over the world for their danger.

1 According to the popular religion of the time, caves sometimes contained underground paradises that were inhabited by immortals.

Concealed boulders crowd the gorges' waters,
Where the currents change a thousand times daily.
I do not worry about the rapids ahead,
For I fear the maelstroms most of all.
People say that they are only ordinary whirpools,
But I know these maelstroms are far more hazardous.
They form on the river when you least expect them,
And are never bound by the laws of nature.

We float calmly on a river smooth as ironed gauze,
When the water suddenly tosses like agitated white silk.
The water seethes as if it were boiling in a cauldron,
And whirls around us, like a mill-stone grinding tea.
At the height of its fury we enter a depression,
Though the river's anger abates, the water swirls dizzily about.
But just when we nearly recover from our shock,
It gyrates around us in more terrifying confusion.
Froth and foam spurt toward the sky,
Spewn from a hidden leviathan's jaws.
Horrid waves leap up in wild fury,
Like monstrous tortoise paws that attack from the river's depths.
The helmsman stands agape in senseless terror;
The river guide gasps, drenched in his sweat.
Our boat hesitates a moment in fear of its enemy,
Then charges bravely forward into the terrible fray.
Luckily the maelstrom does not suck us under,
But we are buffeted about like a tumbleweed in a storm.
We scream in terror when the rudder cracks,
And scramble to keep the cables from snapping.
We almost drown in the battle to save our boat
And with superhuman effort drag it onto the rocks.
Everyone stands about shivering in horror;
We have escaped from death in the nick of time.

Before when I traveled on government missions,
I experienced all the perils of mountain travel.
So now I strike the oar and swear,
I will never again quail before the waves of this river.
Let them roar all the way up the length of the Three Gorges,
Let them toss our tiny boat as furiously as they wish,
Never will I fight to save my life again –
I will sit properly in the boat with my official cap on.[1]

1 Literally, "Neither will I be so frantic that fingers will be in handfuls / Nor will I be disrespectful with uncovered head." The first line alludes to the account of Jin's defeat at the hands of Chu in the Battle of Bi as described in the *Zuozhuan*. When the commander

I have been entrusted with this mission by His Imperial Highness,
And the River God dares not treat me so lightly.
Come! Beat the drums until they roar like thunder!
Help the oarsmen row our boat upstream – posthaste! (215, 154)

"Bamboo branch songs" of Kuizhou (five poems of nine)[1]

The new town's orchard stretches west of the mountain stream;
Loquats weigh down the branches, and apricots fatten.
At morning they set out to sell them, half green, half yellow;
By noon they buy salt and then some wine to take home.

Women with goitres rush downtown to be on time for the market,
Racing in dozens along the south street, where goods are for sale.
Gentlemen, please don't make fun of these ugly women:
Just see how their young boyfriends buy them silver hairpins!

A white-haired old dame has pinned a red flower in her hair;
A young girl with black hair has teased her hair into three buns.
The women carry sleeping babes on their back as they climb uphill;
They finish picking the mulberry leaves – time to pick tea!

The ancient walls have disappeared before White Emperor's Shrine;[2]
Wild grass on the barren mountain arouses yearnings for antiquity.
All that's left behind are the rapids in the gorges,
Which, just like men's hearts, never are still.

The singing girls at the banquet sing bamboo-branch songs;
They repeat the verses three times, and the guests forget home.

of Jin's armies saw that the battle was lost, he announced that the first troops to make it across the river would be rewarded. In the resulting struggle to board Jin's ships, many soldiers lost their fingers, and "in the boats there were fingers in handfuls." See *Zuozhuan*, Xuangong 宣公, twelfth year, sixth month. The second line refers to the fact that in ancient times it was considered disrespectful to go without a cap or hat. According to one story, when Guan Ning 管寧 of the Three Kingdoms period was traveling on the ocean, he met with a storm that nearly sank his boat, and after examining his behavior realized that the storm may have been caused by nature's anger at his not putting on his cap in the morning. Fan is saying that he is not guilty of such improper behavior and that the maelstroms have no reason to act improperly toward him. Zhou Ruchang does not cite the source of this story, and it does not occur in Guan Ning's official biography.

1 "Bamboo Branch Songs" were originally a form of Sichuan folk poetry. See the discussion of these poems in Chapter 6.

2 This is associated with Liu Bei, the heroic ruler of the state of Shu (modern Sichuan) during the Three Kingdoms period, who, after failing in his attempt to conquer Wu, died at this place in 223.

To the Deep South and Far West

At the side of Thousand Mile Bridge a large ship arrives:
Embroidered robes of gauze flash and glitter on its deck. (220, 160)

At Moshuipu it clears in the evening and the moon comes out, but at dawn there is another big downpour. The roof is leaking and the floor is so wet, I can hardly stand it.

In the dim rays of last twilight it was so mild and warm,
The young boys raced here to report the good news.
But then, for no reason, moon and stars shone on wet ground,
And once again rainclouds rose from mountains and streams.*
My dreams froze on the inn's bed, as water oozed from the ceiling;
My traveling coat, drenched, I warmed myself by a cold oven at morning.
I'm certain every traveler is praying the sky will clear quickly,
But then I worry the farmers will sunburn their backs when they plow!
(225, 162)

Toward the end of night I arrive at the summit of Mount Fengding

A sliver of moonlight dangles from the high mountain,
When I commence my ascent of its highest peak.
I raise my hand to reach out and clasp it,
But I fear I'll startle all the lunar fairies.
The moon's cassia tree[1] throbs with heady perfume,
Beads of dew drip earthward, harshly cold.
The Northern Dipper already reclines on the ground;
The Southern Dipper slants toward the end of its journey.
Suddenly I am engulfed by the Absolute's music,
Arising straight from the Primal Heavens[2] above me.
The bright Morning Star also shines on this scene,
And the dawn lights up the east like a glowing banner.
White, silken mist obscures the land beneath me,
And somewhere beyond lies the world of men.
I imagine I can see my friends below,
Rising at dawn to burn themselves out like lamp oil.

* *Author's note*: There is a proverb in Wu: "If the moon and stars shine on wet ground, there will be rain the next day," which is to say that if after a rain it clears a bit and the moon and stars shine brilliantly, it will rain again, something that never fails to happen.

1 According to popular lore a giant cassia tree grows on the moon.

2 Both of these terms are Daoist in origin. *Fuli* (the Absolute) is the highest and purest realm of the universe, and *Shiqing* (Primal Heaven) is the "eastern pole," the origin of the *yang* principle.

The stars all set; the sky's jade vault whitens,
And the rising sun begets clouds of red damask.
The moon's icy orb is still reluctant to leave,
And gazes down upon me – flawlessly round. (225, 163)

In the morning it cleared and I set out from Guang'anjun, staying for the night at the manor of Duckweed Pool Village

Nighttime rain washed away the sultry air,
And a dawn breeze endowed us with clear, mild weather.
The cloud peaks resemble crumbling hills of iron ore;
Sunrays spray down in cascades of gold.
Though it's summer, the road is cool all day long;
Everything's perfect for journeying afar.
This traveler just happens to be in a great hurry,
And one person after another watches him from the roadside.
Luggage in proper order, an official green parasol shades me,
But the spectators walk barefooted, clad in blue skirts.
Life is crude on this northern boundary of the southern lands,
Where nature takes on the semblance of east Sichuan.
Here the bamboo shoots are bitter and green;
The lychees are sour and still not ripe.
The long reeds are dense enough to double as fences;
Straight cypresses stand solemnly like groves of flagpoles.
But the mud has dried and my horse's hooves skip nimbly;
The road is level, and the milestones flash by.
At evening I drop in at somebody's manor,
With windows shaded by long, straight bamboos. (226, 165)

On the third we went to the courtyard of the Inscription Pavilion in the eastern outskirts of Chengdu[1]

We went to sacrifice to the Spring God, and, therefore, held a banquet in the courtyard. According to local custom the people of Sichuan sweep their ancestors' graves on this day.

Purplish mists darken distant willows against a newly cleared sky,
A freezing wind sends pure ripples waltzing over the small river.
Red dust billows as people rush home from ancestors' tombs;
Hungry ravens swoop from perches to trample burnt spirit money.
(232, 167)

1 Fan Chengda has now taken up his position at Chengdu in modern Sichuan Province.

On the twenty-third of the third month I go to Haiyun Temple to hunt for "lucky-stones"[1]

I come again and again to the Pavilion to Encourage Farming,
A sick, old man, who drifts around the world like duckweed.
It seems I just collected winter camelia[2] here in last night's dreams,
But I return to hunt lucky-stones – spring almost ended.
I'm frightened how time flows on like a river to the east;
People stream past me and vanish in a cloud of dust.
Luckily there's enough wheat to keep everyone full this year;
I meet some farmers on the road, and my knitted brow smooths.

(235, 169)

The next day I inspect the militia at Fengong Pavilion, and again I use the rhymes of my previous poem on the western tower

I can see how the clear dew speckled the green moss;
The months and years speed on in a few nods of the head.
I'm so old I forget what I read a moment ago,
But lines for poems still fly at me whenever I'm drunk.
If I hear a cock crow at midnight, I still can dance;
When I shoot pheasants in the west suburbs, I don't need decoys.
I laugh at my feebleness, but I'll make do for a while;
After all, my ambitions haven't all turned to ashes yet! (240)

When I set out from Taicheng, I addressed this parting poem to some of the old peasants[3]

In west Sichuan there had been a summer drought, but for several days before I left, it rained, and the village elders said, "Once again there will be a good harvest."

In the fifth month, seedlings for autumn still aren't planted,
And I'm more depressed than usual as I prepare to leave.
But on the road I meet old peasants who bear good tidings,
Announcing that last night three inches of rain fell!
Although I'm about to leave you, I needn't frown now;
Good sirs, stay in peace, and don't worry about me.

1 On the twenty-first of the third month, the inhabitants of Chengdu went to the Haiyun temple, where they searched for stones in the temple's pool in order to obtain good luck.
2 On the eighteenth of the twelfth month Fan had visited this temple to view the camelias.
3 This poem and those following were written after Fan had left Chengdu to go on a pilgrimage to Mount Emei and then return to his home.

In every field you can hear water gurgle through irrigation ditches;
This autumn you'll feast and drink when they sacrifice chickens and pigs!
(247, 174)

Gazing upon the Snow Mountains from Mount Big-Face's highest peak

Mount Big-Face's peak still freezes in the summer months;
Dawn speckles the mountain's clouds and conceals its mirages.[1]
Suddenly three silver towers loom up in the middle of the sky:
The western frontier's Snow Mountains – or so people say! (250, 176)

After we pass Swallow Ford, I gaze at Mount Emei and see a white vapor shaped like a multistoried tower sticking up from the clumps of clouds

A thousand mountains surround the fields, dim in the summer air,
But Great Emei's mist and fog are rich with color.
A peak of jade suddenly soars up thirty thousand feet –
Surely this is a cloud straight from Buddha's Paradise of Cotton![2] (256)

The mountain litter

I bounce on the litter like a fish hooked on a long rod,
And the bends in the path resemble reflections in a series of mirrors.
And yet I'm grateful to the porters for carrying me uphill –
Stumbling around by yourself in this world is just too hard![3] (258, 179)

1 The Foguang or "Buddha Light," a phenomenon believed to be a manifestation of the Boddhisatva Samântabhadra.
2 See the preceding note and n. 1 on p. 119.
3 This was written at the time of Fan's ascent of the Buddhist holy mountain, Mount Emei. Although this poem is primarily witty, the Buddhist significance of the last line is obvious.

On the twenty-seventh of the sixth month, the fourth year of the Chunxi reign period [1177], I ascended the summit of Mount Emei, which is also named the Peak of Victory. According to Buddhist books, it is the abode of the Buddha Samântabhadra,[1] *and day after day his radiance is manifested there. I wrote this poem to record what I experienced, and then entrusted a stone carver to inscribe it on the mountain, so that it might be an important study case.*[2]

How lofty is this Peak of Victory that soars into the azure sky,
Where white deer guide my ascent into the Magical Realm![3]
The Buddha living in this mountain is delighted a stranger comes,
And welcomes me by wrapping the world in many-hued cotton mist.[4]
A round halo, bright and radiant, stands erect beside a cloud,
So splendid it must have been made from the seven precious gems.[5]
Before one ray of light vanishes, another flashes forth,
And ink-black forms arise, created by my mind alone.[6]
A white feather rises from the earth to penetrate the blue void –
Heavenly bodies flicker like candles, heaven's dragons are terrified.
The Night God's Buddhahood is foretold, and he presents an offering,
Illuminating the entire universe with thousands of lamps.[7]
The next morning this silvery world is all jumbled together,
And lies so close above me, I get dizzy and shudder from the cold.
Suddenly heaven's face and the land's form are clearly revealed,
But then the sky turns so gloomy immortals and gods are depressed.

1 Samântabhadra is the Buddha of Universal Wisdom and is usually depicted as riding on a white elephant. He is closely associated with the Lotus and Avatâmsaka Sûtras and their devotees. Before the Cultural Revolution, Mount Emei in Sichuan was the main center for his worship in China, but unfortunately most of the temples on the mountain were pillaged by the Red Guards. However, even today Mount Emei remains a popular tourist destination, and travelers still enjoy viewing the unusual atmospheric phenomena (traditionally called *Foguang*, or "Buddha light") described in this poem.
2 Literally, a "public case" (Japanese, *Kôan*), or a passage that was used for meditation by the Chan (Japanese Zen) sect of Buddhism.
3 White deer were frequently raised near Buddhist monasteries and are still to be seen in Nara, Japan. The term *huacheng* literally means "magically created city" and refers to a land conjured up by the Buddha.
4 See n. 1 on p. 119.
5 According to the dictionaries, the first word of this line, *fu*, means "angry," which does not make any sense here, so it is likely that it is a mistake for *yan* 艷, or "gorgeous." Different lists are given for the seven precious things (Sanskrit, *saptaratna*), but they include such precious substances as gold, silver, lapis lazuli, crystal, agate, ruby, and cornelian.
6 This refers to the Buddhist idea that the phenomenal world is created by the mind.
7 The term *shouji* (literally, receiving a record) refers to the prophecy of one's future Buddhahood by a Buddha. Fan means that since Samântabhadra has prophesied the Buddhahood of the Night God, he presents his "lamps" or stars as an offering.

People say the Buddha is ready to show his Six Supernatural Powers,[1]
When a heavy downpour washes the mountain clean.
The impression of a great yellow[2] wheel appears on the cliff –
It is made of neither mist nor cloud, nor is it painted either.
Now I seem to stand together with magically created beings;
And we gaze at one other's faces in mirrors that mutually reflect.[3]
A giant round form suddenly wells forth from the mountain before me;
The sun is circled by a halo like the moon and floats in the blue sky.
All the forests, streams, and plants are wrapped within
What people call the radiance of Samântabhadra, the Wise.
A vocabulary vast as the ocean would not suffice to describe
The golden bridge that lies athwart the mountain's northern peak.
The pious monks stand a long time before they finish devotions;
Not one defiled thought arises among these rugged peaks now.
From the beginning there never was a teaching that could be explained,
So even people with ears could never understand it.[4]
The vow that I made during my past three lives
Has been answered with one thought in accordance with my karma.[5]
This journey is deeply imprinted in the depths of my heart;
What more could I seek than these precious pearls on my robe?[6]
I have written a poem, recited a verse, and made a study case,[7]
To allow those who come in the future to know my experience.
I must examine the spiritual powers and teachings of the Buddha –
Let my boiling cup of tea rumble forth like the thunder of spring![8] (261)

1 These are (1) *tianyan* (literally, god eye), instantaneous view of anything, anywhere in the realm of form, (2) *tian'er* (god ear), ability to hear any sound anywhere, (3) *taxin* (other mind), ability to know the thoughts of other minds, (4) *suming* (former lives), knowledge of all former existences of self and others, (5) *shentong* (spirit penetration), power to be anywhere or do anything at will, and (6) *loujin* (outflows exhausted), the waning of vicious propensities.
2 The term *sangcai* does not appear in the dictionaries but seems to mean the same as *sangse* 桑色, "mulberry-colored," or "light yellow."
3 This accords with contemporary descriptions of atmospheric phenomena on Mount Emei, where the faces of people on the mountain are reflected in the sky.
4 Fan is following Buddhist nondualism by denying the possibility of truly expressing the Buddhist teaching in human language, which then can be explained to ordinary people.
5 In other words, after perfecting himself for three lifetimes, his karmic development has reached the point where he can fulfill his vow.
6 In line with Fan's more secular nature verse, the pearls are probably beads of dew, but here Fan is compares to the pearls adorning a Buddhist image with the suggestion that he has achieved some higher form of enlightenment.
7 The word "verse" translates the term gâthâ (Chinese *ji*), which is a kind of Buddhist poetry. For "study case," see n. 1, p. 145.
8 Fan seems to be saying that he is going to enjoy boiling a cup of tea to show his indifference to the material world.

Falling fast asleep while we pass Jiangjin County we fail to attend to the rudder[1]

The west wind assists the oars as if we were floating on a raft;
The river is wide, its reefs lie deep, and the waves are without froth.
In my dreams I hear a fierce snowstorm howl among bamboos –
I awake just as our boat scrapes over a sandbank! (267)

We moor at Yufu Inlet and watch the moon rise from Red Shell Mountain. The mountain is split so that it resembles a hidden crocodile or dragon with open jaws, and the moon rose from that crack up to the mountain's peak.

The moon rose at Red Shell Mountain like a platter of bronze,
Spit out and swallowed again by a crouching dragon's gaping maw.
A great wind from far away finally pried it loose,
And its image fell in the river's middle, where it bobbed up and down.
Heaven is high, the night is still, and the mountains are silent;
All I can hear are the rapids that clamor by Water Gate.
I can't write a poem like Du Fu in his study on high,[2]
So like him I remain sleepless and gaze at the moon the night through.
(270)

1 The following three poems were written on Fan's voyage back home down the Yangzi Gorges.
2 Du Fu wrote some of his most famous poetry in the area of the Yangzi Gorges. Du used the expression *gaozhai* (study on high) four times in his complete works to refer to his study, and here Fan is alluding to his poem "Spending the Night in a Pavilion by the River," *A Concordance to Tu Fu*, vol. 2, p. 487, in which Du describes his sorrow at being unable to improve the political situation in China during the An Lushan Rebellion.

Old age and retirement (1177–1193)

When I had just returned to Stone Lake

Early morning sunshine bakes the mist red and blue,
On my pond's west bank, east of ancient Yue's ruined wall.[1]
Half of a man emerges above the paddy blossoms;
A lone heron flashes among water-chestnut leaves.
I stroll along aimlessly, for I know all the old paths by heart,
But I'm shocked again and again how my neighbors have aged.
In the willow I planted long ago by the arched bridge's side,
Countless cicadas now hum, and the tree sweeps the sky – green.

(280, 185)

Just before autumn there is a rainstorm and it suddenly turns cool

Autumn comes as if by appointment and doesn't need to be rushed;
He invigorates me with his rain's patter and the soughing of wind.
Let the summer's warm sunrays sneak off as if they were bandits;
Then I won't blame old age pouring toward me like an ocean tide.
A wine cup in hand moves my heart to write verse,
A pile of books invites my sickly eyes to read.
Tomorrow it will be colder – I can predict the weather already:
At evening the clouds are jumbled up into big, messy piles! (289, 186)

I rise in the morning and listen to the rain

As I get older I prefer freedom from Demon Sleep;[2]
I can sit still as a stump and listen to the fifth watch's drumbeats.

1 This had been built in the Zhou dynasty during Yue's wars with the state of Wu.
2 See n. 1, p. 133.

Old age and retirement

I pity the dying candle, as its last smoke writhes upwards;
I despise the buzzing mosquitoes that hover arrogantly around me.
The Hill-Climbing Festival[1] finished, rain comes when it likes,
But everyone is rushing to mow his crops and needs some clear weather.
Don't say the autumn harvest is a time free of worry;
Some strong sunshine, please! Help dry the fragrant rice! (290, 186)

Walking at evening by the ancient city wall of Wu[2]

Strolling leisurely, I ignore thornbushes and brambles;
The wind billows my sleeves, and they float like wings in the air.
I lean against my cane, and a pair of pheasants soar up,
A lone hawk glides in circles around the tip of a pagoda.
A drunken, red sun slopes west and wraps the ground in its warmth;
Rivers, smooth as ironed gauze, soak the sky with swollen waters.
I turn around to gaze at hearth smoke rising over the eastern paddies,
A sliver of moon already glistens on the oak grove – red. (293, 187)

Fording Xukou again

From antiquity this place has delighted even uncouth minds like mine;
The sky circles the glistening lake and the sun beams down.
One goose flies level with the clouds, disappearing, reappearing;
Two mountains undulate in the waves, sinking and rising in turn.
My white beard is aging together with the fluff on the reeds,
But my wine-flushed face isn't as crimson as the maple leaves.
Devotees of net and fishing pole come and enquire about my plans:
Am I going to keep the appointment I made with them last year?
(294, 188)

Galloping on horseback past Brocade Hamlet, I am delighted by the clear weather

The rice tassels have just dried and still fear rain;
The sky steams at evening, and a fine mist forms.
If only the west wind would blow these rainclouds clean away,
I wouldn't mind galloping home, cap flapping in the air! (294)

1 On the Double Yang Festival (ninth day of the ninth lunar month), it was the custom to climb a hill to avoid bad luck for the rest of the year.
2 Fan was living close to the modern city of Suzhou, which was the capital of the state of Wu during the Zhou dynasty.

Crossing Hengtang Bridge to Yellow Mountain

Light gusts of cold wind reinvigorate my skinny horse;
A small banner invites customers to a thatched tavern among bamboos.
The spring has already greened up all the water in the south creek;
Now it dyes a thousand willow branches on its south bank the same hue.
(298, 189)

Following the rhyme scheme of Wang Dayou's poem celebrating the rainfall (second of two quatrains)

There's no use worrying about old age's infirmities,
For that will afford scant comfort to the people of this district.[1]
If only I could be certain no one suffers from poverty in the country,
It wouldn't matter if money doesn't roll all over the ground! (301, 189)

Composed ten days before spring

Spring's almost on us, but we still owe winter ten days;
Busy with paperwork, I regret how quickly life passes.
My poems are too weak to fetch me some snow,
And wine has lost its magic to dispel my sorrows.
Yet the season would never bully a sick man like me;
We scholars just like to gripe about our problems all the time.
Why do we fret and worry so much during the short span we're allotted?
After all that fuss and bother, we end up in a dirt hole anyway! (307, 190)

I meet my subordinates at Jade Unicorn Hall to view the peonies and roses[2]

The east wind is still cool enough to preserve what's left of spring;
Our wine warms without fire among perfumed red and violet blossoms.
There's no need to hurry and fetch silver candelabras:
Snow-white roses will light up the dusk, all by themselves! (318, 195)

1 At this time Fan was serving as governor of Mingzhou (modern Ningbo).
2 This poem was written while Fan was serving in Jiankang (modern Nanjing), shortly before his retirement from official life. All the poems that follow were written after Fan retired in 1183.

Old age and retirement

My nephew Zao has recently begun composing pentasyllabic verse that is already charming, and I am greatly pleased. Therefore, in spite of my illness I wrote twelve poems for him, so that he can instruct his brothers to compose poems in reply, which is preferable to spending the whole day doing nothing but eating and sleeping (one poem of twelve)

My vision is so fuzzy, pearls and jewels float before me;[1]
Inside my dull ears, a jade flute drones.
Autumn should sadden me, but even my white hairs have fallen;[2]
I dream at noontime, yet the beautiful goddess does not appear.[3]
I pour out some water to wake the flowers in my vase,
And blow on the firewood, so my medicine cauldron will boil.
Where is the dream realm in which I can live a lifetime each slumber?[4]
Rays of the setting sun have already crept halfway up my verandah.

(338, 198)

A ballad of white whiskers

Four years after forty my whiskers started to gray,
When I was China's ambassador to the northern wasteland.[5]
My sedan chair returned quickly, my body in one piece,
Moreover, the hair on my temples still gleamed like black silk.
In a flash, I arrived at years nine and forty,
Racing a thousand miles south and then a thousand miles west.[6]
My beard was speckled under my chin with Wu's[7] white frost,
But I could still shave it off to fool strangers and friends.
In the flick of a finger, another ten years have passed;
For the last two years I've lain exhausted under the autumn wind.
I'm not certain how long a man can maintain his vital essence,
But I needn't gaze in a mirror to know my hair's white as snow.

1 See n. 2 on p. 120. Fan's vision is worsening.
2 Literally, "Autumn feelings, Pan Yue's temples are bald." For the allusion to Pan Yue, see n. 4, p. 118.
3 Allusion to the Zhou dynasty author Song Yü's "Prose-Poem on the Goddess," in which King Xiang of Chu meets with a beautiful goddess. Fan says that he is getting too old for such sexual dreams.
4 Reference to the famous "Story of the Southern Branch," in which Chunyu Fen sleeps beneath a scholar-tree. After dreaming that he has lived a whole lifetime during which he achieves fame and high position, Chunyu Fen awakes to find that the country in which he passed his life was nothing other than an anthill at the base of the tree.
5 Reference to Fan's embassy to the Jin.
6 Reference to Fan's service in the deep south at Guilin and in the far west in Sichuan.
7 Wu is the region around Fan's native village.

In the capital the younger generation makes light of us oldtimers:
We spend a thousand pieces of gold to buy all sorts of dye for our hair.
Then we wrap it in an irksome sack that prevents us from sleeping,
But, alas, it ends up tinted weirdly like pink clouds at sunset!
This sick, old man lies in bed with his gate locked firmly,
Long snowy hair dangling down, his mortal frame, purified.
The children do not call me a Buddhist layman, as they should –
No, instead I've been nicknamed the Enshrined God of Longevity![1] (342)

New Year's Eve (three poems of four)

Night never comes to the city, where lotus lamps blossom on land;[2]
The plum flowers have just bloomed and the new moon is waxing.
New Year's is by far the best holiday of the year –
Only an old fellow like me sleeps at home, his door shut tight!

Under a lone lamp I boil the herbs in my cauldron,
And squat on my meditation mat like a sickly, old monk.
My children force me to celebrate New Year's and supply all the trimmings,
But the paper moth they give me falls from my disheveled, white hair.[3]

Girls, ripe as plums, celebrate the holiday in fashion,
I resemble a rotten tree on a cliff and yield the springtime to others.
Yet I love our dialect's cadence, how it revives a sick man's hearing,
I listen as a hawker cries "MALT CAKES FOR SALE" on the other side of the wall. (350, 200)

Presented to the flowering crabapples at Stone Lake (second poem of two)

Old and lazy, I live at home like a monk who's left his home;
Spring's colors cloak fields and woods, rain soaks the sand.
I'm not yet in the mood to go see the crabapple flowers,
So why does Buddha's angel scatter them like blossoms of paradise?
(354)

1 The Shouxing or "Star of Longevity" is not a Buddhist deity but plays an important role in folk religion.
2 See n. 2 about the Lantern Festival on p. 162.
3 For the decorations worn on New Year's, see n. 3 on p. 105.

Old age and retirement

Inspired while I was lying in bed

The dawn's new rays light up my window like the moon;
My quilt's warm as an oven, my snoring, even.
Suddenly a peddler who braves the rain passes my wall;
Surely he ought to laugh at a human being like me. (358, 202)

I was moved while I was sitting up at night

In the still of night everyone closes his door and slumbers;
Wind and rain fill the town, and the weather suddenly turns cold.
Somewhere a man shouts "FORTUNES FOR SALE!" –
Hoping to pay for tomorrow morning's meal. (358, 202)

On a snowy day I hear a man peddling fish outside our wall and I am so moved by the desperation in his cry that I write three quatrains

He is driven outdoors with his basket, never a moment of rest;
Ice and snow cover him head to toe, but he's used to the winter.
Of course, he could shut his door and sit at home all day;
It's just that hunger is harder to bear than the cold!

Passions can burn mountains; the sea of karma is bottomless;
We would lick honey from life's sharp knife, but we get cut in the end.[1]
The peddler braves the blizzard so his family can stay warm,
Since he can't express himself in a poem, I'll write one for him!

You cry mournfully like a freezing sparrow or a starving raven,
For the sake of a few pecks of rice to keep body and soul together.
I wonder whatever the Universe ever had in mind,
To trouble you with an existence like the one you lead? (361, 203)

It is cloudy for several days after New Year's Eve

I ask for news about the spring wind's arrival,
But cold fog and freezing mist still imprison ponds and terraces.
Flurries of snow swept the sky clean but then turned into rain;

1 An allusion to the Buddhist scripture *Foshuo sishierzhang jing*: "For men, wealth and sex are like the honey on a knifeblade which a young boy yearns for. Its sweetness is not enough for one meal, and he has to worry about cutting his tongue." *Sishierzhang jing* 四十二章經, *Taishô shinshû daizôkyô* 大正新修大藏經, no. 784, 723a.

We've put away New Year's lamps, but no plum blossoms appear.[1]
The wine cup is poor company for an old man, night after night,
Cloudy weather in spring acts the matchmaker for Dame Sorrow.[2]
Quick! Bring on the tambours! All flowers, report for duty!
Let a hundred drums roar like thunder with frontier rhythms of Liangzhou![3]
(366, 205)

Written extemporaneously one spring evening to keep You Ziming and Wang Zhongxian from leaving

A thousand red blossoms embroider the ground,
And beneath the level bridge, a single boat punts.
The gold-bell's flowers lure yellow croakers[4] to swim over;
Showers of late spring[5] ripen cherries on the trees.
We laugh that I have nothing but dust in my rice cooker,
But I am truly moved by your kind gift of a robe.[6]
Dear friends, can't you stay with me just a little bit longer?
The path before my gate has been overgrown with brambles too long!
(368, 207)

1 In Song times the lamps of the Lantern Festival were taken in on the eighteenth of the first lunar month. The plums (*mei*) should have been blooming by this time.
2 Allusion to Li Bai's lines: "The golden zither and jade pot / Are both matchmakers for sorrow." Hideki Hanabusa, 877, 35.
3 There is a tradition that when the willows and apricots were about to bloom, the Tang emperor Xuanzong (reg. 713–756) beat on the drum causing the trees to bloom immediately. *Jiegu lu* 羯鼓錄, BBCS, 1–2a. In Han times, the frontier area of Liangzhou centered on modern Gansu province was famous for its lively, non-Chinese music.
4 A fish of the genus *Pseudosciaena*, which spends the winter in the deep ocean and migrates to the coastal areas of China in the spring, where it is caught in large numbers.
5 Literally, "of the Grain Rains." The Grain Rains is one of the twenty-four solar periods used in traditional time-reckoning and lasts approximately from April 20 to May 4 on the Western calendar.
6 Allusion to Fan Sui (died 255 B.C.) of the Spring and Autumn period, who served under Xu jia in the state of Wei until Xu Jia drove him away. Later when Fan had become prime minister in the state of Qin, Xu Jia was sent on a mission to Qin, but Fan did not take vengeance on him, because when Xu Jia saw that Fan was wearing light clothes, he presented him with a robe at the time of his audience with Fan. Note that Fan Chengda and Fan Sui have the same surname. *Shiji*, 79, pp. 2401, 2413–4.

Impromptu verses on the four seasons of the countryside

In the *bingwu* year of the Chunxi reign period [1186], my illness became less serious, and once again I could go to my old place of reclusion at Stone Lake. Whenever I found inspiration in the fields, I immediately wrote down a quatrain, and by the end of the year I had obtained sixty quatrains, which I entitled *Impromptu Verses on the Four Seasons of the Countryside.*

Early spring

The soil begins to quicken, urged on by the rain;
Thousands of flowers burst open in a single moment.
Even the fallow plot behind my house is green with life,
Bamboo shoots from my neighbor's yard pop up from under our fence!
(372, 208)

Wheat crops in the high fields merge with verdant mountains;
Low fields near water turn green though still unplowed.
Peach and apricot flowers flood the village, embroidering the springtide;
People sweep their ancestors' graves, dance, drum, and sing. (372, 208)

Homemade brew has fermented in the peasants' old vats,
Just in time to be carried to the fields for spring sacrifices.
Priests and priestesses, don't complain its flavor is too weak:
Government wine sold in the taverns has more lime preservative![1]
(372, 209)

Beneath the altar, spirit money burns and drums roar like thunder;
The sun dips low, and drunken old men are helped back home;
Green twigs litter the ground, blossoms are scattered everywhere –
I know that my boys have been straw-fighting again![2] (372, 209)

Girls adorn their hair with sprigs of flowers at Cold Food Festival,[3]
And ride small barques, dressed in red skirts with green sleeves.
Once every year they worship at the temples in the mountains;
If they don't go to Spirit Cliff, then they climb Tiger Hill.[4] (372, 210)

Town people return home after they sacrifice and sweep the tombs;
Freshly brewed country liquor is served with green plums;

1 In Song times lime was added to wine as a preservative before it was bottled, but the lime was generally considered to be harmful to the health.
2 *Doucao* or "straw-fighting" was a popular children's game in which the players competed in forming different patterns with the stalks of grass.
3 The day before the Qingming or Grave-Sweeping Festival, when no hot food was eaten.
4 Both places are close to Suzhou and were known in Song times for their Buddhist temples, which were popular places of pilgrimage.

The day is long, and the road is pleasant, as we near the city gate;
Someone lends me a thatched pavilion where I can warm my wine.
(372, 210)

In wooden clogs, I stalk the spring season cheerfully;
Rainwater fills the hoofprints, deep as cups, on the road.
The brown dog that follows me trots on ahead;
He races to the streamside, then scurries straight back. (372, 211)

Fruit from the orchards barely repays our labor,
Not to speak of the nuisance from young lads and birds.
We have laid out a thorn hedge to fence the bamboo shoots,
Now we spread out fishnets and snare cherry trees! (373, 211)

Late spring

Pair by pair, butterflies enter the rapeseed blossoms;
No guests arrive at our cottage on this day that never ends,
A hen swoops over the fence and the dog barks in his kennel:
We know an itinerant peddler has arrived to sell tea. (373, 212)

Ocean rain and river winds pile waves on high;
Fresh fish and vegetables follow the spring season's advance.
Reeds bud, bamboos sprout, and the globefish[1] goes upstream;
The chinaberry blooms and the yellow croakers[2] swim over.
(374, 213)

Ravens swoop down on our grove, where passersby are rare;
Mist darkens on the mountain and steals toward our gate.
A young boy rows a boat as flimsy as a leaf;
Ducks waddle home in formation – row upon row. (374, 213)

Summer

Plums turn to gold, and apricots fatten;
Among a blizzard of buckwheat flowers, the rape blossoms thin.
Not a person passes our fence on this eternal day;
Only dragonflies and butterflies flit here and there. (374, 214)

Silk cocoons boil in the vats' frothy surf;
Silk filatures buzz like straw coats pelted by rain.

1 Includes various species of the genus *Fugu*, famous in China and Japan for their delicate flesh, which must be prepared carefully to eliminate a gland that is extremely poisonous. The globefish normally live in the ocean but enter fresh waters to spawn in the spring.
2 See n. 4 on p. 154.

Mulberry-picking maids and spinners congratulate each other:
Spoiled cocoons are rare; prime cocoons abound! (374, 215)

Some hoe in the morning, some plait hemp at night:
Each youth in the village has his own line of work.
Though the toddlers haven't learned how to plow or weave yet,
They study melon planting in the mulberries' thick shade! (374, 216)

Sweat trickles from the dust-begrimed face of the traveler,
Who stops a moment to rinse his mouth in our sweet well water.
We let him sit on the flat boulder in front of our gate,
In the willow tree's shade with its cool, noontime breeze. (374, 217)

I row my boat in delight around the thousand acres of lotus;
Get lost in the dense flowers, and at evening forget to go home.
But my family knows exactly where my boat is headed:
From time to time it frightens ducklings up into the air. (374, 217)

Autumn

Wolfberry and chrysanthemum[1] drip pearls of dew;
Two crickets speak their dialogue in a patch of grass.
Spiders' silk entangles the golden sunflower's leaves:
Its lofty blossoms bow forlornly before the evening wind. (375, 218)

I tranquilly watch a spider weave her web low on my eaves,
Where it needlessly hinders the small insects' flight.
Dragonflies hang upside down, even bees are beleaguered:
I order my servant boy to go and raise her siege – quick! (375, 219)

In autumn we fear an endless drizzle most of all,
But no clouds have marred fall's beginning[2] – a lucky omen.
When the peasants complete the rice harvest, they'll dry the grain;
Please, lots of sunshine, until our crops enter the barns! (375, 220)

On the newly built threshing ground, flat as a mirror,
Each family rushes to work during the cold, clear weather.
A faint rumble like distant thunder underlies their songs and laughter:
All night flails will clatter until the sky brightens again. (375, 220)

1 Wolfberry is still commonly used in Chinese herbal medicine, and both wolfberry and chrysanthemum were used as famine food by poor peasants.
2 Literally, the "*jiazi* day," which was the first day in a cycle of sixty days. According to peasant lore, if there were no clouds on this day, the fall harvest would be good.

Winter

The sun settles on the mountain, a sliver of moon rises;
I take medicine after my nap and stroll by the riverside.
Frosty wind has stripped foliage from one grove after another;
I lean on my cane lazily and count the storks' nests left behind.
(376, 221)

The sun at my eaves toasts my back like an oven,
Intoxicating me with its warmth, making me drowsy and languid.
What official is this, cantering past my gate on his horse,
Hat aslant, hands stuffed in sleeves, at war with the north wind?
(376, 221)

I added another layer of thatch to the roof of my house,
And sealed the walls' mud as tight as a monk's cell.
Let the winter wind roar outside as much as it likes:
I'll lie and listen to it whistle like a jade flute through my fence!
(376, 222)

I burn resinous pine branches in place of candles,
With smoke so dense, they ink up my windows.
In late afternoon, I wipe the southern pane clean,
And I discover that the setting sun is doubly red! (376, 222)

Twigs burn without smoke in the long, snowy evening;
I warm wine on the clay stove, until it simmers like soup.
I shouldn't be angry with my wife for preparing no snacks:
She smiles and points at fragrant chestnuts roasting in the ashes.
(376, 223)

It's in winter that you feel the villagers' warm friendship;
The old man next door politely knocks on our brushwood gate.
The cloth of his long robe resembles frost or snow;
He says he wove it himself on his family's very own loom. (376, 225)

From morning to noon I arrange my daily activities and meals in accordance with the sounds I hear outside my house, and I write four quatrains in jest of this

A monk south of our lane proclaims the last watch with a clapper;
To the north, another monk recites scriptures, plucking a string.
My dreams have already been spoiled by both of these fellows,
When the wind starts ringing the bells on somebody's pet pigeons!

When the vegetable vendor starts shouting, my window is bright;
When the cake seller hawks his wares, I've finished boiling medicine.
I stay idly at home and have no reason to go out;
I hear only the opening of doors and the swish of brooms.

North Garrison's troops finish drilling, and drums rumble far away;
East Chan Temple's breakfasts are cooked, and their chow bell rings.
A small boy calls three times and I climb out of bed,
Sunshine floods my east window – warm as spring.

I rise and sit by my east window, book in hand;
My silver hair is so sparse I don't bother to comb it.
Breakfast is sent in, and I have to bother putting on a cap,
But the fishmonger has already come around the second time today!

(377, 226)

For half a month after the Double Nine Festival[1] the weather is mild but suddenly turns extraordinarily cold, and at the end of the month there is a blizzard, although most of my neighbors have not made preparations for winter

A wild gale blasts our late autumn "spring,"
And scrapes my face like the blade of a sword.
Clouds black as ink splash across the sky,
Benighting my window as if the sun had set at noon.
Hexagonal snowflakes, big as the palm of my hand,
Appear from nowhere to overwhelm the sky.
The Dark Goddess,[2] however, still lies fast asleep,
And neglects to sprinkle fresh frost over the ground.
Mystery enshrouds this change from warmth to cold,
But Snow Spirit and Lord Wind[3] are really too violent.
My neighbors to the south haven't bought any charcoal;
Those on the north haven't even padded their clothes.
Do I dare complain how the price of wine soars,
Or that a bundle of kindling is dearer than cassia?[4]
Of course, everyone knew they must prepare for winter,
But, as a dancer needs long sleeves, they require cash for that.[5]
Year after year, their harvests have been meager,
And nine families of ten have spent their last penny.
They knew they couldn't escape the freezing weather,

1 The Double Yang Festival celebrated on the ninth of the ninth lunar month.
2 Qingnü, the goddess of frost.
3 Tengliu is the god of snow and Sun is the wind god.
4 Allusion to passage from the *Zhanguoce*: "In the state of Chu, food is more expensive than jade and firewood is more expensive than cassia." Although *gui* is usually translated as cassia, strictly speaking it is *Osmanthus*, a southern Chinese tree valued for its blossoms and wood. *Index du Tchan Kouo Ts'o* (Taipei, repr. 1968), 16/191/1b.
5 Reference to a common proverb: "You need long sleeves to dance well and lots of money to be a successful merchant."

But they hate the winter season for rushing like this.
Yet what kind of morning do I wake up to now?
A cloudless sky is suspended high over my roof!
Suddenly winter's curfew lifts for us all,
And little boys laugh as they stroll down the lane hand in hand.
A miracle has turned the weather balmy and warm,[1]
And the people are spared from freezing to death in a ditch.
My neighbors on all sides report they are safe,
And I'm so excited, I chant this poem – just for them! (380, 227)

On the sixteenth of the third month I write about my estate at Stone Lake (one poem of three)

I planted these trees twenty years ago,
Cleared the southern fields with my very own hands.
The months and years have slowly slipped by,
But still I love the ponds and forests of my home.
My estate's low places rule over the surrounding marshes;
And its high spots tower proudly over all the fragrant flowers.
The water chestnut blossoms are always slender;
The shoots of bamboo are as long as before.
I recall when I first began to learn gardening,
I braved wind and frost with reed hat and sickle.
Now that I'm too old to work any more,
I don my cap and walk with others' assistance.
In spite of my feebleness, I manage to come fairly often –
Far better than letting the garden forget me completely! (387, 230)

Rain at night

Candle wax dripping down like wheat tassels befriends my empty study;
Cold, ashen thoughts invade my still vigorous mind.
Feeling old and tired at the last watch, I can sleep very soundly,
Let the rain drip as loud as it wants on my deserted stairway! (393, 234)

1 Literally, "It is mild like the warmth of Mt. Shugu," which refers to a mountain in modern Hebei province, known for its bitterly cold climate that prevented the cultivation of grain in the region. According to tradition, the Zhou thinker Zou Yan lived there and magically transformed the climate by playing on his pitch pipes. The expression was already proverbial by Fan's time and refers to any miraculous change.

Old age and retirement

On the way to Yan Bridge[1]

They have recently repaired each village's fences;
In every field, the harvest comes to a climax.
The rural scenery along this stretch is the finest anywhere:
Farmers stack rice stalks so high they stick up over the rooftops!
(398, 235)

Following the same rhyme as Yuan Shuoyou's three quatrains "On the road to Changshu" (one quatrain)

After a shower, dreary cold oppresses the clear evening;
Water drips from my eaves, first lightly, then heavily.
Ravens soar and whirl among roiling brown clouds,
Long ago they all agreed: it's going to snow! (404, 236)

I make fun of myself

It's spring, but icicles still hang from my eaves troughs,
And even late in the day, my gate is closed.
I idly withdraw from life, startled when a visitor comes calling;
I am lazier and lazier in old age, fearful some letter might come.
Still every day I tell the gardener to water the bamboos,
Morning after morning I send him to check the plum trees for blossoms.
I'm certain the fellow is secretly laughing as he mutters to himself:
"And my master tells everybody he's given up his love of life!" (406, 237)

Ten ballads on the villages and fields at the year's end [six poems of ten]

After my return to Stone Lake, I associated with the peasants, and having noted ten customs they observe at year's end, I selected suitable language to compose a poem about each of them with the intention of explaining our local traditions. I called these poems Village Ballads . . .

The lamp market

This practice reaches a climax on the fifteenth of the first lunar month, but people are already buying lamps a month before at what is called "the lamp market." Several individuals gamble for the most expensive lamp, and the

1 Near the modern city of Suzhou.

person who wins the game gets the lamp, occasioning a racket hardly less than that of the lamp market itself.[1]

Suzhou has flourished from antiquity to present,
And we particularly love celebrating the Lantern Festival.[2]
At winter's end, before spring, the weather turns clear,
And people set up lamp markets along the streets.
Divine labor must have plaited these thousand silk threads like jade;
Human ingenuity strained to snip these million eyelets from the gauze.
People vie for originality and compete in finishing before others,
And don't even wait until the fifteenth to welcome spring.
Weary lads bear their hoes home after planting wheat all day,
And steal away just to take a look around town.
The clatter of dice mingles with singing and shouting from wineshops:
Every night seems as long as in the middle of the first month.
The floods did not harm more than three out of ten families,
So although the weather's cold, the people seem drunk on spring wine.
In Suzhou we're lucky so few fields lie fallow this year:
That's the only way you can enjoy the lamp markets downtown!

(410, 241)

The sacrifice to the Hearth God

On the twenty-fourth of the twelfth lunar month, people sacrifice to the Hearth God at night, saying that the next day he will ascend to heaven to report on everyone's behavior during the year, making it necessary to pray to him beforehand.

On the twenty-fourth of the last month, according to ancient tradition,
The Hearth God returns to heaven to report men's deeds,
But he stays his wind steeds and tarries in his cloud chariot a while,
Until the households present rich offerings in cups and on platters.
Boiled pig heads steam by the side of fresh fish set in pairs,
Sweet, flaky bean paste fills round, fluffy cakes of rice.
The boys present wine, while the girls withdraw;
Wine libations and burnt spirit money delight the Hearth God.
"Lord, please, ignore our bickering maids,
Be not offended by our cats' and dogs' litter.
We send you off drunk and sated to the gates of Heaven:
Say nothing up there about our shortcomings and misdeeds.[3]
Beg for the blessings we'll share with you, when you return!" (410, 241)

1 In this poem and the others of the series, the "preface" to each poem has been taken from the preface to the entire series.

2 The Lantern Festival is celebrated on the fifteenth of the first lunar month, or fifteen days after New Year's.

3 Literally "ladle long, ladle short," local dialect for "right and wrong," with the emphasis here on the wrong!

Lighting the braziers

On the evening when they set off firecrackers, people fill a brazier with firewood that they burn in front of their door, a custom followed by rich and poor, which they call "warming everyone up."

> On the fifth day before spring, after the first watch,
> We open our gates to light fires, brilliant as daylight.
> Wealthy families burn dried firewood in place of beanstalks;
> Humble families light freshly cut branches with leaves still attached.
> Dark smoke fills the town, half of the sky whitens;
> Roosting birds squawk in fear and clatter up into the sky.
> Children sit around the fires, dogs and chickens are busy;
> Neighbors laugh with joy and eye each other from a distance.
> The cold season's Yellow Bell[1] has only reigned two months;
> Dark Winter[2] is still haughty, and its wind is ferocious.
> We welcome the sunrays' return and celebrate spring's arrival –
> The braziers are just what's needed to warm everybody up! (412, 242)

Lighting up the fields and silkworms

This is done on the same day as the lighting of the braziers. The villagers make old brooms or even hemp stalks and bamboo branches into torches, which they tie on the ends of long bamboo poles and use to illuminate the fields brilliantly everywhere, in order to pray for good silk and grain harvests.

> On the twenty-fifth of the last month, people of our village
> Illuminate the south fields with torches on long poles.
> Seen close up, they resemble stars that glitter through a rent cloud,
> From far away, they seem to be fireflies fluttering in a cool breeze.
> Last spring, it hailed much, and silk cocoons were sparse,
> At autumn equinox, it thundered, and our rice was meager.[3]
> All around Suzhou the fires burn brightest tonight,
> Reassuring everyone about the next rice and silk harvests.
> At night's end a breeze blows the flames west and then east –
> Nothing can top this, the luckiest omen of all!
> Mulberry leaves will be cheap and our grain will flourish,
> There won't be joints in the ramie, or any bugs in the vegetables!
> (412, 243)

1 Yellow Bell is the first of the twelve pitch pipes of ancient Chinese musical theory. According to tradition, each pitch pipe "resonates" with a particular period of the year, Yellow Bell corresponding to the period from the first of the eleventh lunar month to the end of the twelfth lunar month.

2 Literally, "the year's *yin*," a reference to the theory of *yin* and *yang*, in which the *yin* force comes to its climax during the winter season.

3 Reference to a folk belief that if it thundered on the autumn equinox, the rice crop would be poor.

Sharing the harvest

After the New Year's Eve sacrifice to our ancestors is finished, young and old gather to drink and depart only after congratulating and toasting each other, which is called "sharing the harvest."

> From antiquity, men have offered these sacrifices in broad daylight,
> But by local custom, in Suzhou, we present them at night.
> The night is yet young when we put the ritual vessels away,
> So we down the libations and then share the harvest with all.
> The clay stove's warm fire distills the fragrance of herbs;[1]
> Candies and tarts are arranged on a platter like cells in a honeycomb.
> The crisp sugar-cakes, prepared especially for this holiday,
> Crackle like frosted ice, between the teeth of our guests.
> Small boys are overjoyed that New Year's Eve has come,
> For in both mind and body they wax stronger each year.
> But an old fellow like me holds his wine cup in a daze:
> As the years roll by, the time allotted me shortens.
> My wife urges me to drink and proposes a toast:
> "A cup to the health and long life of everyone present!
> Just see how many of our oldest friends and relatives
> Are no longer with us to partake of this wine."
> When I finish my cup, I smile, twirl my whiskers, and think,
> "Tomorrow morning I'll return and get plastered on New Year's wine!"

(412, 244)

Selling foolishness

After we finish sharing the harvest, the young boys run around the streets shouting, "Foolishness for sale! Foolishness for sale!" Since, according to tradition, we people of the Wu region are particularly foolish, the young boys are upset by this and want to "sell" our extra foolishness, which action is even more foolish!

> New Year's Eve is nearly finished but still people don't sleep:
> Time to exorcise last year's misfortunes and welcome the New Year.
> Young lads race down the long street and shout out loud,
> "FOOLISHNESS FOR SALE!" to entice some customers.
> Foolishness is hardly in short supply anyplace in this world,
> But here in Suzhou we have more than our share.
> So neither north nor south of my alley can the boys find any takers,
> And amid gales of laughter they poke fun at one another.

1 The Chinese text reads *cangzhu*, which is the name for the rhizome of Chinese atractylodes (*Atractylodes chinensis*), a popular Chinese herb used for medicinal purposes.

Old age and retirement

I sit alone, like a useless log, behind layers of curtains,
But I want to buy some foolishness, so I ask the price.
One boy says, "Good Sir, you don't need to pay cash:
We'll give it to you on credit for ten thousand years!" (413, 245)

Living in reclusion

In my life of reclusion I've always neglected my dress,
And now the autumn heat boils a broth of sweat from my skin.
A lengthy conversation with a guest is a veritable trial,
And I'm lax as always with my household finances.
I sleep too early to await the stars at my window;
I frequently dine with the sun only half down my wall.
But don't say an idle recluse lacks all material desires:
Every morning I count the days until the weather turns cool! (415)

Written in jest after reading Bai Juyi's Luoyang poems[1] *about the infirmities of old age*

Bai Juyi claimed he had penetrated the great Dao,[2]
But even in old age he was always depressed.
He used wine and song to vent his frustrations,
But his mind was still full of vexation and sorrow.
People advised me that before the onslaught of old age,
I'd better drink up, if I expected to enjoy life,
But although I can't forget the warmth of good wine,
What I mainly fear now is isolation and loneliness.
In old age I must observe so many prohibitions,
I'm just like a monk, bound by monastic rules.
My passions' cold ashes will never rekindle,
And it is impossible to drum up my youth's old vigor.
Not only have I renounced both song and dance,[3]

1 Bai Juyi (772–846) is the famous Tang poet mentioned in our study of the evolution of Fan's poetry, who lived in retirement opposite the Buddhist caves at Longmen near Loyang in modern Henan province. Although his earlier poems of social criticism are more popular in China now, Fan seems to have enjoyed the Buddhist-influenced poetry he wrote during his later years.

2 One of Bai's best known poems is entitled "The Ballad of the Enlightened Man Who Takes Joy in Heaven (or Letian, another name for Bai)." Bai Juyi, *Baishi Changqing ji*, SBCK, 69–384c.

3 Literally, "renounced the defilement of sound." According to Buddhist thought, color (Sanskrit *rûpa*, also translated as "form"), sound, smell, flavor, feeling, and *dharma* (here roughly equivalent to "phenomena") are classified together as the six defilements (or dusts). However, in this line it is likely that Fan is using the word "sound" in the sense of music.

But I must also abstain from filling my wine cup.
My daily task is to compose a few lines of poetry,
And before I'm dead, I'll finish off a sackful of medicine.
If I had some way to bring old Bai back to this world,
He would surely get a laugh out of my sad decline.
Am I right? Is he wrong? Now what do you think?
Come on, my friends! Settle this argument for us! (419, 246)

Written extemporaneously at the Shrine of Release (one quatrain of three)

I recover, and Demon Disease surrenders without a battle;
I dream of a thousand acres of White Seagull River stretching before me.
My mind is void, the world quiet, vulgar noise and filth are eliminated;
Most of all I love the flies bumping against my paper window in autumn.
(424)

I was moved after looking at myself in a mirror on a spring day

By habit I never gave old age much thought,
And even now my youthful mind soars like a mountain.
But suddenly I begin to compare ages with my neighbors
And am startled to discover how much older I am than they are!
I never looked at myself carefully before,
And kept bragging about my youthful face, pink like a drunkard.
But today I've met my true self in this mirror –
I'm as wan and sallow as a withered lotus.
My body has somehow been magically transformed,
And I will pass my remaining years in infirmity.
I realize it's too late to get all worried about this,
But now that I know, what, alas, can I do?
The old sun and moon have been playing tricks on me,
But it's not worthwhile laughing at them or getting angry.
I must whet the sword that cuts away sadness,
For the lance that turns back time[1] is useless to me now.
Young lads, who noisily celebrate the fair spring festival,
Call me to come out to dance and sing with them.
The very idea of this sets my blood on fire,
And I rise up, strong, to frisk and gambol about! (429, 248)

1 Allusion to the account of a battle between Duke Yang of Lu and Han Gou described in the *Huainanzi*. When Duke Yang could not finish defeating his enemy before sunset, he waved his lance at the sun, which supposedly moved back toward the east. *Index du Houai Nan Tseu* (Taipei, repr. 1968), p. 61b.

Winter daphnes (one poem of three)

I move the delicately hued flowers from next to the small railing,
And carry them inside to bewitch my meditation room.
A Buddhist like me does not know how to drink;
And yet, I'm always intoxicated by the daphne's heavenly fragrance! (438)

For several evenings strong winds have mistreated the cold plum flowers so that most have already fallen (two quatrains of three)

Just when the flowers of jade are spread evenly over the branches,
A wild wind swirls them across the dusty ground at midnight.
All last spring I didn't get even three nights of good dreams;
This winter I wear myself ragged, hunting for plum blossoms.

Once the snow-white flowers of jade fall, they're no better than mud;
I pity the blossoms, recalling how much I enjoyed them.
When we view flowers, it's forbidden to climb trees or break branches –
My family members are just permitted one small sprig in their hair!
(444, 250)

Notes

Abbreviations

BBCS *Baibu congshu jicheng* 百部叢書集成. Taipei, 1965.
BY Bi Yuan 畢沅. *Xu zizhi tongjian* 續資治通鑑. Beijing, 1957.
CZJ Yang Wanli 楊萬里. *Chengzhaiji* 誠齋集. SBCK. Taipei, 196?.
FCDSX Zhou Ruchang 周汝昌 ed. *Fan Chengda shixuan* 范成大 詩選. Beijing, 1959.
FSHJ Fan Chengda 范成大. *Fan Shihu ji* 范石湖集. Shanghai, 1962.
SBCK *Sibu congkan* 四部叢刊. Taipei, 1965.
SGSJ Huang Tingjian 黃庭堅. *Shangu shiji* 山谷詩集. Taipei, 1969.
SKQS *Siku quanshu zhenben* 四庫全書珍本. Taipei.
SS Tuo Tuo 脱脱 et al. *Songshi* 宋史. Beijing, 1975.
ZBD Zhou Bida 周必大. *Zhou Yiguo Wenzhonggong ji* 周益國 文忠公集. SBCK. Taipei, 196?.

Chapter 1

1 Fan Chengda's official biography is contained in Tuo Tuo et al., *Songshi* (hereafter abbreviated SS) (Beijing, 1975), 385, 11867–70. A similar biography appears in Qian Shisheng, *Nansong shu* (Tokyo, 1973), 33, 218–19. The most detailed account of his life is the epitaph written by his friend Zhou Bida (also the son-in-law of Fan's mentor Wang Bao) in Zhou Bida, *Wenzhongji*, *Siku quanshu zhenben* (hereafter abbreviated SKQS), 2 (Taipei, 1971), 61, 11a–29b (hereafter abbreviated ZBD). Although one would expect such a work to exaggerate the virtues of its subject, it seems to be reasonably accurate and accords with the outline of Fan's life that one can derive from reading his poems, which are fortunately arranged in chronological order. The most important modern sources, based largely on the above, are two versions of Fan Chengda's *nianpu* in Wang Deyi, "Fan Shihu xiansheng nianpu," *Wenshizhe* 18 (1969); and "Fan Shihu nianpu," *Songshi yanjiu lunji*, 2 (Taipei, 1972). Except where noted, all dates in this account of Fan Chengda's life have been expressed in the Chinese lunar calendar.

2 All the relevant material concerning this question has been collected in Zhang Jianxia, *Fan Chengda yanjiu* (Taipei, 1985), pp. 3–5.
3 ZBD, 61-1b. Practically all official terminology has been translated in accordance with Charles O. Hucker, *A Dictionary of Official Titles in Imperial China* (Stanford, 1985).
4 See, for example, "On the Sixteenth of the Third Month . . ." translated on p. 160.
5 For studies of Fan Zhongyan, see J. Fischer, "Fan Chung-yen, das Lebensbild eines chinesischen Staatsmannes," *Oriens Extremus* (1955), pp. 39–85, 142–56; P. Buriks, "Fan Chung-yen's Versuch einer Reform des chinesischen Beamtenstaates in den Jahren 1043–1044," *Oriens Extremus* (1956), pp. 57–80, 153–84; and Denis Twitchett, "The Fan Clan's Charitable Estate," in David S. Nivison and Arthur E. Wright, eds., *Confucianism in Action* (Stanford, 1959), pp. 47–133.
6 The best monograph on Wang's reforms to appear in a Western language so far is James T. C. Liu, *Reform in Sung China; Wang An-shih and His New Policies* (Cambridge, Mass., 1959). See also the collection of essays in John Meskill, ed., *Wang An-shih, Practical Reformer?* (Boston, 1963).
7 The following historical outline, which does not pretend to be original, is based largely on a reading of Bi Yuan, *Xu zizhi tongjian* (hereafter abbreviated BY) (Beijing, 1957). The annals section of SS has also been consulted along with Tuo Tuo et al., *Jinshi* (Beijing, 1975), but Bi Yuan's annals generally give a more detailed account than what one finds in the annals of the SS or *Jinshi*. One modern book that contains an accurate record of the period's political events is Liu Boji, *Songdai zhengjiaoshi* (Taipei, 1971). Another very useful work on Song-Jin relations is Toyama Gunji, *Kinchôshi kenkyû* (Tokyo, 1964). There is a useful biography of Huizong by T. Yoshida in Herbert Franke, *Sung Biographies*, vol. 1 (Wiesbaden, 1976), pp. 461–4. In the history of Chinese art, Huizong is most famous for his compositions in the *ci* 詞 form and his relations with *ci* poets such as Zhou Bangyan 周邦彥 (1056–1121), his development of the "thin, gold" (*shoujin*) style of calligraphy, and his collection of calligraphy and paintings, which led to the compilation of two famous catalogs of calligraphy and painting in the palace collection (*Xuanhe shupu* 宣和書譜 and *Xuanhe huapu* 宣和畫譜, respectively.) On the negative side, Huizong's employment of Cai Jing 蔡京 (1046–1126) as prime minister led to a persecution of the so-called conservative party's adherents, who had opposed Wang Anshi's reforms, and in 1102 the government set up a stele at one of the capital's gates with the names of 120 famous intellectuals accused of participating in the party (BY, p. 2244). Although neither Huizong nor Cai Jing attempted to bring back the new laws that the conservatives had opposed, the proscription was so thorough that the writings of the most famous author of the Northern Song, Su Shi, who had opposed Wang Anshi, were still banned in 1120 (BY, p. 2423). The most serious effect of Huizong's infatuation with art was the public outrage caused by extravagance in collecting unusual plants and stones for the imperial gardens. Such popular discontent brought about the most dis-

astrous revolt of Huizong's reign, that of Fang La 方臘 in 1120 (BY, p. 2424).

8 The decline of the Liao government, which resulted from the emperor's obsession with hunting and falconry, is said to have begun in 1102 (BY 2241). The Jin attack on the Liao was brought about by their anger at the Liao missions through their territory to find rare falcons (BY, p. 2358).

9 Aguda 阿骨打, the first emperor of the Jin, won his victory against the Liao in the eleventh month of 1114, but in spite of the urging of his courtiers, he did not declare himself emperor until New Year's of the next year. BY. pp. 2361–4.

10 This treaty was formed with the assistance of a surrendered Liao general, Zhao Liangsi 趙良嗣. BY, p. 2419. For a detailed discussion of Song-Jin cooperation in the defeat of the Liao, see Tao Jing-shen, *Two Sons of Heaven, Studies in Sung-Liao Relations* (Tuscon, 1988), pp. 87–97.

11 After the Jin captured the Liao Central Capital (Zhongdu) in 1122, the Song imperial favorite, the eunuch Tong Guan 童貫 (d. 1126), led two disastrous expeditions against the Liao in the same year, and after the Jin defeated the Song at the Liao capital of Yanjing, they easily took the city, which was originally to have gone to the Song, according to the treaty. For the capture of Qinzong, see BY, p. 2544.

12 BY, p. 2573. Gaozong had escaped from the Northern Song capital after the first Jin siege, and at the time of the fall of the Northern Song, he did not advance against the Jin from his base in Jizhou (modern Shandong province) but instead retreated to Nanjing, where he set himself up as emperor.

13 After ascending the imperial throne in Nanjing, Gaozong removed to Yangzhou in 1127 (BY, p. 2635), but was forced to retreat to Hangzhou, then Yuezhou (modern Shaoxing), then Mingzhou (in modern Zhejiang province), and finally into the sea all the way to Wenzhou (modern Zhejiang). He was saved by the fact that the Jin were inexperienced in naval warfare and despite their numerous victories over the Song armies their commander was concerned that he would not be able to recross the Yangzi River.

14 Yue Fei has been so revered by later Chinese "patriots" that it is difficult to evaluate his life impartially. One attempt to do this is Hellmut Wilhelm, "From Myth to Myth: The Case of Yüeh Fei's Biography," in D. Twitchett and A. Wright, eds., *Confucian Personalities* (Stanford, 1962), pp. 146–61. See also James T. C. Liu, "Yüeh Fei and China's Heritage of Loyalty," *Journal of Asian Studies* 31 (1972), pp. 291–7. According to BY, Yue's petition was omitted from his biography (intentionally?). See BY, p. 3197.

15 For Qin Gui, see M. Yamauchi's article "Ch'in Kuei," in Herbert Franke, *Biographies*, vol. 1, pp. 241–7. In all fairness to Gao Zong, during a conversation with the generals Zhang Jun and Han Shizhong in 1135, he is supposed to have said, "I can be happy only when I have reconquered the Central Plain [north China] and the two Sages [Huizong and Qinqong] are returned." BY, p. 3049. Yamauchi sees the struggle between Gao Zong and

Qin Gui on one side and Yue Fei and the other generals on the other side as a contest between the Song policy to exercise control over the military and the military's desire to seize more power.

16 BY, pp. 3261, 3300.

17 BY, pp. 3297–9.

18 One of Fan's earliest surviving poems mentions his many cousins, who "had drifted to villages on both sides of the river," suggesting that the members of his family had been dispersed during the turmoil. Fan Chengda, *Fan Shihuji* (hereafter abbreviated FSHJ) (Shanghai, 1962), p. 2; and Zhou Ruchang, ed., *Fan Chengda shixuan* (hereafter abbreviated FCDSX) (Beijing, 1959), p. 1. Whenever a poem occurs both in FSHJ and in FCDSX, the entry will henceforth list the page number of FSHJ first, then the page number of FCDSX, hence, 2, 1 for the preceding entry. The FSHJ was edited by Zhou Ruchang from earlier available editions, of which the most accessible is the *Shihu jushi shiji*, reprinted in the *Sibu Congkan* (hereafter abbreviated SBCK) (Taipei, repr. 196?). Zhou used the Qing dynasty edition of the *Fan Shihu shiji* by Gu Sili as the basis for his text but collated it with the assistance of poems preserved in the most famous Qing anthology of Song poetry, the *Songshi chao* edited by Lü Liuliang et al. For a discussion of the history of the transmission of Fan's works, see Cheng Guangyu, "Shihuji kaolue," *Shixue huika* 8 (July 1977).

19 ZBD, 61-1b.

20 Ibid. Of course, one should always take such accounts of precocity with a grain of salt.

21 ZBD only mentions Fan's caring for his sisters' marriages, but he would also have been responsible for his brothers' education.

22 Unfortunately, we know little about this important period in Fan's life. See Kong Fanli, "Fan Chengda zaoqi shijikao," *Wenxue yichan* 1 (1983), p. 59.

23 See Zhang Jianxia, *Fan Chengda*, p. 14.

24 See, for example, "On the Fifteenth of the Third Month," translated on p. 133.

25 For Fan's relation with Wang Bao, see Yu Beishan, "Fan Chengda jiaoyou kaolue," *Zhonghua wenshi luncong* 25 (1983), pp. 180–1.

26 Fan's journey to the capital was also significant because of the important friendships he made, most notably with Yang Wanli, one of the four greatest poets of the early Southern Song.

27 Nanxu is located near modern Zhenjiang, and Fan wrote this poem on the way to a preliminary civil service examination in Nanjing.

28 Wu refers to the area near modern Suzhou in Jiangsu province, Fan's hometown, while Chu refers to the area near Nanjing; hence, the Chu river is the Yangzi.

29 12, 12. See n. 18 above for this method of citing sources.

30 It is common to compare the small, newly sprouted leaves of the mulberry to eyes.

31 FSHJ, p. 56.

32 ZBD, 61-12a.

33 FSHJ, p. 66.

34 Fan is comparing the smoke from his censer to the characters of the archaic seal (*zhuan*) script of Chinese, which appears strangely contorted to one used to the later forms of the script.

35 Literally, "I idly muse about the magpies filling the River's Drum." The River's Drum (Hegu) is another name for the Oxherd's Star or Altair. According to Chinese legend, the Queen Mother of the West (Xiwangmu) punished the Oxherd and the Weaving Lady (Zhinü or the star Vega) by forcing them to live apart on the two sides of the Milky Way (Yinhe, or "Silver River," in Chinese), allowing them to meet only on the seventh day of the seventh lunar month, when magpies form a bridge between them. According to Zhou Ruchang, the word "Drum" has little or no force here.

36 62, 60.

37 For Fan's relation with the Hong brothers see Zhang Jianxia, *Fan Chengda*, pp. 39–40. There is a biography of Hong Gua in Herbert Franke, *Biographies*, on pp. 466–8 and of Hong Zun on pp. 481–3.

38 ZBD, 61-12b.

39 Unfortunately, we know practically nothing about the men with whom Fan associated in Huizhou. Even Yu Beishan's article on his early friendships is silent about most of his acquaintances during this period. See Yu Beishan, "Fan Chengda jiaoyao kaolue," *Zhonghua wenshi luncong* 25 (1983). Fan's poems from this period are contained in Chapters 5–7 of his complete works.

40 The title *hucao* comes from Fan's biography in SS, 386–11867. According to ZBD, 61-12b, Fan's specific duty was to oversee the Pharmacy Service (*hejiju*).

41 FSHJ, p. 119. For an account of Hong Mai's mission see his biography in Franke, *Biographies*, pp. 469–78.

42 The Song victory at Caishi was not as glorious as it may seem because the Song army was on the verge of collapse before Yu Yunwen, the commander who led the Chinese to victory, arrived on the scene. If there had been any delay in his assuming command, the Chinese forces would have been unable to fight the Jin. Still, the Song victory was disastrous for the Jin, and their ruler was murdered by his followers shortly after their army was defeated. BY, pp. 3588–9. There is a detailed study of the Jin expedition against the Song in Tao Jingshen, *Jin Hailingdi de fa Song yu Caishi zhanyi de kaoshi* (Taipei, 1963).

43 BY, pp. 3665–5.

44 Zhang Jun was the only important military leader left over from the purges of Gaozong's reign. Yang Wanli regarded him as his mentor and wrote a biography of him in Yang Wanli, *Chengzhaiji* (hereafter abbreviated CZJ), SBCK (Taipei, 196?), 115-1a. See also Y. Satake's biography of Zhang in Franke, *Biographies*, vol. 1, pp. 13–16.

45 The main disagreements were between Li Xianzhong and Shao Hongyuan. Shao seems to have been consumed by jealousy for Li, and his refusal to assist Li at the siege of Suzhou sealed the fate of the Song army. See BY, pp. 3668–9. Also Franke, *Biographies*, vol. 2, p. 561.

46 There was a slight improvement in the terms of the treaty that sealed the peace between the Jin and Song at this time. The tribute that the Song had to pay was reduced, and in official communications the Song court had to address the Jin as "uncle" rather than "sovereign." BY, p. 3696.

47 ZBD, 61-13a.

48 According to Chang Fu-jui, Hong's retirement in 1166 was occasioned by prolonged rains, which made him suspect that the Song government had lost the favor of heaven. It is even more likely that he had lost favor in court or had reasons to doubt his continued tenure in office. See Franke, *Biographies*, p. 467.

49 ZBD, 61-13b.

50 Ibid., 61-14b. See also Wang Deyi, *Fan Shihu nianpu*, pp. 196–208.

51 According to Han Biao, one ambassador to the Jin during Gaozong's reign discovered that most of the Song royal tombs had been violated and that the emperor Zhezong's bones had been exposed, so he used his own clothes to cover them. Han Biao, *Jianquan riji*, BBCS, 1-5b.

52 This ritual would have necessitated the Song ruler rising from his throne and behaving as if he were not the supreme ruler of the civilized world, and not remaining seated and facing south as a Chinese ruler normally did. An account of this ritual is found in Yue Ke, *Tingshi, Baibu congshu jicheng* (hereafter abbreviated BBCS) (Taipei, 1965), p. 1.

53 Chen Junqing's objections to the mission are found in SS, 383, 11788–9.

54 See Wang Deyi, "Fan Shihu nianpu," p. 209. Li Tao is most famous as a historian. See Franke, *Biographies*, pp. 585–91 for a detailed biography of Li, which, however, does not mention this less appealing side of Li's career.

55 ZBD, 61-16ab. Feeding on "snow and felt" refers to exile among the "barbarians," the non-Chinese people on the northern frontier, where the weather was colder and felt was used for making yurts.

56 According to Zhou Bida, Fan asked to submit both requests to the Jin court but was refused. See ZBD, 61-16b.

57 Ibid., 61, 16b–17b.

58 This has been translated with a detailed scholarly commentary in James Hargett, "Fan Ch'eng-ta's Lan-p'ei lu: A Southern Sung Embassy Account," *Tsing Hua Journal of Chinese Studies*, n.s. 16 (1984), pp. 119–77. An excellent study of Fan's travel diaries is found in James Hargett, *On the Road in Twelfth Century China: The Travel Diaries of Fan Chengda (1126–1193)* (Stuttgart, 1989).

59 ZBD, 61-17b, 18a.

60 In addition to the account in ZBD, there is a somewhat more detailed version by Yue Ke. According to Yue, Fan Chengda confronted the emperor face to face, and after the emperor listened to Fan's remonstrance, "he abated his anger and muttered, 'I will think about it,' and the next day Zhang withdrew." Yue also records that the emperor tried to keep Fan in the court. However, he reappointed Zhang shortly after Fan left. Yue Ke, *Ting Shi* 4-10b-11b.

61 ZBD, 7-6ab.

62 FSHJ, p. 164.

63 The following four lines are an example: "Human life was originally without sadness; / You must first become familiar with adverse conditions. / If you don't experience misfortune and trouble, / How will you understand that the level way is fortunate?" FSHJ, p. 170.

64 See his "Ballad on Floating on the Xiang River" and "Visiting the Southern Peak" FSHJ, pp. 166, 167, respectively.

65 Fan Chengda, *Canluan lu, Congshujicheng* (Shanghai, 1936). This has been discussed briefly with a translation of one passage in James Hargett, "Some Preliminary Remarks on the Travel Records of the Song Dynasty," *Chinese Literature, Essays, Articles, and Reviews* 7 (July 1985), pp. 87–8.

66 This has been edited with a commentary in Fan Chengda, *Guihai Yuheng zhi jiaobu* (Liuzhou, 1984).

67 ZBD, 61-19ab.

68 One scholar mentions the benefits that accrued from Fan Chengda's dredging of a new channel for the diversion of the Li River's waters. Zhou Qufei, *Lingwai daida*, BBCS (Taipei, 1966), 1-11b.

69 Literally, "My post is called Agricultural Development Commissioner [*quannongshi*]," which according to Hucker was originally "a special delegate from the central government to stimulate agriculture in a designated area," but which after 1006 became "a concurrent title for officials of Circuits (*lu*) and sometimes smaller units of territorial administration who bore similar responsibilities." Hucker, *A Dictionary*, p. 199. Fan's official title was not actually *quannongshi*, but in accordance with the system of his age, he was fulfilling the duties of the post.

70 182, 131.

71 ZBD, 61-22a.

72 Wu Jing, *Zhuzhouji*, Ming Hongzhi ed., p. 5.

73 Lin Guangchao, *Aixuan ji, Siku quanshu zhenben chuji* (Shanghai, 1934–1935), 6-12a.

74 ZBD, 61-21b.

75 For Fan's friendship with Lu You, see Yang Yunzhi, "Wenzijiao de dianxing: Lu You yu Fan Chengda," *Yiwenzhi* 170 (November 1979). See also Zhang Jianxia, *Fan Chengda*, pp. 34–6. For a biography of Lu You and a study of his literary activities, see Michael Duke, *Lu You* (Boston, 1977).

76 Duke, *Lu You*, pp. 65–80.

77 The diary has been translated into English with annotations in Chun-shu Chang and Joan Smythe, *South China in the Twelfth Century: A Translation of Lu Yu's Travel Diaries,* A.D. *July 3d–December 6th, 1170* (Hong Kong, 1980).

78 Lu You, *Lu Fangweng quanji, Weinan wenji* (Taipei, 1970), 18-103.

79 Ibid., 14-78.

80 Ibid.

81 Ibid., *Jiannan shigao*, 8-131.

82 SS uses the term *tuifang* (decadent) to describe Lu's behavior (SS 395-12058) but does not refer to any action being taken against him. However, see Yu Beishan, *Lu You nianpu* (Shanghai, 1985), p. 203. For Lu's drinking see Duke, *Lu You*, pp. 101–15.

83 Two of these are preserved in Chapter 8413 of Xie Jin, ed., *Yongle dadian* (Beijing, 1960).

84 This has been translated in Delphine Weulersse, "Journal de voyage d'un lettré chinois en 1177, Wu-ch'uan lu de Fan Ch'eng-ta" (dissertation, Université de Paris, 1967).

85 "Lun Shubing pinfa zhazi" (Discussion of the lack of Sichuan soldiers), in Xie Jin, ed., *Yongle dadian* (Beijing, 1960), 8413-16a.

86 ZBD, 61-24a.

87 For Fan's relation with Yang see Zhang Jianxia, *Fan Chengda*, pp. 36–7. For a study of Yang Wanli, see J. Schmidt, *Yang Wan-li* (Boston, 1976).

88 See Schmidt, *Yang Wan-li*, pp. 26–8.

89 CZJ, 82–680.

90 Yang Wanli compared Fan to such disparate poets as Xie Lingyun, Li Bai, and Liu Zongyuan. See the discussion of the narrower range of style ascribed to Fan by other critics in Chapter 3.

91 ZBD, 61-24b.

92 Ibid., 61-25a.

93 Ibid., 61-25b.

94 Ibid., 61-26b.

95 For a study of the *Wujunzhi*, see Cheng Guangyu, "Wujunzhi kaolue," *Shixue huikan* 7 (July 1976).

96 For Fan's relation with Jiang Kui, see Zhang Jianxia, *Fan Chengda*, pp. 43–4. There is a study of Jiang Kui's contributions to *ci* poetry in Shuen-fu Lin, *The Transformation of the Chinese Lyrical Tradition: Chiang K'uei* [Jiang Kui] *and Southern Sung Tz'u* [Ci] *Poetry* (Princeton, 1978).

97 Fan's *ci* poetry is the subject of Huang Shengyi, "Shihu ci yanjiu ji jianzhu" (Master's thesis, Taiwan Normal University), n.d.

98 ZBD, 61-26ab.

99 For Zhou's relations with Fan see Zhang Jianxia, *Fan Chengda*, pp. 33–4.

100 See Yang Wanli's preface to Fan's works in n. 89. According to what Fan's son told Yang when he requested Yang to write the preface, Fan Chengda had been "personally editing his works day and night for several years" before his death.

101 Not many years later in the Song dynasty, the scholar Chen Zhensun reported that Fan's villa Stone Lake "is in ruins today, and after a few years I am afraid that no traces of it will remain." Chen Zhensun, *Zhizhai shulu jieti*, BBCS, 18-22a. Recently the Chinese authorities reconstructed the villa, which is open to the public.

Chapter 2

1 The transmission of Fan Chengda's poetry and the loss of his prose works have been dealt with in Cheng Guangyu, "Shihuji kaolu," *Shixue huikan* 72 (July 1977). There is also a convenient summary of the history of Fan's prose works in Zhang Jianxia, *Fan Chengda*, pp. 55–7, which also contains a catalog of his surviving prose writings on pp. 65–75. Practically all the surviving

prose works have been collected in Kung Fanli, *Fan Chengda yizhu jicun* (Beijing, 1983). Unfortunately for the purposes of our study, practically all of Fan's surviving prose works deal with political problems. See the list of books with prose works by Fan in the bibliography.

2 FSHJ, pp. 143–4. Fan's footnote on p. 143 states that there are fifteen poems, but only twelve poems follow. Also, it is not clear if the last six poems of the chapter, which Fan says were written about dreams, are to be included among the fifteen. Since the footnote does not indicate any date, we cannot be certain when the original poems were written.

3 The plant referred to here is the tawny day lily (Chinese *xuancao*), which is also known as *wangyou* (forgetting sorrow), because of its supposed power to relieve melancholy, and *danji*, or "cinnabar thorn."

4 The plant alluded to is the silk tree, or *hehuan* (uniting happiness), which is also known as *qingtang* (green crabapple).

5 The first two words of the fourth line of this poem do not seem to make sense, but since they are parallel with the words *manao* (agate) in the previous line, it is likely that they refer to some mineral. The first word *long* (dragon) is frequently written with the jade radical to describe various gems. FSHJ, 1.

6 Two poems from the series are translated in Wu-chi Liu and lrving Yucheng Lo, *Sunflower Splendor* (New York, 1975), p. 68.

7 Li's poems of this title are in *Li Taibai ji* 李太白集, *Wanyou wenku huiyao* 萬有文庫薈要 (Taipei, 1965), 2, 17–19.

8 FSHJ, 4. Bai's poem has been translated in Cyril Birch, ed., *Anthology of Chinese Literature* (New York, 1965), p. 266.

9 FSHJ, 7. In his introductory comments about Tao Qian's quadrasyllabic poems, Hightower comments: "Inevitably these poems strike a reader as contrived, mannered, and archaizing – all the things T'ao Ch'ien's [Tao Qian's] poetry is usually praised for not being." Since Tao was imitating the *Shijing*, which had been written more than a thousand years before his own time, one can imagine how archaic Fan's imitations of Tao seemed to his readers in the Song dynasty, about six centuries after the age of Tao Qian. See James Robert Hightower, trans., *The Poetry of T'ao Ch'ien* (Oxford, 1970), p. 12.

10 FSHJ, 29. Li He's complete poems have been translated in J. D. Frodsham, *The Poems of Li Ho (791–817)* (Oxford, 1970).

11 FSHJ, p. 79.

12 In discussing Chen's admiration of Du Fu, Yoshikawa writes: "Chen was aware that the age of Su Tung-p'o [Su Shi] and Huang T'ing-chien [Huang Tingjian] had come to an end and that new efforts were needed if one was to continue, like the men of the past, to draw inspiration from Tu Fu [Du Fu]." Here Yoshikawa seems to accept Chen's view that Su Shi and Huang Tingjian were imitating Du Fu themselves but that their supposed imitations had arisen from a failure to imitate all aspects of Du's work. Burton Watson trans., Yoshikawa Kôjirô, *An Introduction to Sung Poetry* (Cambridge, Mass., 1967), p. 141. It is a common phenomenon in Chinese culture that a thinker or literary figure provides an alternative to the creations of the previous

generation by claiming that they do not imitate some ancient model correctly and that he has only returned to the orthodoxy of the past.

13 11, 11.

14 According to Zhou Ruchang, this echoes Huang Tingjian's line: "Birds cry, flowers are startled, I had better go home." It is interesting to note that both Huang's and Fan's lines contain the colloquialism *zhime*, because although Huang Tingjian is usually regarded as a "difficult" author, colloquialisms are actually fairly common in his work.

15 Chen Yuyi, *Chen Yuyi ji* (Beijing, 1982), p. 379. Judging from his description of Chen's verse, Yoshikawa would seem to take this type of poetry as representative of his work. Hargett writes that after 1126 [when the Northern Song fell and Chen became a refugee], "his poetry underwent a significant change in subject matter, diction, and tone as a result of this situation; the lackluster verse of leisure and contentment found in his juvenilia now gave way to an emotionally charged poetry that expressed intense feelings of patriotic indignation, moral outrage, hope, and despair (*chüan* 12–29 in his works)." It is interesting to note that the poem just translated comes from *juan* (*chüan*) 24 of Chen's works and, hence, falls within the later period suggested by Hargett, for although Hargett is correct in saying that Chen wrote much fine political poetry in his later years, his earlier poetry of leisure and contentment occupies a prominent position in his post-1126 creations, and this poetry seems to have had the greatest impact on authors such as Fan Chengda. Of course, the influence of his patriotic verse on other Southern Song authors such as Lu You is highly probable. See James Hargett, "Ch'en Yü-i" in William H. Nienhauser, Jr., ed., *Indiana Companion to Traditional Chinese Literature* (Bloomington, 1986), pp. 241–2. See also Hargett, "The Life and Poetry of Ch'en Yü-yi" (Ph.D. diss., Bloomington, 1982).

16 What Pauline Yu calls Wang Wei's "impassive depictions of tranquil nature scenes" closely resemble Chen Yuyi's more typical work. See Pauline Yu, trans., *The Poetry of Wang Wei* (Bloomington, 1980), p. 155, which is followed by an analysis and translation of the types of poems by Wang that probably influenced Southern Song authors.

17 Stephen Owen suggests that Tang readers "were attracted to a sense of freedom in his [Meng Haoran's] work; reading the man through the poetry, they concluded he was 'wild' and 'did as he pleased.'" However, it is doubtful that Song readers would have had the same reaction to his work, and the attraction that Meng had for Chen Yuyi and his generation is more likely a result of what Owen calls Meng's ability to "describe a landscape changing through time, showing a sensitive awareness of subtle gradations in light and movement." See Stephen Owen, *The Great Age of Chinese Poetry: The High T'ang* (New Haven, 1981), pp. 79–80.

18 Burton Watson, trans., *An Introduction to Sung Poetry*, p. 143.

19 In spite of the obvious differences between Chen Yuyi and Huang Tingjian, perhaps one reason that traditional critics frequently speak of Chen in the same breath as the Jiangxi School is this skill in constructing couplets, which, as we shall see, is one link between Fan Chengda and Huang Tingjian. Even

the most complete collection of primary materials on the Jiangxi School includes Chen with the Jiangxi school. See Fu Xuancong, ed., *Huang Tingjian he Jiangxi shipai juan* (Beijing, 1978), pp. 791–852.

20 One is reminded of such a painting as *Grass and Insects* by Xu Di 許迪, slide B-7 in the National Palace Museum Collection, Taipei.

21 Chen Yuyi is quoted to this effect in a preface to his works written by an unidentified scholar named Huizhai. See Chen Yuyi, *Jianzhaishi waiji*, SBCK, 1a. For examples of echoes of Chen Yuyi's poetry see FCDSX, p. 61, n. 2, and p. 85, n. 4.

22 The only book that has appeared in a Western language on Huang Tingjian so far is Lutz Bieg, *Huang Tingjian, Leben and Dichtung* (Heidelberg, 1971), but unfortunately for the purposes of our study, this study concentrates mostly on biographical and textual problems. There are also two Ph.D. dissertations: Paul Panish, "The Poetry of Huang T'ing-chien" (University of California, 1975); and Michael Workman, "Huang T'ing-chien: His Ancestry and Family Background as Documented in His Writings and Other Sung Works" (Indiana University, 1982).

23 Yang describes his burning of his earlier works in the preface to his earliest surviving collection of poems. See CZJ, 80-672a.

24 As one might expect, twentieth-century East Asian scholars differ on the influence of Huang Tingjian on the major Southern Song poets. Yoshikawa speaks of the "new direction" in which Chen Yuyi was moving from Northern Song poetry and does not even mention Huang in his discussion of Fan Chengda. See Yoshikawa, *An Introduction to Sung Poetry*, pp. 139, 159–61. The most extensive history of Song verse in Chinese stresses the great contrast between Southern Song verse and Huang's creations but says that Fan Chengda "began life [*chushen*] in the Jiangxi School" but was not "restrained" by it, and then devotes the rest of its discussion to Fan's imitations of Tang authors. See Hu Yunyi, *Songshi yanjiu* (Hong Kong, repr. 1959), pp. 136–7, 158–60. Among the general historians of Chinese literature, Zheng Zhenduo states that Lu You, Yang Wanli, and Fan Chengda were "somewhat" influenced by Huang but does not elaborate, while Liu Dajie recognizes Jiangxi influence on Fan and quotes Ji Yun on this matter but maintains that Fan totally abandoned Jiangxi style poetry later in life, which, as we shall see, is not true. See Zheng Zhenduo, *Chatuben Zhongguo wenxueshi*, vol. 3 (Beijing, 1959), pp. 601–3; and Liu Dajie, *Zhongguo wenxue fazhanshi*, vol. 2 (Beijing, 1962), p. 160.

25 FCDSX, pp. 289–91.

26 Although Lü Benzhong included Chen Shidao in the Jiangxi school, Yang seems to concur with most other critics in distinguishing him from Huang Tingjian and his followers. See also Yoshikawa's discussion of Chen Shidao, in Watson, *An Introduction to Sung Poetry*, pp. 130–3.

27 Wang Anshi's poetry has little in common with Huang Tingjian, but unfortunately no monographs on his work have appeared in European languages yet. See Yoshikawa, *An Introduction to Sung Poetry*, pp. 85–97.

28 Zhou Ruchang says that "Tang poets" refers to late Tang poets. See n. 5 in

Zhou Ruchang, ed., *Yang Wanli xuanji* (Beijing, 1964), pp. 167–8. All these influences have been discussed in some detail in the dissertation by Chen Yicheng, *Yang Wanli yanjiu*, Zhongguo wenhua daxue (Taipei, 1982).

29 CZJ, 80-672.

30 Ibid., 26-251b.

31 Although Zhang Lei's work amply repays the effort to read him, he is a strangely neglected author, and there is not even an entry on him in the *Indiana Companion to Traditional Chinese Literature*. His complete works are contained in *Keshan ji*, SKQS, 4 (Taipei 1973).

32 Fat Immortal was Zhang Lei's *hao*, or literary name. CZJ, 40-382a.

33 There is a discussion of the relation between Zeng Ji and Lu You in Qi Zhiping, *Lu You* (Shanghai, 1978), pp. 12–14. See also Michael Duke, *Lu You* (Boston, 1977), pp. 42–5.

34 In line with the Jiangxi concern with literary orthodoxy, Lu is ranking Zeng with the most famous poet and prose writer (Du Fu and Han Yu, respectively) of the Tang dynasty.

35 Lu You, *Lu Fangweng quanji, Jiannan shigao* (Taipei, 1970), 1-1.

36 Lü drew a diagram of twenty-six poets belonging to the Jiangxi school, most of whom are minor authors. One version of his list is contained in Huzi, *Tiaoxi yuyin conghua*, vol. 1 (Beijing, 1981), 48-327.

37 One of Lu You's earliest datable poems is another work presented to Zeng Ji, "Sending Off Master Zeng to the Capital," which was written in 1157. See You Guo'en and Li Gaizhi, eds., *Lou You Shixuan* (Beijing, 1961), pp. 2–3.

38 Lu You, *Lu Fangweng*, 25-418.

39 Ibid., 78-1076.

40 CZJ, 72-610b.

41 Huang came from Shuangjing (literally, Matched Wells) in modern Jiangxi province. In typical Jiangxi fashion, Yang is making a pun on the place name.

42 CZJ, 7-72ab.

43 Ibid., 114-989a.

44 Ibid.

45 Ibid., 114-994a.

46 Lu You's comments about Huang Tingjian mostly involve his appreciation of Huang's talent for calligraphy. In one case, however, he tells us that his father "sighed over the marvelous qualities" of another poem by Huang, "Begging for a Cat." See Lu You, *Laoxue'an biji*, BBCS, 8-9b.

47 FSHJ, pp. 254, 255. In the preface to these four poems after Huang Tingjian, Fan writes that he has used the same rhymes "respectfully (*jing*)," which suggests the high admiration he had for Huang's artistry. FSHJ, p. 265.

48 Jiang Kui, *Baishi daoren shiji*, SBCK (Taipei, 196?), p. 11a. You Mou was included with Fan Chengda, Lu You, and Yang Wanli among the four greatest poets of the early Southern Song, but unfortunately most of his poetry has been lost.

49 Song Lian, *Song Xueshi quanji, Congshu jicheng chubian*, vol. 15 (Changsha, 1939), p. 1052.

50 FSHJ, pp. 29–30.
51 Ibid., p. 30.
52 Ibid., p. 1.
53 Ibid., p. 3.
54 Unfortunately, Ji does not indicate what late Tang or Five Dynasty poets he thinks Fan is imitating in these works, and the three poems entitled "Spring Evening" seem to resemble Chen Yuyi more closely than any late Tang authors.
55 Ji Yun, *Siku quanshu zongmu tiyao*, vol. 31 (Taipei, 1965), p. 12.
56 In addition to the works already mentioned, the best shorter work about Huang's theory of literature in a European language is Adele Rickett, "Method and Intuition: The Poetic Theories of Huang T'ing-chien," in Adele Rickett, ed., *Chinese Approaches to Literature from Confucius to Liang Ch'i-ch'ao* (Princeton, 1978).
57 Translated in Rickett, *Chinese Approaches*, p. 110.
58 According to a memorial recorded in the biography of Ma Yuan, "When the King of Wu liked knights-errant, most of the commoners had scars [from practicing sword-fighting], and when the King of Chu favored slim waists, many [ladies] in the palace starved to death. . . . When people in the city like high chignons, everyone in the four directions makes her hair a foot higher. When people in the city like broad eyebrows, everyone in the four directions covered half her forehead with them." *Houhanshu* 漢書 (Beijing, 1965), 827-853.
59 *Shangu shijizhu* (hereafter abbreviated SGSJ), *waiji*, BBCS (Taipei, 1969), 12-6b.
60 As an example of a twentieth-century Chinese critic whose methodology still resembles traditional scholars, see Hu Yunyi's discussion of Huang's poetry in Hu Yunyi, *Songshi yanjiu*, pp. 90–1. Although he does a bit more analysis than what one finds in the pre-twentieth-century *shihua* literature, Hu still discusses Huang's poetry largely in connection with its use of allusions.
61 Huang Tingjian, SGSJ, *neiji*, 3-16b-17b. Although I have translated the word *xingxing* as "orangutan" in line with modern Chinese, it is probably some other ape-like creature, the identification of which is not clear.
62 Quoted in Chen Yungzheng, ed., *Huang Tingjian shixuan* (Hong Kong, 1980), p. 106.
63 According to this book, the orangutan loves to drink and to wear clogs. See Chang Ju 常璩, *Huayang guozhi* 華陽國志 (Chengdu, 1964), 4-430. Huang has also drawn on a Tang essay on the orangutan entitled "Xingxing ming (Inscription on the Orangutan)" from *Tang wencui* 唐文粹, SBCK, 78, 523b-524.
64 "The orangutan is able to talk, but it does not leave the birds and beasts." *Liji* 禮記, *Quli* 曲禮, SBCK, 1-6a.
65 Found in Ruan's biography in *Jinshu* 晉書 (Beijing, 1974), p. 1365.
66 *Concordance to Chuang-tzu [Zhuangzi]*, Harvard Yenching Institute Sinological Index Series (Harvard, 1956), 93/33/69.
67 At least the commentary in SGSJ says that this is the origin of this allusion,

but the only source found for it was in a commentary by Kong Zhao (fourth century), although it is possible that Kong based his commentary on Zheng Xuan. See the chapter *Wanghuijie* 王會解 in *Yi Zhoushu* 逸周書, *Hanwei congshu* 漢魏叢書 (Shanghai, 1925), 7-5b.

68 The Stone Channel Pavilion (*Shiqu ge*) was founded by the first emperor of the Han dynasty (Gaozu 高祖, reg. 206–194 B.C.) to keep maps and books from the previous Qin dynasty. Under Emperor Xuandi 宣帝 (reg. 73–48 B.C.) famous scholars were invited to edit the Confucian classics there, and under Emperor Chengdi 成帝 (reg. 36–2 B.C.) it became the site of the imperial library.

69 *Concordance to Meng-tzu [Mencius]*, Harvard Yenching Institute Sinological Index Series, (Taipei, 1966), 53/7A/26.

70 There is a complete translation of Xie's poetry in J. Frodsham, trans., *The Murmuring Stream* (Kuala Lumpur, 1967). Unfortunately for the purpose of this study, the extensive discussion of Xie focuses almost entirely on biographical considerations. See Kang-i Sun Chang, *Six Dynasties Poetry* (Princeton, 1986), pp. 47–78 for a discussion of Xie's "new descriptive mode."

71 James Liu's characterization of Li Shangyin as a "Baroque" poet would seem to distinguish him immediately from Huang Tingjian and his followers. See James J. Y. Liu, *The Poetry of Li Shang-yin* (Chicago, 1969). Although Liu's article on Li in the Indiana Companion refers to his use of irony, this would seem to be different from the wit that lies behind many of Huang's allusions (see discussion in Chapter 2). See "Li Shang-yin" in Nienhauser, *Traditional Chinese Literature*, p. 552.

72 FCDSX, pp. 264–6.

73 See Ji Yun's comments translated above.

74 The fifth poem in Fan's complete works already resembles Chen Yuyi. See FSHJ, p. 2.

75 Allusion to Han Yu's line, "Administrative Assistant is such a low position it is not worth speaking of," according to Zhou Ruchang, but this could not be located in the standard edition of Han Yu's poems, *Han Changli shi xinian jishi* 韓昌黎詩繫年集釋 (Shanghai, 1957).

76 Allusion to Han Yu's line, "The blazing officer's hot underlings with red caps and trousers." Ibid., p. 300.

77 During Tang times the Liangzhou area (modern Gansu Province) was known for its vigorous non-Chinese music.

78 The idea is based on Du Fu's lines: "The air is intoxicated, the sun sets, and west wind comes / I wish it would blow the water in the fields to fill my golden cup." *A Concordance to Tu Fu*, 63/6/21.

79 Allusion to Zhao Lin's (fl. 836–46) *Yinhua lu*, a Tang work that contains much valuable information on official life: "The Bureau of Sacrifices is called an ice hall, because it is so cold." Zhao Lin 趙璘, *Yinhua lu* 因話錄, *Congshu jicheng* 叢書集成 (Shanghai, 1939), pp. 5–31.

80 Allusion to the *Shijing*, "When you sing, I answer." See *A Concordance to the Shi Ching*, Harvard Yenching Sinological Index Series (Tokyo, 1962), 18/85/1.

81 According to the *Zhuangzi*, when Zengzi lived in dire poverty in the state of Wei, he was still able to sing the odes of Shang. In later times this story was used as an example of an intellectual who was not discouraged by adversity. See *Zhuangzi*, 78/28/50 (66, 62).

82 For example, see "Following the Rhymes of Tang Wenbo's 'Planning to Return Home,'" in which practically every line has an allusion or echoing of some earlier work (66, 61).

83 It is probably fair to say that Huang Tingjian's absorption with this theme narrowed the scope of his poetry when compared with Su Shi and earlier Song poets. In any case, the frequent complaints to be found in Huang's works resemble the themes of such Tang authors as Du Fu.

84 According to Zhou Ruchang, the first line echoes Du Fu, "The evening mist is as long as rain," but this line could not be found in the concordance to his works. Malarial clouds and mist are conventional images in poetry about the deep south where Yang Wanli was serving at the time. Much of the population in the Guangdong area was not Han; hence, Fan's reference to treating the "barbarians" like men of China.

85 In a poem sent to Li Bai, Du Fu had written: "When your writing brush descends, it startles wind and rain; / When your poem is finished, it makes ghosts and gods sob." *A Concordance to the Poems of Tu Fu*, Harvard-Yenching Sinological Index Series (Taipei, 1966), 339/44/4.

86 Reference to Yang Wanli's recent repulsion of bandit incursions in Guangdong and southern Fujian provinces.

87 In the north of modern Qujiang County of Guangdong province there are thirty-six rocks called Shaoshishan (Shao Rocks Hill), which the semi-mythical sage emperor Shun is supposed to have climbed to play the so-called Shao music on his panpipes.

88 Allusion to the Six Dynasties poet Lu Kai 陸凱 who sent some plum blossoms from south China to his friend Fan Ye 范曄 together with a poem, a story that later became an example of good friendship. Yu Range is a rugged range of mountains in Guangdong province. See *Xianqin Han Wei Jin Nanbeichao shi* 先秦漢魏晉南北朝詩, vol. 2. (Beijing, 1983), p. 1204.

89 The red-stringed zither is said to be appropriate for the imperial ancestral shrine in the Zhou dynasty ritual text, the *Li Ji*. See *Li Ji*, 19/1(37)/11a.

90 The roc is a gigantic mythical bird that was believed to be able to soar up to heaven. Fan is urging Yang to maintain his moral purity (like a zither in the imperial ancestral shrine) and not be tempted to rise to high position. 314, 190.

Chapter 3

1 Burton Watson, trans., Yoshikawa Kôjirô, *An Introduction to Sung Poetry* (Cambridge, Mass., 1967), pp. 21–4.

2 Hu Yunyi remarks that "the two men's talents were so disparate that any relation involving mutual influence was extremely shallow." See Hu Yunyi, *Songshi yanjiu* (Hong Kong, repr. 1959), p. 88.

3 Watson, *An Introduction to Sung Poetry*, pp. 104–6.
4 Su Shi, *Jizhu fenlei Dongpo xiansheng shi*, SBCK (Taipei, 196?), 6-138b.
5 Ibid., 23-1a.
6 As might be expected, Su Shi loves to use clever puns in his poetry. For example, see his famous poem on an excursion to Gushan near modern Hangzhou that he undertook to visit two monk friends. Su puns on the word *dao*, which he uses both literally in the sense of "road" and in the sense of "religious path," and on the word *gu*, which he uses in the place name Gushan and in its original sense of "lonely." Ibid., 17-307b.
7 FSHJ, p. 27.
8 SGSJ, *neiji*, 16-6a.
9 Huang Tingjian, *Yuzhang xiansheng wenji*, SBCK (Taipei, 196?), 26-298a.
10 Ibid.
11 SGSJ, *neiji*, 10-8b.
12 FSHJ, p. 35.
13 Mei Yaochen's poetry has been studied and translated in J. Chaves, *Mei Yao-ch'en and the Development of Early Sung Poetry* (New York, 1976).
14 A poet by the name of Minzhan could not be found, so the character *min* is possibly a mistake for *zi*, in which case this may refer to Su Shi, who has the courtesy name Zizhan, which, however, is written with a different character.
15 Sun Yi, *Lüzhai shi'er bian*, BBCS, 10-14b.
16 Quoted in *Huang Tingjian shixuan*, p. 140.
17 SGSJ, *neiji*, 7-17a. The notes in *neiji* indicate that the term "cock's head" can also mean lotus seeds, probably because the two are similar in shape. If this is the case, the lines become even more complex.
18 26, 31.
19 Zhou Ruchang occasionally analyzes examples of the complex diction of Fan's early works. See FCDSX, p. 9, n. 3.
20 Fang's comments are scattered in the notes he wrote to the poems by Fan that he included in his anthology, the *Yingkui lüsui*. For his comment on a couplet of Fan see Fang Hui, *Yingkui lüsui, Siku quanshu zhenben* (hereafter abbreviated SKQS), 8 (Taipei, 1978), 21-121b.
21 Zhou Zhilin, "Shihu xiansheng shichaoxu," *Song simingjia shichao*, Kangxi reign period edition.
22 Cai Zhengsun, *Shilin guangji*, vol. 2 (Taipei, 1973), 5-19/527.
23 Zhang Jie, Suihantang shihua, *Congshu jicheng*, 1-13.
24 SGSJ, *neiji*, 2-7b.
25 Ibid., 6-9a.
26 Watson, *An Introduction to Sung Poetry*, p. 123.
27 Allusion to a story in the *Zhuangzi* in which a hunchback is skillful at catching cicadas because he is able to make his body like a withered tree and his arm like a withered branch. Huang has transformed this allusion by leaving out the hunchback and comparing the players' bodies to cicada shells on a withered branch. See *Concordance to Chuangtzu*, 48/19/18.
28 Reference to the King of Xiangdong (later Emperor Yuan of the Liang dynasty [reg. 552–555]). He had only one eye, and when he was fighting

with the rebel Hou Jing, Wang Wei made the disparaging remark that he would not be able to defeat Hou because of his disability. See *Nanshi* 南史 (Beijing, 1975), 80-2018. In Chinese chess (*weiqi*) a piece is considered to be "dead" if there is only one free space (i.e., "eye") to which it can be moved. The emphasis here is obviously on the specialized use of the word "eye" in chess parlance.

29 SGSJ, *waiji*, 2-4ab.

30 FSHJ, p. 50.

31 Translated in Cyril Birch, ed., *Anthology of Chinese Literature* (New York, 1965), p. 169–73.

32 One good example is the poem "To the Rhyme: Appreciating Plum Blossoms" in SGSJ, *waijibu*, 3-3a.

33 One of the most striking examples in Han Yu's poetry is his second poem on "Plum Flowers," Han Yu, SBCK (Taipei, 196?), 5-1b, translated in Erwin von Zach, *Han Yü's poetische Werke* (Cambridge, Mass., 1952), pp. 121–2.

34 FSHJ, p. 56.

35 Ibid., p. 49.

36 Ibid., p. 301.

37 Su Shi, *Jizhu*, 13-255b.

38 Ibid., 11-227a.

39 Shi Yannian (Manqing) was a well-known poet of the early Northern Song period, whose work was highly praised by Ouyang Xiu. Only one chapter of his works survives in the *Shi Manqing ji*, contained in *Liang Song mingxian xiaoji*, SKQS (Taipei, 1976); the poem to which Su alludes seems to have been lost.

40 Su Shi, *Jizhu*, 14-266a.

41 Although the "character" of the plum flowers in Han Yu's poem referred to in no. 33 is not as consistently developed as in Su Shi's work, Su's indebtedness to Han Yu is quite clear.

42 J. D. Schmidt, *Yang Wan-Li* (Boston, 1976), pp. 103–35.

43 CZJ, 35-330b.

44 SGSJ, *neiji*, 7-10a.

45 FSHJ, p. 11.

46 Although not identical, this poem has a number of traits in common with the work of Cao Cao, the famous leader of the Three Kingdoms period. See, for example, "Duange xing" (Ballad of the short song) in Cao Cao, *Cao Cao ji* 曹操集 (Beijing, 1962), p. 5.

47 FSHJ, p. 64.

48 Ibid., p. 134.

49 The problem of Huang Tingjian's use of color words is discussed in Li Yüanzhen, *Huang Shangu de shi yu shilun* (Taipei, 1972), pp. 79–82.

50 FSHJ, p. 77.

51 Huang Tingjian, *Huang Shangu*, *neiji*, 1-8b.

52 SGSJ, 16-10b.

53 FSHJ, p. 61.

54 Ibid., p. 49.

55 Ibid., p. 140.
56 Ibid., p. 200.
57 Ibid., p. 259.
58 SGSJ, 8-16b.
59 Su Shi, *Jizhu*, 1-55a.
60 SGSJ, 3-14b.
61 For the influence of Li Shangyin on the Xikun school, see "Hsi-k'un [Xikun] ch'ou-ch'ang chi" in William H. Nienhauser, Jr., ed., *Indiana Companion to Traditional Chinese Literature* (Bloomington, 1986), pp. 412–13. According to the authors of the article, although some Northern Song poets such as Ouyang Xiu expressed admiration for the Xikun poets' imitations of Li Shangyin, few Song authors followed in their footsteps, and the collection of their works was not reprinted until the sixteenth century.
62 One can see the connection between Fan's decorated style and Buddhist scriptures most closely in his poem on his ascent of Mount Emei (translated on p. 144), where many of his decorative images come from the general stock of such images found in Chinese translations of Indian Buddhist Sûtras.
63 Yang's description of Fan's styles includes both his prose and poetry. He compares Fan's writing to such disparate authors as the Han historian Sima Qian (145 B.C.?–85 B.C.?), the Period of Division poet Bao Zhao, and the Tang poet Li Bai. Although a certain amount of exaggeration is expected in such a preface, Yang would not have been likely to write what he did if he did not feel that there was a great variety of styles to be found in Fan's work. See CZJ, 82-681.
64 Jiang Kui, *Baishidaorenji*, p. 11a.
65 Song Lian, *Song Xueshi quanji*, vol. 15, p. 1052.
66 Zhu Yizun, *Pushuting ji*, SBCK (Taipei, 196?), 39-330a.
67 FSHJ, p. 71.

Chapter 4

1 Translated by Lu K'uan Yü (Charles Luk), *The Transmission of the Mind* (London, 1974).
2 Translated by Thomas and J. C. Cleary, *The Blue Cliff Record* (London, 1977).
3 *The Blue Cliff Record* was compiled by the eminent Song monk Xuedou Chongxian (980–1052), who added verses to each of the Tang stories. Later the Song monk Yuanwu Keqin (1063–1135) added his commentaries to this compilation, and only then did the text reach its present form. See also Yampolsky's discussion of the complex textual history of the *Platform Sutra*, the most revered text of the Southern School of Chan, in Phillip Yampolsky, trans., *The Platform Sûtra of the Sixth Patriarch* (New York, 1967), pp. 89–110.
4 One edition of Su's poems, which is arranged according to themes, lists fifty-six poems under the category *Shilao* (Buddhism and Daoism), fifty-nine under *siguan* (temples) and four under "pagodas," not to mention all the other

poems in which Buddhist concepts and imagery figure. See index to Su Shi, *Jizhu fenlei Dongpo xiansheng shi*.

5 A selection of Hanshan's verse is contained in Burton Watson trans., *Cold Mountain* (New York, 1962).

6 Wei Qingzhi, *Shiren yuxie* (Shanghai, 1959), 1-8.

7 Yan Yu, *Canglang shihua jiaoshi* (Beijing, 1962), p. 10. The entire work has been translated into German in Günther Debon, *Ts'ang Lang's Gespräche über die Dichtung* (Wiesbaden, 1962).

8 J. D. Schmidt, *Yang Wan-Li* (Boston, 1976), pp. 38–78.

9 Zhang Zi, *Nanhuji*, SKQS, 4 (1975), 6-10b.

10 Lou Yue, *Gongkuiji*, BBCS (Taipei 1969), 72-7b.

11 FCDSX, pp. 268–9, 292.

12 FSHJ, p. 9.

13 Ibid., p. 39.

14 "Wuxu Miyinsi," FSHJ, p. 41.

15 Ibid., p. 114.

16 Ibid., p. 252.

17 For the complete translation of this poem, see p. 144. Ibid., p. 261.

18 Ibid. p. 239.

19 In the eighth poem of the series on p. 335 of SHSJ, Fan compares himself to both of these sages.

20 Ibid., p. 262.

21 For the poetry of the *bianwen* texts, see Cheung, Samuel Hung-nin, "The Use of Verse in the Dun-huang bian-wen," *Journal of Chinese Linguistics* 8.1 (January 1980), pp. 149–62. Another useful study is Richard Strassberg, "Buddhist Storytelling Texts from Tunhuang," CHINOPERL 8 (1978), pp. 39–991.

22 See Wolfgang Kubin's article "Han-shan" in William H. Nienhauser, Jr., *Indiana Companion to Traditional Chinese Literature* (Bloomington, 1986), p. 394, for a discussion of the influence of the *jiyu*.

23 For a discussion of Wang Wei's more purely Buddhist verse, see Pauline Yu, trans., *The Poetry of Wang Wei* (Bloomington, 1980), pp. 112–31. Poem 51, "Kulapati Hu Lay Ill in Bed, So I Sent Some Grain and Presented This Poem to Him," translated on pp. 131–33, is a good example of Wang's *gâthâ*-style poetry.

24 FSHSJ, p. 44.

25 Ibid., p. 358.

26 Ibid., p. 13.

27 One is reminded of the descriptions of leisure in Tao's famous series "Returning to the Farm to Dwell." See James Robert Hightower trans., *The Poetry of T'ao Ch'ien* (Oxford 1970), pp. 50–6. Hightower translates the third line from the end of the first poem, "Within my bare room I have my peace of mind," which conveys the general meaning correctly, but the literal meaning is "in my empty room there is extra leisure." See Tao Qian, *Jianzhu Tao Yuanming ji*, SBCK, pp. 2–16.

28 FSHSJ, p. 323.

29 Ibid., p. 40.
30 Ibid., p. 238.
31 Ibid., p. 357.
32 Ibid., p. 354.
33 Ibid., p. 244.
34 Ibid., p. 200.
35 Ibid., p. 377.

Chapter 5

1 For a discussion of these two painters' contribution to landscape painting, see James Cahill, *Chinese Painting* (Cleveland, 1960), pp. 79–87.
2 FSHSJ, p. 49.
3 Ibid., p. 176.
4 Ibid., p. 89.
5 Fan's estate was located close to the former capital city of the state of Wu during the Warring States period, over eight centuries before his own time.
6 FSHSJ, p. 35.
7 Ibid., p. 167.
8 Fang Hui, *Yingkui lüsui*, 4-217ab.
9 Lu You's diary of his journey through the Gorges, which is generally regarded as the best travel diary of Song times, has been translated in Chun-shu Chang and Joan Smythe, trans., *South China in Twelfth Century: A Translation of Lu Yu's Travel Diaries* (Hong Kong, 1980). For a detailed discussion of Song travel diaries, see James M. Hargett, "Preliminary Remarks on the Travel Records of the Song Dynasty," *Chinese Literature, Essays, Articles, Reviews*, 7 (July 1985), pp. 67–93.
10 The most famous example of such poetry by Li Bai is his "Shudao nan," in Li Bai, *Li Taibai ji* 李太白集, *Wanyou wen ku hui yao* 萬有文庫薈要 (Taipei, 1965), 2-3. This has been translated in Wu-chi Liu and Irving Lo, *Sunflower Splendor*, p. 105.
11 FSHSJ, p. 274.

Chapter 6

1 The poem from the *Shijing* is contained in *A Concordance to the Shi Ching*, Harvard Yenching Sinological Index Series (Tokyo, 1962), 31–32/154.
2 Translated in James Robert Hightower, trans., *The Poetry of T'ao Ch'ien* (Oxford 1970), pp. 50–6.
3 The last line in the first poem of the series of poems just mentioned is translated by Hightower: "And now I have my freedom back again," but the literal meaning is "Again I can return to naturalness (*ziran*)," which Hightower interprets as "things as they are of themselves," *The Poetry of T'ao Ch'ien*, pp. 50–1, 47.
4 A good example is "Watching the Wheat Reapers," translated in Wu-chi Liu, *Sunflower Splendor*, p. 202.

5 In Bai Juyi, *Baishi changqing ji*, SBCK, 3-17a.
6 Liu Yuxi, *Liu Mengde wenji*, SBCK (Taipei, 196?), 9-64b.
7 Ibid., 9-65a.
8 Ibid., 9-65a.
9 This follows the interpretation given in Huang Yu, ed., *Liu Yuxi shixuan pingzhu* (Hong Kong, 1979), pp. 33–4.
10 Wang Jian, *Wang Sima ji*, SKQS, 10 (Taipei, 1980), 2-5b.
11 86, 74.
12 Literally, "Both of us have lost our sheep," which is an allusion to a story from *Zhuangzi*, in which one man loses his sheep while he is reading and another man loses it while he is gambling. It would seem that the actions of the man who was reading are more forgivable than those of the gambler, but Zhuangzi reminds us that both have lost their sheep. The sheep, of course, is a metaphor for Daoist truth. *Concordance to Chuangtzu*, 22/8/22.
13 81, 69.
14 An example of this tendency in Bai's work is his well-known poem "Maitanweng" (The old charcoal seller), in which the white snow contrasts grimly with the blackened face of the oppressed old man. See Bai Juyi, *Baishi changqing ji*, 4-23a.
15 FSHSJ, p. 220.
16 Gerald Bullet, *The Golden Year of Fan Ch'eng-ta* (Cambridge, 1946). James Hargett's new translation appeared just before the final version of this book was prepared. See James M. Hargett, "Boulder Lake Poems: Fan Chengda's Rural Year in Suzhou Revisited," *Chinese Literature, Essays, Articles, Reviews* 10 (July 1988). The Qing scholar Song Changbai was so impressed by the series that he wrote: "Fan Chengda's 'Impromptu Poems on the Four Seasons established a new literary realm distinct from Tao Qian, Liu Zongyuan [773–819], Wang Wei, and Chu Guangxi," who were among the most famous poets who wrote bucolic verse before the Song dynasty. See Song Changbai, *Liuting shihua, Zhongguo wenxue zhenben congshu* (Shanghai, 1935), 22-507.
17 FSHSJ, p. 372.
18 375, 217.
19 376, 221.
20 See, for example, the humor in the last poem of the summer season, FSHSJ, p. 375.
21 The last two lines of the ninth poem of late spring read: "The peonies buds burst, and the cherries ripen; / They don't permit flying petals to diminish the spring yet." FSHSJ, p. 373.
22 The most notable exception is poem 12 of autumn: "Only the orange grove presents a different scene: / In their green clumps hang ten thousand pieces of gold." FSHJ, p. 376. Also notice the comparison of the silk cocoons in the poem below to "straw raincoats."
23 See, for example, Fan Hui, *Ying Kui lüsui*, 13-15a.
24 Tao Qian, *Jianzhu Tao Yuanming ji*, p. 29.

25 Poem 5 of the series is particularly famous for its philosophy of life. Hightower discusses some of the ideas expressed by Tao in ibid., pp. 130–2.
26 372, 208.
27 376, 223.
28 373, 212.
29 375, 219.
30 An interesting contrast can be made with a similar poem by Yang Wanli:

> I can see only a few flowers from afar as I gaze up at the trellis,
> But when I go upstairs and look down, they stand out beautifully.
> There's no way to distinguish these roses from butterflies;
> You know they're not flowers – when they fly away!

Although this poem is basically *dan* in style, the surprise is left to the last line, as one would expect in a quatrain. CZJ, 25–235a.
31 FSHSJ, 372.
32 Ibid., 373.
33 372, 210.
34 375, 220.
35 FSHSJ, p. 409.
36 The first one of the series. Ibid., p. 410.
37 See Fan Chengda, *Wujunzhi*, BBCS (Taipei, 1968).
38 Burton Watson, trans., Yoshikawa Kôjirô, *An Introduction to Sung Poetry* (Cambridge, Mass., 1967), p. 161.

Chapter 7

1 SS, p. 5595b.
2 Duke touches on the Han Tuozhou affair on pp. 19 and 22 of his study. See Duke, *Lu You* (Boston, 1977). Lu You was already eighty years old when he cooperated with Han. However, his currying of Han's favor by composing the "Nanyüanji" (Record of the southern garden) has caused historians to criticize him for consorting with a man whom many consider a "wicked" minister. See also Liu Weichong, *Lu You pingzhuan* (Taipei, 1966), pp. 112–13 and Qi Zhiping, *Lu You* (Shanghai, 1978), pp. 47–51. Both Liu and Qi take a lenient view of Lu's actions, suggesting that he was motivated solely out of patriotism.
3 Although this is the case with most of the selections of Lu's verse published in the People's Republic, You Guoen and Li Yi, ed., *Lu You shixuan* (Beijing, 1957), is more extreme than others.
4 See Duke's discussion of Lu's "patriotism" in Duke, *Lu You*, pp. 65–80.
5 FSHSJ, p. 102. An account of Hong Mai's unsuccessful mission is given in Chang Fu-jui's biography of Hong in Herbert Franke, *Sung Biographies* vol. 1 (Wiesbaden 1976), pp. 471–3.
6 Fan's travel diary has been translated with detailed notes in James Hargett, "Fan Ch'eng-ta's Lan-p'ei lu: a Southern Sung Embassy Account," *Tsing*

Hua Journal of Chinese Studies, n.s. 16 (1984), pp. 119–77. For a discussion of this group of poems, see also E. A. Serebrjakov, "On the Rational and Emotional Sources in the Poetry of Fan Ch'eng-ta (1126–1193): The Cycle of Quatrains Written by the Poet during an Ambassadorial Mission to the State of Chin," *Ucennye Zapiski Leningradskogo Universiteta* 396 (1977).

7 Qian Qianyi, *Muzhai chuxue ji* (Shanghai, 1985), 1, 2b-3a.

8 Pan Deyu, *Yangyizhai shihua*, Saoye shanfang, ed. (Shanghai, early twentieth century), 9-8b.

9 Zhang Xun and Xu Yuan are two heroes who were faithful to the Tang dynasty during the An Lushan Rebellion. When the city they were guarding was besieged, food ran so low that they finally slaughtered their beloved concubines to feed their soldiers. When the enemy finally captured them, they suffered torture and execution rather than submit to rebel demands that they collaborate. *Xintang shu* 新唐書 (Beijing, 1975), 192, 5538–40.

10 Reference to the events that led to the collapse of the Northern Song dynasty after it was attacked by the Jin. The Northern Song capital Bianjing's (modern Kaifeng's) location south of the Yellow River was supposed to render it impregnable. Fan's poem does not specify who is to blame for the Northern Song debacle, but the emperor Huizong is one of his more obvious targets (146, 107).

11 See Zhou's discussion in FCDSX, pp. 271–2.

12 152, 114.

13 145, 107.

14 Lu You, *Lu Fangweng quanji*, 4–70.

15 Fan's diaries follow his poems so closely that they can almost be read as a commentary on them or vice versa, and the poems provide material which the present editions of the diary have lost.

16 156, 120.

17 154, 115.

18 The first painting is about Fan's mission to the Jin, while the second is about his journey to Guilin, Cassia Sea being a phrase he took from the poetry of Jiang Yan 江淹 (444–505) and used for the region of modern Guangxi province in spite of the fact that there are no seas nearby.

19 Fan refers to the failure of his diplomatic mission to the Jin to accomplish its objectives.

20 Allusion to Du Fu's line, "Snow buries my brocade saddle blanket." *A Concordance to Tu Fu*, 330/33/8. Here Fan is dreaming of his mission to the north, although none of his poems written during that period mention an encounter with snow.

21 Literally, "I cannot put things in order among the mulberries and elms; I am old." According to a Chinese proverb, "If you lose something at sunrise [literally, "eastern edge"], you can get it back at sunset [literally, "mulberries and elms," i.e., the trees behind which the sun sets]. Fan is saying that he is too old to improve the situation even during the "sunset" of his life.

22 184, 132.
23 Although many of Lu You's later dream poems treat Daoist experiences, according to Duke, twenty-three of his dream poems involve patriotism. See Duke, *Lu You*, pp. 132–41.
24 See Schmidt, *Yang Wan-li*, chapter 1.

Bibliography

Please see the list of abbreviations at the beginning of the Notes (p. 168). Items marked with an asterisk contain works that survive from Fan Chengda's lost collected prose. Most of the works used only to identify allusions in Fan's poetry have been omitted but can be found in the relevant notes.

Primary sources

Bai Juyi 白居易 (772–846). *Baishi Changqing ji* 白氏長慶集. SBCK.
Bi Yuan 畢沅 (1730–1797). *Xu zizhi tongjian* 續資治通鑑 Beijing, 1957.
*Cai Chengshao 蔡呈韶 (fl. 1798). *Lingui xianzhi* 臨桂縣志. Taipei, 1967.
Cai Zhengsun 蔡正孫 (13th century). *Shilin guangji* 詩林廣記. Taipei, 1973.
*Cao Lunbin 曹綸彬 (*jinshi* 1709). *Chuzhou fuzhi* 處州府志. Taipei, 1987.
*Chen Jiru 陳繼儒 (1558–1639). *Bihanbu* 辟寒部 Taipei, 1965.
Chen Yuyi 陳與義 *Chen Yuyi ji* 陳與義集. Beijing, 1982.
Chen Jianzhai shiji hejiao huizhu 陳簡齋詩集合校彙注. Taipei, 1975.
Chen Zhensun 陳振孫 (fl. 1211–1249). *Zhizhai shulu jieti.* 知齋書錄解題 *Baibu congshu jicheng* 百部叢書集成 (BBCS).
Fan Chengda 范成大 (1126–1193). *Canluan lu* 驂鸞錄. *Congshu jicheng* 叢書集成. Shanghai, 1936.
Kong Fanli 孔凡禮, ed. *Fan Chengda yizhu jicun* 范成大遺著輯存. Beijing, 1983.
Zhou Xifu 周錫輹, ed. Fan Chengda shixuan范成大 詩選. Hong Kong, 1986.
Fan Shihuji 范石湖集. Shanghai, 1962; repr. Hong Kong 1974.
Guihai Yuheng zhi jiaobu 桂海虞衡志校補. Liuzhou, 1984.
Lanpei lu 攬轡錄. BBCS. Taipei, 1966.
Shihuci 石湖詞. BBCS. Taipei, 1966.
Shihu jupu 石湖菊譜. BBCS. Taipei, 1960.
Shihu meipu 石湖梅譜. BBCS. Taipei, 1965.
Shihu Jushi shiji 石湖居士詩集. *Sibu congkan* (SBCK). Taipei, 196?.
Shihu Shiji 石湖詩集. BBCS. Taipei, 1965.
Wuchuanlu 吳船錄. *Congshu jicheng*. Shanghai, 1937.
Wujunzhi 吳郡志. BBCS. Taipei, 1968.

Fang Hui 方回 (1227–1307). *Yingkui lüsui* 瀛奎律髓. *Siku quanshu zhenben* 四庫全書珍本 (SKQS), 8. Taipei, 1978.
Tongjiang ji 桐江集. Taipei, 1970.
Fu Xuancong 傅璇琮, ed. *Huang Tingjian he Jiangxi shipai juan* 黃庭堅和江西詩派卷. Beijing, 1978.
*Gu Yanwu 顧炎武 (1613–1682). *Tianxia junguo libing shu* 天下郡國利病書. *Sibu congkan xubian* 四部叢刊續編. Taipei, 1966.
Han Biao 韓淲 (1160–1224). *Jianquan riji* 澗泉日記. BBCS.
Hong Gua 洪适 (1117–1184). *Panzhou wenji* 盤州文集. SBCK Taipei, 196?.
Hu Zi 胡仔 (fl. second half of twelfth century). Tiaoxi yuyin conghua 苕溪漁隱叢話. Beijing, 1981.
*Huang Huai 黃淮 (1367–1449). *Lidai mingchen zouyi* 歷代名臣奏議. Taipei, 1964.
**Huang Song zhongxing liangchao shengzheng* 皇宋中興兩朝聖政. *Songshi ziliaocui bianji* 宋史資料萃編輯. Taipei, Yungho, 1967.
Huang Tingjian 黃庭堅. Edited by Chen Yungzheng 陳永正. *Huang Tingjian shixuan* 黃庭堅詩選. Hong Kong, 1980.
Shangushi jizhu 山谷詩集注. BBCS. Taipei, 1969.
Yuzhang Huang Xiansheng wenji 豫章黃先生文集. SBCK. Taipei, 196?.
Huang Zhen 黃震 (*jinshi* 1256). *Huangshi richao* 黃氏日鈔. SKQS, 2. Taipei, 1971.
Ji Yun 紀昀 (1724–1805) et al. *Siku Quanshu Zongmu tiyao* 四庫全書總目提要. Taipei, 1965.
Jiang Kuei 姜夔 (ca. 1155–1235). *Baishidaoren shiji* 白石道人詩集. SBCK. Taipei, 196?.
Liangsong mingxian xiaoji 兩宋名賢小集. SKQS.
Lin Guangchao 林光朝. *Aixuan ji* 艾軒集. *Siku quanshu zhenben chuji* 四庫全書珍本初集. Shanghai, 1934–1935.
Liu Yuxi 劉禹錫. *Liu Mengde wenji* 劉夢得文集. SBCK.
Huang Yu 黃雨, ed. *Liu Yuxi shixuan pingzhu* 劉禹錫詩選評注. Hong Kong, 1979.
Lou Yue 樓鑰 (1137–1213). *Gongkui ji* 攻媿集. BBCS. Taipei, 1969.
*Lu Xiong 盧熊 (fl. 1379). *Suzhou fuzhi* 蘇州府志. Taipei, 1983.
Lu You 陸游 (1125–1219). *Laoxue'an biji* 老學菴筆記. BBCS.
Lu Fangweng quanji 陸放翁全集. Taipei, 1970.
You Guo'en 游國恩, and Li Gaizhi 李改之, eds. *Lu You Shixuan* 陸游詩選. Beijing, 1957.
Lü Liuliang 呂留良 (1629–1683) et al. *Songshi chao* 宋詩鈔. Shanghai, 1935.
*Ni Tao 倪濤. *Liuyi zhi yilu* 六藝之一錄. Harvard Yenching Sinological Indexes. Peiping, n.d.
Pan Deyu 潘德輿 (1785–1839). *Yangyizhai shihua* 養一齋詩話. Saoye shanfang 掃葉山房 ed. Shanghai, early twentieth century.
Qian Qianyi 錢謙益 (1582–1664). *Muzhai chuxue ji* 牧齋初學集. Shanghai, 1985.
Qian Shisheng 錢士升 (Ming). *Nansong shu* 南宋書. Tokyo, 1973.

Song Changbai 宋長白. *Liuting shihua* 柳亭詩話. Zhongguo wenxue zhenben congshu 中國文學珍本叢書. Shanghai, 1935.
Song Lian 宋濂 (1310–1381). *Song Xueshi quanji* 宋學士全集. *Congshu jicheng chubian* 叢書集成初編. Changsha, 1939.
Su Shi 蘇軾 (1037–1101). *Jizhu fenlei Dongpo xiansheng shi* 集注分類東坡先生詩. SBCK. Taipei, 196?.
Sun Yi 孫亦 (12th c.). *Lüzhai shi'er bian* 履齋示兒編. BBCS.
Tang Guizhang 唐圭章 , ed. *Quan Songci* 全宋詞. Beijing, 1967.
Tao Qian 陶潛 (365–427). Jianzhu Tao Yuanming ji 箋注陶淵明集. SBCK.
Tuo Tuo 脱脱 (1313–1355) et al. *Jinshi* 金史. Beijing, 1975.
Songshi 宋史. Beijing, 1977.
*Wang Ao 王鏊 (1450–1524). *Gusuzhi* 姑蘇志. SKQS, 10. Taipei, 1980.
Wang Jian 王建 (*jinshi* 775). *Wang Sima ji* 王司馬集. SKQS, 10. Taipei, 1980?.
*Wang Keyu 汪珂玉 (b. 1587). *Shanhuwang* 珊瑚網. Chengdu, 1985.
*Wei Qixian 魏齊賢 (fl. 1190). *Wubaijia bofang daquan wencui* 五白家播芳大全文粹. SKQS, 10. Taipei, 1980.
Wei Qingzhi 魏慶之 (fl. first half of thirteenth century). *Shiren yuxie* 詩人玉屑. Shanghai, 1959.
Wu Jing 吳儆 (1125–1183). *Zhuzhouji* 竹洲集, SKQS, 4. 1973.
*Xie Jin 解縉 (1369–1415), ed. *Yongle dadian* 永樂大典. Beijing, 1960.
*Xie Weixin 謝維新 (Ming). *Gujin hebi shilei beiyao* 古今合璧事類備要. Taipei, 1971.
*Xu Song 徐松 (1781–1848), ed. *Song huiyao jigao* 宋會要輯稿. Beijing, 1957.
Yan Yu 嚴羽 (12th century). *Canglang shihua jiaoshi* 滄浪詩話校釋. Beijing, 1962.
Yang Shen 楊慎 (1488–1559). *Quanshu yiwen zhi* 全蜀藝文志 , n.d.
Yang Wanli 楊萬里 (1127–1206). *Chengzhaiji* 誠齊集. SBCK, Taipei, 196?.
Yue Ke 岳珂(1183–1234). *Tingshi* 桯史. *Baibu congshu jikan* 百部叢書集刊. Taipei, 1965.
Zhan Zhi 湛之 , ed. *Yang Wanli Fan Chengda juan* 楊萬里范成大卷. Beijing, 1965.
Zhang Duanyi 張端義 (1179–ca. 1235). *Gui'er ji* 貴耳集. Taipei, 1966.
Zhang Jie 張戒 (12th c.). *Suihantang shihua* 歲寒堂詩話. *Congshu jicheng.*
Zhang Lei 張耒 (1054–1114). *Keshan ji* 柯山集. SKQS, 4, 1973.
*Zhang Mingfeng 張鳴鳳 (*juren* 1552). *Guisheng* 桂勝. SKQS, 4. Taipei, 1973.
Zhang Zi 張鎡 (b. 1153). *Nanhuji* 南湖集. SKQS, 1975.
*Zheng Huchen 鄭虎臣 (13th century). *Wudu wencui* 吳都文粹. SKQS, 6. Taipei, 1976.
Zhou Bida 周必大 (1126–1204). *Wenzhong gong ji* 文忠公集. SKQS, 4. Taipei, 1971.
Zhou Zhilin 周之麟 . *Song simingjia shichao* 宋四名家詩鈔. Kangxi reign period edition.
Zhou Mi 周密 (1232–1308). *Qidong yeyu* 齊東野語. BBCS. Taipei, 1965.
*Zhou Qufei 周去非 (*jinshi* 1163). *Lingwai daida* 嶺外代答. BBCS.
Zhou Ruchang 周汝昌, ed. *Fan Chengda shixuan* 范成大詩選. Beijing, 1959. New edition, Beijing, 1984.
ed. *Yang Wanli xuanji* 楊萬里選集. Beijing, 1964.
Zhu Yizun 朱彝尊 (1629–1709). *Pushuting ji* 曝書亭集. SBCK. Taipei, 196?.

Secondary sources in Chinese and Japanese

Chen Yicheng 陳義成. "Yang Wanli yanjiu" 楊萬里研究. Ph.D. diss., Zhongguo wenhua daxue 中國文化大學. Taipei, 1982.

Cheng Guangyu 程光裕. "Shihuji kaolue" 石湖集考略. *Shixue huikan* 史學彙刊 8 (July 1977).

"Shihu jixing sanlu kaolue" 石湖紀行三錄考略. *Huaxue yuekan* 華學月刊 72 (December 1977).

"Wujunzhi kaolue" 吳郡志考略. *Shixue huikan* 史學彙刊 7 (July 1976).

Fei Haiji 費海璣. "Fan Chengda fangwen ji" 范成大訪問記. *Changliu* 暢流 53.9 (May 1976).

Gôyama, Kiwamu 合山究. "Ryo Honchû no Kôsei shisha shûhazu ni tsuite" 呂本中の江西詩社宗派圖について. *Kyûshû Chûgoku gakkaihô* 九州中國學會報, 16 (1970).

Guo Shaoyu 郭紹虞. *Zhongguo wenxue pipingshi* 中國文學批評史. Beijing, 1979.

Hu Yunyi 胡雲翼. *Songshi yanjiu* 宋詩研究. Hong Kong, 1959.

Huang Shengyi 黃聲儀. "Shihuci yanjiu ji jianzhu" 石湖詞研究及箋注. Master's thesis, Taiwan Normal University, n.d.

Kong Fanli 孔凡禮. "Fan Chengda zaoqi shijikao" 范成大早期事蹟考. *Wenxue yichan* 文學遺產 1 (1983).

and Qi Zhiping 齊治平, eds. *Lu You juan* 陸游卷. Shanghai, 1962.

Li Yuanzhen 李元貞. *Huang Shangu de shi yu shilun* 黃山谷的詩與詩論. Taipei, 1972.

Liu Boji 劉伯驥. *Songdai zhengjiaoshi* 宋代政教史. Taipei, 1971.

Liu Dajie 劉大杰. "Huang Tingjian de shilun" 黃庭堅的詩論. *Wenxuepinglun* 文學評論 1, (1964).

Zhongguo wenxue fazhanshi 中國文學發展史. Beijing, 1962.

Liu Weichong 劉維崇. *Lu You pingzhuan* 陸游評傳. Taipei, 1979.

Luo Genze 羅根澤. *Zhongguo wenxue pipingshi* 中國文學批評史. Shanghai, 1957.

Qi Zhiping 齊治平. *Lu You* 陸游. Shanghai, 1978.

Tao Jingshen 陶晉生. *Jin Hailingdi de fa Song yu Caishi zhanyi de kao shi* 金海陵帝的伐宋與采石戰役的考實. Taipei, 1963.

Toyama Gunji 外山軍治. *Kinchôshi kenkyû* 金朝史研究. Tokyo, 1964.

Wang Deyi 王德毅. "Ji Hong Mai shi Jin shimo" 記洪邁使金始末. *Daxue shenghuo* 大學生活, 4.3, 1958.

"Fan Shihu nianpu" 范石湖年譜. *Songshi yanjiu lunji* 宋史研究論集, 2. Taipei, 1972.

"Fan Shihu xiansheng nianpu" 范石湖先生年譜. *Wenshizhe* 文史哲 18 (1969).

"Siku Zongmu Fan Shihu shiji tiyao shuhou" 四庫總目范石湖詩集提要書後. *Wenshizhe* 文史哲 18 (1969).

Yang Yunzhi 楊允之. "Wenzijiao de dianxing: Lu You yu Fan Chengda" 文字交的典型一陸游與范成大. *Yiwenzhi* 藝文誌 170 (November 1979).

Yokoyama Iseo 橫山伊勢雄. "Kô Teiken shironkô" 黃庭堅詩論考. *Kokubungaku kambungaku ronsô* 國文學漢文學論叢 16, (1971).

Yoshikawa Kôjirô 吉川幸次郎. *Sôshi gaisetsu* 宋詩概說. *Chûgoku Shijin Senshû* 中國詩人選集. Tokyo, 1962.

Index